Measurement and Statistics for Teachers

Written in a student-friendly style, this modestly priced text shows teachers how to use measurement and statistics wisely in their classes. Although there is some discussion of theory, emphasis is given to the practical, everyday uses of measurement and statistics such as how to develop and use effective classroom tests, how to carry out informal assessments, performance assessments, portfolio assessments, and how to use and interpret standardized tests. Part II provides a more complete coverage of basic descriptive statistics and their use in the classroom than any text now available.

Malcolm Van Blerkom has been teaching various college courses in Psychology and Educational Psychology for the past 28 years, and is currently at the University of Pittsburgh at Johnstown. He has also published research on topics as varied as cognitive styles, class attendance, and study strategies.

Measurement and Statistics for Teachers

Malcolm L. Van Blerkom

University of Pittsburgh at Johnstown

Routledge
Taylor & Francis Group

NEW YORK AND LONDON

First published 2009
by Routledge
270 Madison Ave, New York, NY 10016

Simultaneously published in the UK
by Routledge
2 Park Square, Milton Park, Abingdon, Oxon OX14 4RN

Routledge is an imprint of the Taylor & Francis Group, an informa business

© 2009 Taylor & Francis

Typeset in Minion by
RefineCatch Limited, Bungay, Suffolk
Printed and bound in the United States of America on acid-free paper by
Edwards Brothers, Inc.

Library of Congress Cataloging in Publication Data
Van Blerkom, Malcolm L.
  Measurement and statistics for teachers / Malcolm L. Van Blerkom.—1st. ed.
     v. cm.
  Includes bibliographical references and index.
  1. Educational tests and measurements. 2. Educational statistics. I. Title.
  LB3051. V25 2008
  371.26—dc22

                                                    2008020571

ISBN10: 0–415–99565–5 (hbk)
ISBN10: 0–805–86457–1 (pbk)
ISBN10: 0–203–88786–7 (ebk)

ISBN13: 978–0–415–99565–8 (hbk)
ISBN13: 978–0–805–86457–1 (pbk)
ISBN13: 978–0–203–88786–8 (ebk)

Dedication
For my wife, Diane,
for all of her love, help,
and encouragement

CONTENTS

PREFACE

This text is designed to give prospective and practicing teachers those skills required that will allow them to make intelligent decisions about testing and grading. My personal experiences have led me to conclude that many teachers feel that they are out on their own when it comes to testing and grading, having often had very little formal training in measurement and statistics. This text is not designed to turn teachers into either statisticians or psychometricians. However, it is designed to give you a basic understanding of both statistical and measurement principles and specific skills that will allow you to make intelligent choices about testing and related issues.

This text will be partly theoretical and partly practical. It will be theoretical in that you will learn about the basic principles of measurement and statistics. This will allow you to know when it will be appropriate and useful to use certain techniques. An understanding of statistics is also necessary for an understanding of measurement. This text will also be practical in that you will learn how to calculate means, standard deviations, correlation, and other statistics, and will learn how to develop frequency distributions and graphs. In addition, you will learn how to develop good test items and use a variety of measurement techniques.

I have had several goals in mind as I planned and wrote this book. First and foremost, I want teachers to be able to make intelligent choices about using testing and grading in their classrooms. What type of test would be the most appropriate given the material that was covered, your goals, and the age of your students? I also want teachers to be able to defend their methods to colleagues, supervisors, parents, and students. You must be able to explain logically why you use those methods, and why they are better than the alternatives. Finally, I hope that the readers of this text will be leaders in their respective school systems promoting the better use of measurement. Schools are constantly faced with a variety of measurement dilemmas. We need educators who are knowledgeable about measurement if we expect schools to make good choices.

This textbook is fairly unique. Most statistics texts include both descriptive and inferential statistics. However, very few teachers, unless doing research, ever have the need to use inferential statistics in their classrooms. Therefore, this text will be limited to covering only descriptive statistics. Many measurement texts go into great detail in building theoretical rationales for various measurement procedures, and, at times, the theory can become quite complex. Most classroom teachers, however, require only an understanding of the basic theoretical issues involved. Instead, teachers frequently need considerably more assistance with the many practical aspects of measurement. They need to know how to develop and evaluate classroom tests so that they can have the most effective tests that are possible. Although this text will not neglect theory, it will place heavy stress on the practical aspects of measurement.

Students sometimes avoid statistics courses because the courses involve mathematics. Although statisticians can use some very sophisticated mathematical methods such as calculus and matrix algebra, those are rarely necessary. Most of the mathematics required for statistics is addition, subtraction, multiplication, division, squares, square roots, and simple algebra. Actually, the most difficult part of statistics is that it frequently requires you to engage in logical/mathematical thinking. Statistics is extremely logical and I stress the logic. Once you understand the basic logic of statistics, the concepts and calculations are quite simple.

This text is intended for undergraduate education and related majors. However, it could also be used in some Master's level programs.

Organization of this Text

Some measurement textbooks exclude any material on statistics. Others contain an appendix that includes a brief review of statistics. However, in my experience, students who lack any background in statistics have difficulty understanding many measurement concepts. Since very few of my students have taken any statistics course, I spend the first few weeks of the class teaching basic descriptive statistics. Therefore, this text is divided into two parts. Part I includes 17 chapters on measurement, and can stand alone as a measurement text. Part II includes five chapters on descriptive statistics. Although I teach the statistics chapters first, we set up the text in this way to allow instructors flexibility. They can choose to use the chapters on statistics as optional supplemental material; they can use those chapters for a very quick review, or they can teach them as they would the other chapters. I hope that instructors will find this organization useful.

Part I is divided into four sections. Section I includes the first five chapters and includes an introduction to measurement, a chapter on ways to interpret test scores, a chapter on objectives, a chapter on reliability, and finally a chapter on validity. Section II includes six chapters on developing and using classroom tests. There are chapters that describe how to build each of the four types of test item typically found in the classroom. In addition, there is one chapter on producing and administering classroom tests and a chapter on analyzing classroom tests. Section III includes three chapters on alternative assessment techniques. There is one chapter on informal assessment, another on performance assessments, and a third on portfolios. Section IV includes three additional chapters. Chapter 15 discusses how to teach students test-taking skills. Chapter 16 describes and discusses standardized tests typically used in schools. Finally, Chapter 17 discusses alternative ways to report test scores.

Part II includes five chapters on descriptive statistics. Chapter 18 discusses the language and logic of statistics. Chapter 19 discusses how to develop and graph frequency distributions. Chapter 20 discusses several various measures of central tendency.

Chapter 21 then discusses a number of measures of variability. Finally, Chapter 22 discusses correlation.

Features of this Text

Measurement and Statistics for Teachers is clearly written and student friendly. There is minimum use of education jargon. Each chapter includes important terms which are isolated as boxed definitions. There are many examples used within the text that will help make the concepts clear to the students. Each chapter includes a scenario titled "Spotlight on the Classroom" which describes a classroom application. Each chapter includes exercises and practice questions. In addition, seven of the chapters include a study tips appendix designed to help students who might have difficulty with this type of course.

ACKNOWLEDGEMENTS

As is true with many textbooks, most of the ideas presented in this text are not my personal discoveries. Rather, they are my interpretations of knowledge developed by generations of scholars and teachers. I hope that I have presented their ideas well. I am deeply indebted to several of my most influential mentors on these subjects, Paul Games, William Rabinowitz, and Dennis Roberts. I have also relied heavily on the recent writings of scholars in this field, especially Albert Oosterhof from Florida State University and Steven J. Osterlind of the University of Missouri at Columbia.

I thank my many colleagues at the University of Pittsburgh at Johnstown who offered help on various subject areas. These included Melonie Dropik, Nina Girard, Jean James, Donna Kowalczyk, Mark Previte, and Karen Scanlon. I thank other colleagues, Karen Clites and Robert Eckenrod, as well as a student, Brad Rogers, who offered assistance with computer graphics. I thank Jennifer Bonislawski and Kristie Carozza who proof-read all of the chapters and gave significant assistance with the development of most of the chapter exercises and Spotlights on the Classroom. I thank the several reviewers of this manuscript who each took a considerable amount of time to offer helpful suggestions, many of which have been incorporated into this book. I thank my daughter, Sharon Smith, who provided some examples. I especially thank Diane, my wife, who encouraged me to undertake this project, provided many ideas and examples, assisted with the Study Tips, and carefully copyedited the entire text.

Part I
Measurement

Section I

BASIC ISSUES IN MEASUREMENT

This part is divided into four sections. Section I includes four chapters that will introduce you to basic measurement principles. Chapter 1 will introduce you to the various roles that measurement plays in the classroom, to basic terminology, to the difference between formal and informal assessment, to the ways in which you can use assessment in the classroom, and finally to the difference between maximum performance and typical performance measures. Chapter 2 will introduce you to various approaches that you can use to interpret test scores, how to choose a particular approach, and finally to the desired characteristics of both criterion-referenced and norm-referenced tests. Chapter 3 will introduce you to the use of standards, goals, and objectives as an approach to decide what to teach and what to assess. You will learn about several approaches to how to prepare objectives and how to use them in the classroom. In Chapter 4 you will learn about reliability, both from a theoretical perspective and a practical classroom perspective. In addition, you will learn how to interpret reliabilities and how to make your classroom assessment techniques more reliable. Finally, in Chapter 5 you will be introduced to validity, how you can go about obtaining evidence of validity, and how reliability and validity are related to one another.

1

INTRODUCTION TO MEASUREMENT

INTRODUCTION

In this chapter we will begin to look at the various ways in which we use measurement in the classroom. We will differentiate between the terms assessment, measurement, and evaluation as well as differentiate between formal and informal assessment. We will look at the various roles of assessment including preliminary, diagnostic, formative, and summative assessment. We will also differentiate between maximum and typical performance measures. Finally, we examine a brief overview of the remaining chapters on measurement.

THE ROLE OF MEASUREMENT

Measurement plays many different roles in our lives. During the past week I have had to rely on measurement in many different ways. The other day, while at the grocery store, I had to locate a can of diced tomatoes that was 14.5 ounces for a recipe for Spanish rice. Each morning I rely on my alarm clock to wake me at 6:45 a.m. (I get to sleep-in late this year!) I have recently anxiously watched the price for a gallon of gasoline rise and fall. When a student asked me for a recommendation, I reviewed his performance in my class by checking my grade book, paying special attention to his test scores. These examples represent only a few of the many ways that I use measurement on a daily basis.

You will also use measurement a great deal in your classrooms. You may give students diagnostic tests to assess how well they are reading, spelling, writing, counting, and so on. You will give tests to assess how well your students have learned and mastered the material that you have been teaching. You will use informal assessment on a daily basis to judge how well your lessons are progressing: Do your students appear to be comprehending your instruction? You will collect homework to assess if your students are actually able to apply the new skills that they have been learning. As you will see, measurement will play many different roles in our classrooms.

In the five chapters of Part II we discuss statistics. That discussion is designed primarily to give you sufficient background to be able to examine and comprehend the many measurement concepts that we will be discussing in the remaining 17 chapters. Those statistical concepts that will be most often used in the discussions of measurement include the mean, the standard deviation, the variance, correlation, and z-scores. You will see how we use these and other statistical concepts to build good measurement practices.

MEASUREMENT, ASSESSMENT, AND EVALUATION

There are many terms that describe the processes that we use to judge student performance. The three terms most commonly used are measurement, assessment, and evaluation. Although I will provide you with specific definitions for each term, I must warn you that there is no international law or agreement on how these terms should be used. I have seen many instances where these three terms are freely used interchangeably as if they all meant exactly the same thing. However, I will give you specific definitions for each according to the ways that each term is used most frequently in education.

Assessment

The most general term is assessment. *Assessment* is a very general term that describes the many techniques that we use to measure and judge student behavior and performance. Although in some professional circles the term assessment sometimes means something more specific, in relation to the classroom, it is typically a very general, very generic term. When in doubt about how to label a technique, the safest label to use would be assessment.

Measurement

Over the years, I have seen many definitions of measurement. However, here is the one that I find the most useful. *Measurement* is the process of assigning meaningful numbers (or labels) to persons or objects based on the degree to which they possess some characteristic.

Let's look at some examples and start with how we could take measurements of an object. What are some characteristics of a classroom to which we could assign meaningful numbers or labels? The first thing that we generally think of is the classroom's dimensions, especially its length and width. A second important characteristic is the classroom's seating capacity. Some classrooms may be designed to hold 20 students, whereas others could accommodate 35 to 40 students. This becomes important when we are assigning classes to certain rooms. Still another characteristic that I find important is board space. I tend to use the board a great deal, especially in some classes, and want classrooms with plenty of board space (perhaps measured in square feet). What about the room number? For example, let's say that we are in room 231. Is the room number a form of measurement? It may be! The room number is frequently used as a substitute for a name and can be considered measurement at the nominal (naming) level (see Part II, Chapter 18). If room numbers are assigned to rooms randomly and don't assist a stranger in finding the room, then I would argue that in that case the room number was not a form of measurement. In that case the room number was not very meaningful. However, if room numbers are assigned in some logical order (as they are in most buildings) and they assist a stranger in finding the room, then I would argue that they are measurement, if only at its least sophisticated level. In this case the room number has some meaning and tells you something about the classroom, where it is located.

For another example, let's use a student. What are some characteristics of a student that can be described with meaningful numbers or labels? Of course, many of the student's various physical characteristics such as height, weight, and age can all be described with meaningful numbers. Even describing other characteristics such as gender are frequently considered meaningful at the nominal level. Other characteristics to which we can ascribe meaningful numbers would include the student's score on the last social studies quiz, the student's score on an I.Q. test, or her score on the standardized math achievement test. There are many student characteristics that we can measure in a meaningful way.

Measurement is primarily a mechanical process. When we score a test, count up the number of points that the student earned, and record that number, we are using measurement.

Evaluation

The third term is evaluation. *Evaluation* involves the use of measurement to make decisions about or to determine the worth of a person or object. Evaluation is frequently the step that follows measurement. Let's say that Dana earned 87 on a 100-point science test. When we scored Dana's test and determined that she earned 87 out of 100 points we were using measurement. It was a mechanical process. If we then decide that Dana's test score of 87 translates to a letter grade of B, we are now using evaluation. Deciding on a grade was dependent on a judgment of worth. A letter grade is typically a statement of worth: A is excellent, B is good, C is average, and so on. So, scoring a test is measurement, but assigning a grade is evaluation.

Evaluation comes in many forms. One obvious form is the use of letter grades. However, we sometimes run courses on a pass/fail basis. If your mean test score is 75% or higher, you pass. If it is below 75% you fail. At other times teachers may prepare a narrative statement concerning how well the student is performing and use terms like "making satisfactory progress," or "still needs more work in this area." These are also forms of evaluation.

Definitions

Assessment is a very general term that describes the many techniques that we use to measure and judge student behavior and performance.

Measurement is the process of assigning meaningful numbers (or labels) to persons or objects based on the degree to which they possess some characteristic.

Evaluation involves the use of measurement to make decisions about or to determine the worth of a person or object.

There are several measurement issues that it would be helpful to address in this chapter. First, we will differentiate between formal and informal assessment. Then we will look at the various ways in which we use assessment in the classroom. Finally, we will differentiate between maximum and typical performance measures.

FORMAL vs. INFORMAL ASSESSMENT

Generally, when you think about assessment in the classroom, I would guess that tests and quizzes are probably the first things that come to mind. Tests (both standardized and teacher-made), quizzes, and other similar devices are referred to as *formal* assessment devices. With formal assessment you, the teacher, are able to complete the assessment in a relatively standardized manner and are able to control many aspects of the process. With formal assessment all students are given the same questions to answer, typically have exactly the same amount of time to respond, and complete the device in a relatively consistent fashion. Formal assessment is important in the classroom; it is not, however, the only type of assessment that we use.

A much more common type of assessment is what we refer to as *informal* assessment. It involves the many observations that we make about students and the many questions that we ask students throughout the day. It may involve having a child read aloud and attempting to note and remember which reading processes are still giving this child problems. It could involve having children go to the board to work out math problems and looking for which students are performing well and which students appear confused. It can involve the many questions we ask students throughout the day and noting how each student responded to those questions. Many times we are using informal assessment to determine if our students are displaying competency with the skills which we have been teaching. Are we ready to move on to the next topic? Clearly, we do a great deal of informal assessment in the classroom. In fact, I have heard educators estimate that perhaps as much as 90% of the assessment that we do in the classroom is informal assessment, especially in the early grades.

CLASSROOM ASSESSMENT

Preliminary or Placement Assessment

We use assessment in the classroom to serve a variety of purposes. Sometimes we use *preliminary* assessment. Sometimes, at the beginning of the school year we are ready to move ahead with our curriculum, but are uncertain as to how well the students are prepared. Let's say that a 5th-grade teacher has learned from previous experiences that she cannot always begin the school year with the prescribed 5th-grade math curriculum. She has found that sometimes her students came from classes in the previous year where the 4th-grade teacher did not complete the prescribed materials or that some students forgot a great deal over the summer. Therefore, within the first two weeks of the school year, our 5th-grade teacher gives her students a test of the prerequisite math skills, the skills that they need to be prepared to master the new skills that she plans to teach them. If her students perform well on this preliminary test then she knows that she can safely move ahead with the prescribed lessons. However, the test is likely to reveal that there are a few skills that she will need to teach first, or at least review, before she can begin the prescribed curriculum.

A variation of this is the *placement* assessment. Placement assessments are very commonly used in colleges where incoming freshmen are often given placement assessments in a variety of subjects. For example, many colleges require students to take one or more math courses and frequently require proficiency with basic algebra. Therefore, they give mathematics placement tests to their incoming freshmen. If students' scores are high enough, they are frequently exempt from taking the freshman algebra class and can take a higher-level mathematics class. These placement tests are especially important in fields like science and engineering where students are typically expected to take a calculus sequence. Are students ready to take Calculus I or do they need to take the Pre-Calculus course first? Placement tests are also used in other areas such as English and foreign languages, where sequenced courses are often available. Placement tests are also used in elementary schools, middle schools, and high schools. Sometimes they are used at the end of the school year to help determine next year's placements.

Definition

Preliminary or **placement** assessments are assessments performed within the first two weeks of the semester that are designed to measure students' prerequisite skills.

Diagnostic Assessment

A second type of assessment is the *diagnostic* assessment. We use diagnostic assessments when we recognize that students are not performing well, but are uncertain of the exact problem. For example, Ms. Kindya, a 2nd-grade teacher, notices that Tim is struggling with reading, yet she is unable to identify clearly which skills are giving Tim the greatest problems. Luckily, Ms. Kindya is familiar with and skilled at using a variety of reading diagnostic tests. She chooses the test that appears most appropriate, administers it, and is able to identify the specific skills that are giving Tim trouble. She now can provide Tim with the specific help that he needs. We are likely to use diagnostic tests most frequently in the areas of elementary reading and mathematics. However, we also have diagnostic tests in a number of other fields.

Although some diagnostic tests are designed for classroom teachers to administer, others require considerable training. In those cases, you may need to call on a specialist, like a reading specialist, a speech-language pathologist, or a school psychologist, to administer such tests.

Definition

A **diagnostic** assessment is any type of assessment used to identify an individual student's learning decrements.

Formative Assessment

The third type of assessment that we use is known as *formative* assessment. Formative assessment is any type of assessment device that we use while an instructional unit is in progress. It is used primarily to give the teacher feedback on how the unit is progressing. Let's say that you are a 5th-grade teacher and are teaching a six-week unit on adding and subtracting fractions. You might recall that in order to add or subtract fractions, you must first find a common denominator. For example, to complete this problem 1/2 + 1/4 you must convert the 1/2 to 2/4. Therefore, the first two to three weeks of the unit are dedicated to teaching the students this prerequisite skill, finding the common denominator. Before you move into the part of the unit where the students actually learn to add and subtract fractions, you want to make certain that they are doing very well with this prerequisite skill. Therefore, at the end of week two you give your students a pop quiz that requires them to complete 10 common denominator problems. Over the weekend you score the quizzes. In this case, you are using the quizzes primarily as a feedback device for yourself. You want to find out if the class is showing sufficient proficiency with this skill to move to the next step? If they performed well enough on the quiz, then you can move to the next step early next week. If, however, they are still not performing well with the task, it means that you need to spend several more days working with common denominators before you can move on. Formative assessments are designed to give you, the teacher, feedback. Therefore, most psychometricians argue that formative assessments should not be used to give students grades. Others, however, claim that unless assessments are graded students may not take assignments seriously.

Besides pop quizzes, there are many other techniques that can be used for formative assessment. If we continue with the math instruction example, some other techniques that could be used would include having the students perform seat work while you walk around the room looking at their work. You could also have them come up to the board and solve problems there. You could play a game where they have to find the common denominator. There are a large variety of techniques that you can use to gauge students' progress. Many formative assessment techniques involve informal assessment.

Definition

Formative assessment is any type of assessment device that we use while an instructional unit is in progress and is used primarily to give the teacher feedback on how the unit is progressing.

Summative Assessment

The fourth type of assessment is *summative* assessment. Summative assessments are performed at the end of chapters or units to determine the students' level of competency with the material and to assign grades. Many of you may have assumed that summative assessment was the only type of assessment used in school. It is the type that we probably recall most often and with which we have had the most experience. Not all teachers use preliminary or diagnostic assessment. Even when our teachers were using formative assessment we, as students, were not always aware of why they were doing it. However, we were typically keenly aware of summative assessment.

Definition

Summative assessments are performed at the end of chapters or units to determine the students' level of competency with the material and to assign grades.

All four types of assessment play important roles in the classroom. However, in many classrooms formative assessment is the most common type of assessment, as it should be. Elementary school teachers tend to use formative assessment often, especially with the youngest students. As students move into the higher grades, however, there is a tendency to use it less often, which may be a mistake. Many college instructors hardly use it at all. At times, after working with my class on a difficult topic, I find myself asking them this question, "Is that clear to everyone?" As they nod their heads, I feel satisfied that they understand the material and move on to the next topic. I often think that I've completed an effective formative assessment. In the last few years, I have come to recognize that when I do that, I am using a very ineffective approach. How many times, in your experiences, has someone asked you a question like that after teaching you something fairly complex? You may have responded in the affirmative, only to discover later, when you tried to apply the new learning, that you really did not understand. It is much more effective to actually have students try out the new learning to assess if they can use it correctly.

MAXIMUM vs. TYPICAL PERFORMANCE MEASURES

When we measure some skills and abilities we want to assess how well our students can perform. We want to assess them at their best. However, when measuring other types of traits, we are more interested in students' typical behaviors. Classroom tests designed to measure a student's level of competence with some skill should be geared toward measuring the student's maximum performance. We want to assess them doing as well as they can do. However, personality tests or career interest inventories and similar measures work best when they measure a student's typical behavior or interest.

There are differences in how we design the most effective maximum performance measures compared to how we design effective typical performance measures. If this text were designed to be used in a course on psychological measurement, we would spell out those differences. However, since this text is designed primarily for classroom teachers, that is not really necessary. The tests and other measures that classroom teachers use will, almost exclusively, be maximum performance measures. That will be our focus in this book.

Definitions

Maximum performance measures are used when we want to assess how well our students can perform.

Typical performance measures are designed to assess a student's most common, or typical, behavior.

USES OF MEASUREMENT

Since this chapter is introducing the section in this part on measurement, this might be the appropriate place to let you know what to expect in the remaining chapters. Chapter 2, Frames of Reference, will introduce you to the various ways in which we can interpret test scores. Chapter 3, Developing Objectives, covers the various approaches that educators have used to establish goals and objects. We use objectives to help you decide what you will teach and what you will test. Chapter 4, Reliability, will introduce you to the concept of reliability, consistency within tests. What is reliability? How do we measure it? How can we develop tests that are reliable? Chapter 5, Validity, deals with the issue of whether a test is actually measuring what we think it should be measuring.

Chapters 6 through 11 deal with building effective classroom tests. Chapter 6 discusses short-answer and completion items. Chapter 7 deals with essay items. Chapter 8 deals with multiple-choice items. Chapter 9 deals with true–false items and other alternative choice variations. Finally, Chapter 10 discusses how to assemble the individual items into a test. Chapter 11 is a follow-up on the earlier chapters on classroom testing. It deals with how to analyze your tests to assess if they are performing as you had hoped they would.

Chapters 12, 13, and 14 deal with alternative forms of assessment. Chapter 12 delves into informal assessment, which was briefly introduced in this chapter. Chapter 13 deals with performance assessments, which we use when we need to rate a student's actual performance as a judge would do when rating an athletic competition such as gymnastics. Chapter 14 discusses how to use portfolios effectively.

The last three chapters deal with other important topics. Chapter 15 deals with teaching students to be effective test takers. Chapter 16 describes the various types of standardized test you are likely to encounter in schools. Finally, Chapter 17 deals with many alternative ways to report test scores and why many of these are, at times, better than reporting raw scores.

SUMMARY

In this chapter we examined the various roles that measurement plays in the classroom. We also differentiated among three commonly used terms: assessment, measurement, and evaluation. We differentiated between formal assessment and informal assessment. Classroom tests, quizzes, and similar devices are frequently referred to as formal assessment, whereas teacher questions, observations, and many other techniques are often referred to as informal assessment. We differentiated among four ways that we use assessment. We use preliminary or placement assessment to identify students' prerequisite skills. We use diagnostic assessment when students are experiencing learning problems. We use formative assessment to judge how well our instruction is proceeding. We use summative assessment to judge our students' competence with the material that they have been taught. Finally, we differentiated between maximum and typical performance measures. In the classroom we typically use maximum performance measures because we want to assess how well our students can perform the new skills that they have learned. In other settings, especially when examining concepts like personality, we use typical performance measures which will identify the individual's typical, or usual, behavior.

EXERCISES

Identify the type of assessment being used.

Formal or Informal?
1. A 5th-grade standardized reading test.
2. Verbally asking a group of 3rd graders comprehension questions about a story they just read.
3. A pop quiz in a 7th-grade math class.
4. Observing the students as they work in small groups.
5. Using a checklist while a 4th-grade class gives oral presentations.

Preliminary or Placement?
1. A 3rd-grade teacher asks her students multiplication facts before starting a unit on multiplication to assess if they have any experience in working with that operation.
2. In a 2nd-grade classroom, the students take a reading test to find their reading level so the teacher can accurately place the children in ability groups.
3. College freshmen at the University of Oklahoma are required to take a writing test. The test is evaluated by a group of professors and the students are then put in the appropriate composition classes.

Diagnostic, Formative, or Summative?
1. At the end of a unit on weather, Mrs. Jones gives her 4th-grade class a test to assess how much they have learned. This test is 20% of their semester grade.
2. Mr. Gregory is a 1st-grade teacher. He is introducing his children to bar graphs. He is not sure that all of the students understand the material. He has the students work in groups to create a simple bar graph. He observes the children as they work and collects the graphs to check for accuracy.
3. Joey is struggling in all subject areas. He is a bright child and therefore his teacher, Mrs. Buckwalter, believes it is a reading disability. She gives him multiple reading evaluations to assess where the problem lies.
4. Each week Mr. Grables' students receive 15 spelling words. At the end of the week they take a test on the words and their scores are recorded.
5. Mrs. Bacco is teaching a lesson on social studies. She plays a review game a week before the unit test. She observes the students as they answer questions and makes notes on the concepts they will need to review before the test.

SPOTLIGHT ON THE CLASSROOM

Miss Anderson is a first-year 3rd-grade teacher at Wilkins Primary. She is beginning to teach a unit on measurement. Measurement is not directly taught to students in her school before 3rd grade but she knows that some students have picked a few things up on their own. Before she begins, Miss Anderson gives the students a worksheet to complete. The worksheet questions their basic knowledge of measurement. She uses the information to plan her lessons based upon what the students already know.

Miss Anderson decided to introduce a new unit of measurement—such as temperature, length, and weight—one at a time every few days. At the end of each lesson she gives the students a small quiz before moving on to another unit of measurement.

At the end of the unit, Miss Anderson plays a measurement review game with her students. She asks the students questions and they work in groups to come up with answers. She uses this game the day before their unit test. Miss Anderson's unit test covers all of the units of measurement she has taught. She records the students' scores on the test. The test is worth 100 points. A score of 90–100 is an A, 80–89 is a B, 70–79 is a C, 60–69 is a D, and below 60 is considered failing. The scores are 10% of the students' final math grade for the semester.

1. What forms of assessment were used in the above scenario?
2. What changes, if any, would you make if you were teaching this unit?

STUDY TIPS

Setting Effective Academic Goals

Researchers such as Locke and Latham (2002) have demonstrated that one of the most effective ways for students to stay motivated and complete tasks is for them to set effective academic goals for themselves. Perhaps, at the beginning of a term, you may have said to yourself that you wanted to achieve a 3.25 grade point average (GPA) this term or that you wanted a earn an A or a B in a particular course. If you have ever said something like that you were on your way to developing a goal. However, unless you developed a plan concerning how you would achieve that end, you only took the first step in setting an effective academic goal. I have even heard it suggested that such a statement is merely a wish and not a real goal. Goals require planning.

Whenever you begin any activity, it often helps if you spend some time setting goals. Goals can serve many different purposes, but here you will be using goals to help you maintain your motivation. Locke and Latham (2002) point out that when it comes to effective academic goals, the best goals have three characteristics. They are specific, proximal, and moderately challenging.

At the beginning of this term you may have said to yourself, "I would like to do better this term than I did last term." Although there is nothing intrinsically wrong with that goal, it is quite general. If you earned a 2.25 GPA last term, would you be satisfied with a 2.26 GPA this term? After all, you would have met your goal! However, it is more likely that you really wanted to see a more substantial improvement in your academic record. Therefore, it would be even more effective if you set a more specific goal. Perhaps you could set a goal to earn a 2.75 GPA this term. You could then determine what grade you would need to earn in each course to achieve that goal. A specific goal is more motivating than a very general goal.

You set some goals for the distant future (distal goals). Perhaps you decided that you want to be a millionaire by the time that you are 50. There is nothing wrong with that goal. However, if you are currently 22, then you could easily decide that you don't even have to start worrying about that goal until you are closer to 40 and, therefore, it is not an effective motivator for you at the present time. You can set other goals for the near future (proximal goals). For example, you may decide to finish reading this chapter by 7:00 p.m. this evening. When you set proximal goals (also sometimes known as "near" goals) they can be very motivating. Although there are other tasks that you could perform this evening, it is very likely that you will complete this task first.

A third characteristic of effective motivational goals is that they are moderately difficult or moderately challenging. If you set goals that are not challenging, even when you achieve them, you get no sense of satisfaction. On the other hand, if you set goals that are extremely difficult or challenging, or goals that are simply unrealistic, then you may fail to achieve those goals and will feel like a failure. The best goals are moderately challenging, but achievable. With those types of goal, you have a good chance of being successful and will have a sense of accomplishment once the goals are completed.

Having goals that are specific, proximal, and moderately challenging is a good start. However, it is not enough! You then need to plan the steps that you will need to take to achieve those goals. For example, if you set a goal to earn an A in this course, you will need to develop a plan to make that goal achievable. How much study and preparation time do you need to allocate to this course on a weekly basis in order to achieve that A? Do you have all the prerequisite skills required to earn an A or will you need to arrange for some assistance? Should you arrange for a tutor, join a study group, or do some additional preparation for this course?

With effective goal setting and planning you are much more likely to stay motivated and are also much more likely to reach your academic goals.[1]

NOTE

1.   This material has been adapted from Van Blerkom (2009).

2

FRAMES OF REFERENCE
Interpreting Test Scores

INTRODUCTION

In the previous chapter we differentiated between measurement and evaluation. When you score a test, a quiz, or a similar device you are using measurement. You come up with a number or score that represents how well the student performed on that particular instrument. The next step is to find some way to interpret that score. Did the student perform well, about average, or poorly on that instrument? Was the student's score acceptable? This chapter will describe several frames of reference that you can use to interpret test scores. We will be discussing four frames of reference: ability-referenced, growth-referenced, norm-referenced, and criterion-referenced interpretations. We will discuss the advantages and disadvantages of each approach.

FOUR FRAMES OF REFERENCE

Whenever you give your students a test, quiz, or any other form of assessment instrument, you need to score that instrument. Many of our scoring systems result in a number. Let's say that one of your students, Charisa, received 76 points on her last math test. Of course, Charisa may want to know what that 76 stands for. Does it mean that she did well, about average, or poorly? There are a number of ways of looking at her test performance. Did she do about as well as we could expect based on her ability with mathematics? Does this test score reflect a growth in her skills since she took her last math test? How did she do in comparison to the other members of her 8th-grade math class? Does the test tell you specifically what new skills Charisa has mastered? Each of these questions reflects a different frame of reference, a different way to interpret her test score.

Ability-Referenced Interpretations

One approach used to interpret a test score is known as ability-referenced interpretations. With *ability-referenced* interpretations the student's test performance is compared to what we believe the student should be able to do based on his or her ability. We expect a high-ability student to perform better on a test than would an average-ability student. Although this approach sounds quite reasonable, it is highly problematic.

> *Definition*
> With **ability-referenced** interpretations the student's test performance is compared to what we believe the student should be able to do based on his or her ability.

The primary difficulty with this approach is that it is very difficult to obtain a good estimate of a student's ability. Many of us grew up believing that I.Q. tests and other ability tests are able to somehow magically tap into our innate abilities and measure them accurately. It is likely that in the early years when we first started using ability tests, even psychologists felt that those tests could very accurately tap into and measure our abilities. However, now that we have had over 100 years of experience with ability testing, we have come to recognize that scores on ability tests need to be interpreted cautiously. There are many variables that affect our performance on an ability test besides our abilities. For example, such tests generally assume that a student has had the same developmental experiences as other students. Your performance on a math ability test assumes that you have had typical educational experiences with mathematics. We know, however, that not all elementary teachers emphasize mathematics instruction equally. Especially in the very early grades, some elementary teachers spend less than 30 minutes a day teaching arithmetic whereas they spend nearly 3 hours teaching language arts skills (Stevenson, Stigler, & Lee, 1986). If you are dealing with a 3rd-grade student who has had relatively little arithmetic instruction in the past, that student's score on a mathematics ability test will surely underestimate that student's ability with math. Other variables that tend to depress ability test scores include poverty, disabilities, and language. Students who grow up in poverty or who have even a minor disability (or an illness) frequently score too low on ability tests. Students who grew up speaking another language, and only later learned English, tend to do less well than they should on a test given in English. For these students, their test scores frequently do not accurately reflect their abilities. The advice we frequently give today is to interpret ability tests cautiously. With many students, ability tests will underestimate a student's ability.

There is an additional problem with the ability-referenced approach. Many skills we teach in school are dependent on several different abilities. There is no single ability involved in performing well in social studies. We do not really know all of the skills involved with effective learning in social studies and many other areas. Therefore, we have no real way to estimate how a student should perform in most subject-matter areas.

Because of these and other problems we do not typically recommend that teachers use ability-referenced test interpretations.

Growth-Referenced Interpretations

A second approach to interpreting test scores is a comparison approach. With *growth-referenced* interpretations we compare the student's test score after instruction with the score from a similar test given prior to instruction. Essentially, it is a before-and-after approach, sometimes known as a pre-test/post-test approach. The first test is given prior to instruction and demonstrates what the student is able to do before being taught the new material. The second test is given after the instruction. A comparison of the two tests should, therefore, provide a clear picture of what the student has learned. Sometimes we even use the same test on each occasion and then compute a difference score. We assume that a student who scored 37 points more on the second test than the first test learned more than the student whose score only improved by 22 points. This appears very logical and sounds like a reasonable way to interpret test scores.

> **Definition**
> With **growth-referenced** interpretations we compare the student's test score after instruction with the score of a similar test given prior to instruction.

In reality, however, there are several serious problems with this approach. The first problem arises because difference scores are notoriously unreliable. All test scores contain what we refer to as measurement error (for more details on measurement error see Chapter 4). Essentially, measurement error involves all those factors that cause a student to perform on a test in a way other than that in which he or she should have performed. All tests contain some measurement error. When we compute a difference score, as we frequently do with growth-referenced interpretations, we are computing the difference between two test scores. Unfortunately, the difference scores inherit the measurement error from each test and contain even more error than either original test did individually. This additive property of the measurement error is even more severe if the two tests are positively correlated with one another, as they often are since they are each measuring the same skill. As a result, difference scores frequently have so much measurement error that we can have little confidence in what they are telling us.

The second problem with growth-reference interpretations has to do with the nature of the learning curve. The learning curve tends to be non-linear; it is S-shaped. If the learning curve were linear—a straight line—each day, as we were taught a new skill, our performance would improve by the same amount from one day to the next. However, that almost never happens. With just about any type of learning that we have studied over the years we get something quite different. When we start learning a new skill the daily increments in our performance are quite small. It frequently takes us a while to really catch on. After a while we see the learning curve accelerate and we seem to make tremendous strides in our performance from day to day. Finally, the learning curve

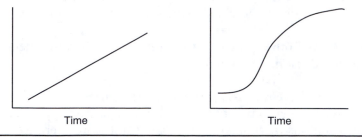

Figure 2.1 A comparison of a linear learning curve with an actual S-shaped learning curve.

begins to flatten out and we reach what has sometimes been referred to as a plateau. We seem to improve very little from day to day.

If we try to compare two students using a growth-referenced interpretation, the learning curve can make interpretations problematic. Let's say that we have two 10th-grade science students. George showed a 37-point improvement from his pre-test to his post-test. His friend, Rick, only displayed a 22-point improvement. We might be inclined to suggest from these test scores that George has learned more than Rick. However, if George and Rick started out at different points on the learning curve, such an interpretation is problematic. Let's say that George was at the acceleration point in the learning curve. We should expect to see substantial growth in his performance. On the other hand, if Rick were approaching the plateau part of the learning curve we should expect much less growth. Each student may have grown exactly as much as we should have expected him to grow. In reality, we never really know where a student is on the learning curve.

Since these two problems interfere with our ability to make good, sound interpretations of growth scores, we tend to use them very little.

Norm-Referenced Interpretations

A third way to interpret test scores is to compare a student's score on a test to the scores of other students who took the same test. With *norm-referenced* interpretations we compare the score a student received on a test with the scores from some norm group. In the case of a nationally standardized test, that norm group typically consists of a random selection of hundreds of other similar students who took the same test. For a classroom test, that norm group typically is the other students in the class. With norm-referenced interpretations, essentially the students who took the test are ranked from those with the highest scores to those with the lowest scores. The student's letter grade (or other evaluative index) is based on where he or she is on the list. If a student is near the top of the list, he or she gets an "A" or some other positive evaluation. If the student is near the bottom of the list, he or she receives a lower grade or some other lower evaluation (e.g. unsatisfactory).

Definition

With **norm-referenced** interpretations we compare the score that a student received on a test with the scores from some norm group.

Educators in the United States have used norm-referenced interpretations for several centuries. Until the 1970s, the vast majority of classroom tests and other instruments were evaluated with a norm-referenced interpretation. Although criterion-referenced interpretations have gained popularity and are used much more often today than they were in the past (for reasons that we will discuss later), norm-referenced interpretations are still considered the most appropriate approach in many situations.

Unfortunately, teachers who use norm-referenced interpretations frequently fail to take an important step. When making a norm-referenced interpretation, it is extremely important to fully describe the norm group. Since it is based on a comparison, it is essential that you describe the group with whom the student is being compared. For example, if Tanya received an "A" for language arts that was based on a norm-referenced interpretation, it could mean that Tanya is one of the very best students in language arts in a class where most of the students are quite competent. However, it could also mean that Tanya was one of the best students in a class where the vast majority of the students actually displayed low levels of competence. Descriptions of the norm group would be especially important if the norm group is small. Larger norm groups are more likely to mimic the population. Unfortunately, norm-reference interpretations frequently do not tell us very much about what skills the student has mastered.

Criterion-Referenced Interpretations

The fourth way to interpret test scores is to compare each student's score to some pre-set standard or criterion. This is known as *criterion-referenced* interpretation. This could be a set of criteria such as those we used when I was in high school. To earn an "A" you needed to score between 93% and 100%; any score from 85% to 92% resulted in a "B"; scores between 78% and 84% resulted in a "C", and scores from 70% to 77% resulted in a "D." The standard could also be set up on a pass/fail basis. On the college campus where I work, our algebra review course is set up so that a final average of 75% is required to pass the course. Any student who scores below 75% fails the course. The Praxis test is used as a teacher certification test in many states. In Pennsylvania, college students must earn a score of 173 on the mathematics test to pass.[1] There are many different ways in which we can set up criteria.

Definition

With **criterion-referenced** interpretations a student's test score is compared to some pre-set standard or criterion.

Criterion-referenced interpretations started to become more popular in the United States in the 1970s, largely in response to the criticisms leveled at norm-referenced interpretations. The major advantage of criterion-referenced interpretations is that they provide a clearer view about which skills the student has mastered. Since many educators found that this was highly desired, they were persuaded to use criterion-referenced interpretations more frequently. We will compare norm-referenced and criterion-referenced interpretations later in this chapter.

Many teachers believe that they are using criterion-referenced interpretations, but fail to meet an essential requirement to do so. When using such interpretations, it is vital to spell out clearly the domain that the test is covering. For example, if you were to give your 6th-grade class a test based on the last chapter that you covered on the economy of the Great Lake states, you would first have to develop a list of objectives from that chapter. The list would have to include all of the topics, terms, and concepts that were covered in that chapter.

When a student earns 75% on a criterion-referenced test, it is expected to mean more than that the student correctly answered 75% of the questions. The test score should let the teacher know that the student has successfully mastered 75% of the objectives from the material that was covered by the test. In order to do that teachers have to develop a list of objectives and then make sure that each objective is being measured by, at least, one item on the test. It is only when we have completed each of these steps that we are using a criterion-referenced interpretation.

A Comparison of Norm-Referenced and Criterion-Referenced Interpretations

Today, teachers use both norm-referenced and criterion-referenced interpretations most of the time. Each approach has advantages and disadvantages. Let's look at some of them.

Advantages of the Norm-Referenced Approach

One advantage of the norm-referenced approach is that students are not disadvantaged (at least, in terms of their grades) by poor instruction. If everyone in the class gets a low score because the material was not taught well, students can still earn reasonable grades. In a similar manner, with the norm-referenced approach students are not really disadvantaged if the test was more difficult than the teacher had intended, because the grades are typically adjusted by the mean score for the class. So, if a student earned a low test score but did well in comparison to the other students who took the test, then that low test score could still translate to a relatively high letter grade.

Disadvantages of the Norm-Referenced Approach

One disadvantage of the norm-referenced approach is that it is based on competition. No matter how well a student does with material in class, only the brightest, most talented, and hardest-working students will earn good grades. If you are not one of the brightest students in the class and you work hard and master the material well, you still can be destined to earn a mediocre grade. For example, I have known some high school students who elected not to take a higher-level class, such as advanced mathematics, in their senior year simply because they knew that they would be in a class of highly talented students. They feared that, in comparison to their highly talented classmates, they would not fare well and would earn a lower grade. Instead, they chose to enroll in a less challenging class where they would be one of the brightest students and would earn a high grade.

A second disadvantage of the norm-referenced approach is that a test grade frequently does not tell others what the student has learned. If one of your high school students earned an A in Algebra I the previous year in a class where grades were based on norm-referenced interpretations, you really do not know how well the student mastered algebra. The only thing that you really know is that the student was one of the better students in the class. If the class consisted of only students with poor math skills, or if the level of instruction was poor, then the student may have earned an A, but still learned very little algebra.

Advantages of the Criterion-Referenced Approach

One of the clear advantages of the criterion-referenced approach is that when it is applied appropriately a student's grade is highly reflective of the student's level of mastery of the material. In some instances the approach tells us exactly which skills the student has mastered. In fact, it is this characteristic of criterion-referenced interpretations that has made them so popular over the past 40 years.

Another advantage is that students typically have a better sense of how they are performing in the class. Students are better able to monitor their own progress in a class. Am I doing well or do I need to get some extra help with this material?

A third advantage is that this approach is non-competitive. One student's grade on the test is not dependent on how other students performed. Over the past 30 years, American education has moved away from using primarily competitive classroom practices to using more and more cooperative practices. Criterion-referenced approaches fit in nicely with cooperative classroom practices.

Disadvantages of the Criterion-Referenced Approach

One disadvantage of this approach is that students may be penalized for poor instruction. If the teacher does an inadequate job of teaching the material, then the students are likely to perform poorly on the test, which will result in low grades. In a similar manner, if a teacher designs a test that is more difficult than was intended, the students may perform poorly on the test and earn low grades. From the students' perspective, these are disadvantages. However, some educators might argue that these issues make teachers more accountable to provide good instruction and appropriate tests.

Another disadvantage of the criterion-referenced approach is that it cannot be applied to all testing situations. If a teacher is giving a test on a single chapter with a relatively small number of objectives, then it is possible to design a criterion-referenced test. However, on a unit exam that covers four chapters, it is likely that there are too many objectives to develop a test that covers all of them in the time the teacher has scheduled for the test. In that case the only reasonable approach is to develop a test that samples the objectives and apply a norm-referenced interpretation.

There is still another disadvantage of the criterion-reference approach. Many teachers believe that they are using a criterion-referenced approach simply because they have developed some pre-set standards. However, they fail to develop a list of objectives and they fail to design their test to make certain that they have appropriately covered those objectives on the test. Without that second step these teachers frequently have developed tests that are difficult to interpret appropriately.

CHOOSING A FRAME OF REFERENCE FOR ASSESSMENT

As I mentioned earlier, psychometricians do not typically recommend that teachers use either ability-referenced or growth-referenced interpretations because of the problems involved with each. However, there are times when working individually with students when each of these approaches might be useful. Sometimes students incorrectly believe that they are incapable of performing a task because they think that they lack the necessary skills. Using the pep-talk approach, "I know that you can do it," is rarely all that helpful by itself. However, teachers can also work with students to help them develop the necessary skills that they need to be successful with that task. Once the students are more successful, they frequently change their opinion about their abilities and show continued improvement.

The growth-referenced approach can also sometimes work when teachers meet individually with students. Showing Susie two samples of her work, one from earlier in the year as well as a recent sample, can sometimes demonstrate to Susie how much her skills have improved. Both approaches can be used to help motivate students who are convinced that they are not progressing.

Clearly, the norm-referenced and the criterion-referenced approaches are most often recommended by psychometricians. Criterion-referenced interpretations are the most appropriate in situations where there is a clear set of information or objectives that the test is expected to cover. With many types of assessment that is the case. When you give a preliminary or placement assessment you have a certain set of skills that you wish to measure. Are your students already proficient with these skills, or are there skills that you will need to review? Clearly, criterion-referenced interpretations will work best here since they are skill specific. When you use diagnostic assessments, you are asking, "With which particular skills is this student having difficulty?" Again, this calls for criterion-referenced interpretations. When you use a formative assessment, you are asking, "Are my students displaying enough progress with these particular skills that we are ready to move ahead to the next topic?" Once again, this calls for the criterion-referenced approach: You want to identify particular skills. So, as you can see, criterion-referenced interpretations are the most appropriate with preliminary assessments, with diagnostic assessments, and with formative assessments. In each case, you are attempting to identify student proficiency with particular skills, something that the criterion-referenced approach does well.

That leaves us with summative assessments, such as chapter, unit, and final exams. Here we have more choices. If the test is covering a single chapter with relatively few objectives, you can often design a test that will measure each objective. In that case, using a criterion-referenced approach seems most appropriate. However, if the test is covering a relatively large number of objectives, then it is frequently impossible to develop test items to measure each objective and expect students to be able to complete the test in the time available. In that case, you have to choose a sample of objectives from each chapter and develop test items for them. Once you have done that, it is no longer reasonable to apply a criterion-referenced interpretation. You must then use a norm-referenced approach, which works quite well in such situations.

There are other situations where we also might want to use a norm-referenced approach. Let's say, for example, that Laurel Green High School found that it could offer an advanced math class to 20 students and knew in advance that there would be more students wanting the class than could be accommodated. One reasonable approach to choosing which students to accept would be to use their scores from a recent math achievement test. In that case they would choose the 20 students with the highest math achievement scores, believing that they are the students who will benefit the most from the class. Any time you would need to rank students, a norm-referenced approach is appropriate.

CHARACTERISTICS OF NORM-REFERENCED AND CRITERION-REFERENCED TESTS

Should we design norm-referenced and criterion-referenced tests in the same way? The typical answer to that question is, "no." There are many tests that are well designed and that could be appropriately interpreted with either approach. However, if you have one of these two approaches in mind when designing a test, there are several characteristics that you should keep in mind.

Item Difficulty

When using a norm-referenced approach you essentially want to rank students from those who know the material well to those who are less prepared. You want to differentiate among the students, to separate the best prepared and the least prepared students. In order to do this reliably you need to see a large standard deviation, a large spread among the scores. If all of the scores bunch up together, then it is difficult to tell whether differences in student performance on the test are because of differences in the various students' skills or as a result of simple measurement error. However, if the scores are spread out further, you can feel more confident that the test is truly differentiating among the students based on their skills.

The amount of spread that you obtain in the test scores is often related to the average item difficulty. For example, if all of the items are relatively easy, most students will do quite well on the test and there will be little spread in the scores. The same will happen if the items are all very difficult. Most students will do poorly on the test and, again, there will be little spread in the scores. You can frequently obtain the greatest spread of scores (the largest standard deviation) when most of the items are of moderate difficulty. Therefore, when using a norm-referenced interpretation, you frequently want the majority of your test items to be moderately difficult. In that case you will obtain a large standard deviation and will be able to differentiate reliably among students. However, if you plan to use a criterion-referenced interpretation, then you do not need to differentiate among the students and item difficulty is somewhat less important.

Number of Items on the Test

In general it is a good idea to use as many test items as time allows. Longer tests (those with more items) are almost always more reliable (as discussed in Chapter 4) and have greater content-related evidence of validity (as discussed in Chapter 5). That being said, we can now look at differences between norm-referenced and criterion-referenced tests.

The number of items needed on a criterion-referenced test is dependent primarily on the number of objectives covered by the test. You need at least one item for each objective. With a fairly large number of objectives, the test will typically have only one item for each objective. Time restrictions will simply not allow for more items. However, having only one item per objective is not the ideal situation as greater reliability and accuracy can be achieved by having more than one item for each objective. If the number of objectives is relatively small, then it might be feasible to have two or more items for each objective.

With norm-referenced interpretations there are no hard and fast rules for the number of items required. In this case you will be sampling objectives to cover on the test and will not need to measure each and every objective. You could, theoretically get away with fewer items. However, it is best to include as many items as time will allow.

Although many test items can be used appropriately on either norm-referenced or criterion-referenced tests, there are times when teachers might want to design items specifically based on the type of interpretation they plan to use. When planning on the number of items to use on the test they also may want to keep in mind how the test scores will be interpreted.

SUMMARY

In this chapter we identified four approaches that teachers use to interpret test scores. With ability-referenced interpretations, teachers compare a student's test score with some estimate of how well the student should be able to perform. With growth-referenced interpretations, the teacher compares a student's performance on a particular skill with how that student performed earlier in the year. With norm-referenced interpretations, the teacher compares the student's performance on a test with the performance of some norm group, often the other members of the class. Finally, with criterion-referenced interpretations, the teacher compares the student's performance on a test with some pre-set standards. Since there are problems associated with the first two approaches, they are not used very often. Norm-referenced and criterion-referenced interpretations, however, are more commonly used for classroom tests.

There are differences between norm-referenced and criterion-referenced interpretations so that in certain situations one has advantages over the other. The two approaches also have different requirements in terms of item difficulty and the number of items required.

EXERCISES

1. Name the type of reference being used in the following examples. Choose from *ability, growth, norm,* or *criterion.*

   a. Amanda's parents were concerned about how well she was doing in biology class. When they contacted her teacher, Mr. Hower, he reported that she had done better than 70% of her classmates on their last exam.
   b. Mrs. Pierce gave her students a pre-test before she began teaching a unit on fractions. Two weeks later, at the end of the unit, she had given her students the same test to see what they had learned.
   c. Mr. Lin has a rule in his classroom that every student must score at least 90% on a spelling test or the student has to retake it the next day.
   d. Because her students learned about the planets last year, Miss Gates expects them to do very well on the solar system exam.
   e. In order to be placed in the Advanced Reading Program at North Hills Elementary, a student must score 170 or better out of 200 on the placement test.
   f. Carlos scored 552 on the math section of the SATs. With that score, he is placed in the 58th percentile, which means that he did better than 58% of all the students who took the SATs at that time.

2. Write your own example of each type of interpretation for a grade or content area that you plan to teach:

   a. Ability-referenced
   b. Growth-referenced
   c. Norm-referenced
   d. Criterion-referenced

SPOTLIGHT ON THE CLASSROOM

Mrs. Neville is a reading teacher at Blue Ridge elementary school. At the beginning of the year, she gave her students a test that contained questions focused on various topics that she planned to cover during the year. She wanted to see what her students already knew. She also wanted to compare the reading levels of each of her students for grouping purposes.

In January, Mrs. Neville feels that she needs to start to focus on preparing her students for the upcoming California Achievement Tests (CATs), which are given in this particular school district. She gives her students the same test that they had taken at the beginning of the year to see what they have learned in the past four months. She looks at each student's test individually and compares the two scores to see how much each has learned and the areas that she needs to review.

Mrs. Neville designed a test that is similar to the CATs. Two weeks before the students were scheduled to take the CATs, she gave her test to the students. She calculated the scores in much the same way that the CATs are scored. She identified areas where students scored poorly and emphasized instruction in those particular areas. When it was time for Mrs. Neville's 3rd-graders to take the CATs, she felt they were fully prepared. After all of this practice, she expects her students to do very well.

Name and discuss the frames of reference that Mrs. Neville used in her classroom.

STUDY TIPS

Time Management

For many college students good time-management skills are as essential for success as they are for most adults in demanding jobs. If you know how to manage your time well, you can typically avoid many last-minute rush jobs or that sinking feeling in your gut when you go in to take a test knowing that you did not allow yourself enough time for adequate preparation. However, good time management requires planning. Because many college students work either part time or full time and have family responsibilities, it can be especially challenging to develop a good time-management plan.

Dianna Van Blerkom (2009) recommends that a good first step in developing a time-management plan is to develop a *fixed commitment calendar*. This is an hour-by-hour calendar for one week which begins when you first wake in the morning and continues until you go to sleep. You begin by filling in all of your fixed commitments, which include meal times, classes, work time, exercise time, and so on. Include any activity that you perform at the same time daily or weekly. If you are uncertain about how you use your time, you could keep a *time log* for a week. In this you record all of your activities on an hour-by-hour basis for a full week. That should help you further complete your fixed commitment calendar which, once completed, should tell you how much time you have left for study and leisure.

A second step is to determine how much study time you actually need. For many college courses students typically need two to three hours out of class for every hour that they are in class. A highly demanding class may require more time, whereas a less demanding class could require somewhat less. During weeks when you are preparing for exams or working on class projects, you will often require extra time. In most instances college students can find enough time for study and preparation. Frequently, when students run out of time, it is because they are spending too much time on leisure activities. Students sometimes discover from their time logs that they are spending an inordinate amount of time playing video (or computer) games, watching TV, or just hanging out with their friends. Of course, some college students work full time and still try to carry a full load in school. That type of commitment requires a great deal of discipline.

Another important time-management skill involves keeping up with your work. That means keeping up with reading your textbook and other out-of-class assignments. If you tend to procrastinate, put off tasks that need to be completed, you have to work especially hard to stay on schedule. One of the best ways to avoid procrastination is to begin a task as soon as it is assigned. It also helps to have daily and weekly *to-do lists*, which are especially effective when you have multiple tasks to complete in a limited time. For complex tasks it often helps to break them down into a number of smaller steps, each of which is less daunting. Once you have filled out your to-do list, it can frequently reduce that debilitating anxiety many people experience when faced with seemingly insurmountable tasks. That anxiety can actually cause people to delay starting the tasks, but, once the to-do list is written, that anxiety is often greatly reduced and you can immediately complete some of the tasks.

There are many time-management skills that can make your college experience more positive. You can get your work done, obtain better grades, and still have adequate time for leisure. If you are looking for additional time-management help, you could consult your college learning center.[2]

NOTES

1. In 2005 Pennsylvania introduced a more flexible pass/fail criterion. A college student can pass several of the basic skills tests (reading, writing, and mathematics) with a somewhat lower individual test score as long as her or his composite score from the three tests meets a certain criterion.
2. This material has been adapted from Van Blerkom (2009).

3

DEVELOPING OBJECTIVES

INTRODUCTION

This chapter will describe how to go about deciding what you will teach and, therefore, what you will test. From the many topics that you could cover in any class, how do you go about picking and choosing which of those you will teach? We will discuss standards as they have been developed by national professional organizations and by the various states. We will discuss how these standards are turned into goals and objectives. Finally, we will describe several approaches to developing and using instructional objectives, especially as they apply to classroom testing.

I should point out that the terms that I am using in this chapter are not always used in a standardized way. Different authors sometimes use these terms in different ways. For example, Impara (2007) points out that what we used to refer to as goals and objectives are now frequently called content standards. However, many in the field of educational measurement tend to view these terms in more specific ways. For example, most content standards are set at the federal, state, or school district level, whereas goals and objectives are often set by individual teachers for use in their classrooms.

STANDARDS

How do we go about deciding what to teach and test? Typically teachers are guided by curriculum standards that are set up by the school system in which they teach. For example, a 6th-grade teacher at Smitherton Middle School, which is a part of the Norwalk School District, is likely to be guided by a booklet entitled *The Norwalk Sixth-Grade Curriculum*. The booklet describes what 6th-grade teachers are expected to cover in the areas of language arts, social studies, mathematics, science, and health. The booklet does not tell the teacher what he or she is expected to teach on a daily basis, but does list the topics that are to be covered by the end of the school year.

The next question to ask is, "How was the Norwalk School District able to determine what is most appropriate for the 6th-grade curriculum?" The school district most likely referred to a set of curriculum standards developed by the state. At one time most school districts were on their own when it came to deciding what was appropriate to teach at each grade level. However, over the past few years most states have embarked on massive projects to develop statewide curriculum guidelines, in part, to improve education within their states. If you go to your state's Department of Education website, you should be able to download the current content standards.

How do the states decide what is appropriate curriculum at each grade level? Sometimes they have been able to rely on the numerous professional organizations for assistance. For example, in 2000, the National Council of Teachers of Mathematics (NCTM, 2000) published a set of principles and standards for school mathematics for kindergarten through 12th-grade education. This was a project on which the NCTM had worked for a number of years and has been widely disseminated. Many states have since incorporated the NCTM standards into their own curriculum standards. Other examples of standards include the American Association for the Advancement of Science *Benchmarks for Science Literacy* (AAAS, 1993) and curriculum standards from the National Council for the Social Studies (NCSS, 1994).

Since 2002, the federal No Child Left Behind (NCLB) law (discussed again in Chapter 16) has had a significant impact on standards in many states. The law has forced many states to develop or adopt new tests that are expected to measure and demonstrate adequate yearly progress for students. In addition, many educators believe that the potential ramifications of not demonstrating adequate yearly progress are so negative that many schools now teach to the tests. That is, in many ways, the content of the tests is driving the curriculum and standards have sometimes taken on a less important role.

As a result of these many efforts, classroom teachers today frequently have a set of standards or guidelines that help them choose what they will be teaching throughout the year for each subject area. However, they still have to develop their own daily lesson plans. How do they accomplish that?

PLANNING BY USING GOALS AND OBJECTIVES

One of the most important and time-consuming planning activities for teachers is the development of daily lesson plans. Over the years there have been many approaches to lesson planning, some which have been more effective than others. Lesson planning efforts made major strides when, in the late 1940s and 1950s, the United States military moved to revamp its training programs (Miller, 1962). Until that time the military had been unhappy with its training. In combat situations many soldiers did not actually know how to complete some of the tasks for which they had been supposedly trained. With the help of training consultants, the military adopted a program that incorporated the use of goals and objectives in their training. The new approach was so effective that word spread quickly and educators throughout the country were soon planning by using goals and objectives.

Goals vs. Objectives

What are the differences between goals and objectives? *Goals* are general statements of anticipated outcomes. They are general statements of what the teacher hopes to accomplish. For example, Sally Rodgers might have set a goal today to teach her 5th-grade students about the Great Lakes. Goals are general! Objectives, on the other hand, are much more specific. *Objectives* are specific statements, in behavioral terms, of what the students will be able to do once the lesson is completed. Ms. Rodgers' goal to teach her students about the Great Lakes might involve several objectives. For example, the students might be expected to be able to name all five Great Lakes, name the states that border the Great Lakes, and describe three reasons why the Great Lakes are so important.

Definitions

Goals are general statements of anticipated outcomes.

Objectives are specific statements, in behavioral terms, of what the students will be able to do once the lesson is completed.

Task Analysis

Objectives are based on what is known as a task analysis. The idea behind a task analysis is for you, the teacher, to start by clearly describing the end product—exactly what it is you want the students to be able to do once instruction is completed. Once you have described the end product, it is often fairly easy to be able to establish the prerequisite skills and behaviors that are required. The result is that, once a teacher has developed a clear objective, it is often much easier to determine the steps that are required for the students to successfully perform the desired behavior.

An example might prove helpful. Let's say that Jack Worrell, a driver's education teacher, wants to teach his students to change a flat tire. His objective could be, "At the end of the lesson each student will be able to successfully and safely change a tire in less than 20 minutes following the prescribed steps." Since Mr. Worrell is very familiar with tire changes, he can easily list the steps that he needs to teach the students. These steps could include the following:

1. Park the car on a level surface.
2. Put the car in gear and set the parking brake.
3. Chock two appropriate tires.
4. Get the new tire and assemble the jack.
5. Place the jack in the appropriate spot and raise car partly.
6. Remove the wheel cover and loosen the lug nuts.
7. Raise car until the tire is off the ground.
8. Remove the lug nuts, storing them in a safe place.
9. Remove the old tire and replace it with the new tire.
10. Replace lug nuts, and tighten.
11. Lower the jack part of the way.
12. Finish tightening lug nuts and replace the wheel cover.
13. Finish lowering the jack.
14. Remove chocks.
15. Store the jack, chocks, and the old tire.

After Mr. Worrell completes his task analysis it is fairly easy for him to plan how to teach each step. In this case Mr. Worrell also recognizes that there are too many steps in changing a tire to complete the task in one 48-minute class period with the 20 students in his class. Therefore, he decides that the lesson is likely to take three class periods. The first class will be devoted to preparing the car, assembling the jack, and raising the car. The other two class periods will be devoted to removing the flat tire and replacing it with the spare. In each case he could develop appropriate objectives for each step in changing the tire.

By the late 1950s and early 1960s, planning by the use of goals and objectives was becoming popular. However, at the time there were still no clear guidelines on how to do this. Fortunately, a number of educators tackled the task to make planning with goals and objectives more systematic.

BENJAMIN BLOOM'S TAXONOMY OF OBJECTIVES

In the 1950s, planning by the use of goals and objectives was not only popular in K to 12 education, it was also becoming popular with college professors. Benjamin Bloom, a well-known developmental psychologist from the University of Chicago, began a project in 1949 to develop a classification system for educational objectives. Eventually, the project included input from more than 30 other college faculties from throughout the country and resulted in what became known as Bloom's *Taxonomy of Educational Objectives* (Bloom, 1956).

Bloom and his colleagues eventually recognized that educators are generally interested in developing objectives in three separate domains. The most obvious area is the *cognitive* domain. We, as educators, are frequently concerned with what our students know, remember, comprehend, and so on. A second area was labeled the *affective* domain, which deals with interest and feelings. Frequently, we would like to get our students interested in and even excited about the subject matter. We not only want them to be able to do math, but want them to enjoy math. The third area applies only to those who teach some specific subject material. It involves physical skills and is referred to as the *psychomotor* domain. Those who would be especially interested in the psychomotor domain would include those who teach physical education, driver's education, typing, industrial arts, and similar subjects. However, elementary teachers are also concerned with psychomotor skills when they are teaching handwriting and similar skills. Science teachers incorporate psychomotor objectives when they need to teach laboratory classes. In fact, many teachers do teach some psychomotor skills. Bloom and his colleagues set as a goal to eventually develop a classification system—a taxonomy—of objectives for each domain.

For the majority of classroom teachers, the taxonomic domain that is most directly applicable to classroom testing is Bloom's *Taxonomy of Cognitive Objectives*. Bloom (1956) and his colleagues included six levels of cognitive objectives.

Knowledge
Comprehension
Application
Analysis
Synthesis
Evaluation

Figure 3.1 Bloom's *Taxonomy of Cognitive Objectives.*

An important aspect of Bloom's taxonomy is that each successive level is more sophisticated than the previous level. Comprehension is cognitively more sophisticated than knowledge. In addition, when we move to the higher-level objectives, such as analysis, they often involve using the lower-level skills. For example, when we are expected to perform an analysis, in the process we are often using knowledge, comprehension, and application.

Knowledge Level Objectives

Knowledge level objectives involve knowing, memorizing, and remembering. We are expected to be able to recite our alphabet in kindergarten, our math facts in 3rd grade, or the atomic weight of the most common elements in high school chemistry. Knowledge level objectives involve being able to remember a list or a definition, but do not necessarily imply comprehension. For example, when my grandson was in the 1st grade, he could recite the pledge of allegiance, although I am certain that he did not understand what it meant. He had achieved a knowledge level objective. Of course, knowledge level objectives are not very sophisticated. However, to become proficient in almost any field, there is a great deal of material that we simply need to memorize.

Comprehension Level Objectives

The second level is *comprehension*. The students can not only recite a definition given in class, they can rephrase it—put it into their own words. They can, in some way, demonstrate that they understand what it means. On the exams that I give in my classes I frequently phrase a concept in a somewhat unique way. At times, a student may complain that my wording on the exam was different from what was in the book or even different from what I used in class. My reply is that with that question I am testing for understanding (comprehension), rather than just memorization (knowledge).

Application Level Objectives

The third level is *application*. After you teach your students how to follow a procedure or algorithm, they need to be able to use that procedure on their own. For example, if you teach your 4th-grade students how to solve an area problem by multiplying length times width, you have taught them an algorithm—a step-by-step approach to solve a problem. If you then ask them to solve a new problem at their seats, you are asking them to apply the algorithm to a new situation or problem.

Analysis Level Objectives

The fourth level is *analysis*. Analysis involves breaking something down into its component parts. After teaching her 7th-grade class about subjects and predicates, Amanda Cho gives her students 10 sentences and asks them to identify the subject and the predicate in each sentence. After Marion Skeill teaches her 10th-grade students about all of the various parts of speech, she gives them 10 sentences and asks that they label each word or phrase. Both of these examples demonstrate how students may be expected to use analysis.

Synthesis Level Objectives

The fifth level is *synthesis*, which involves putting together various pieces of information in a unique or creative way to form a new whole. Most creative efforts are considered to be synthesis. Godfrey Jackson has assigned his 12th-grade Problems of Democracy class a term paper. They are expected to pick a topic, find a number of sources, and develop a paper that will integrate the material from the various sources.

Evaluation Level Objectives

The sixth level is *evaluation.* With evaluation a student is expected to choose a product or idea and determine whether it is either good or bad. The student is expected to choose criteria and then rate the product or idea on each criterion. Obviously, this is a very complex cognitive process. We simply cannot expect our elementary school students to use evaluation very often. However, as our students grow cognitively, we do expect them to use evaluation in more situations.

Bloom's taxonomy is widely used in education. I have heard educators from a variety of different fields refer to it. Obviously it is widely used in planning instruction. In addition, it is very useful when planning and developing a classroom assessment, something that will be covered later in this chapter.

In recent years there have been some attempts to update Bloom's six levels of cognitive objectives (Anderson & Krathwohl, 2001). However, since most educators are so comfortable with the original list, the new versions have not yet received a great deal of attention.

ROBERT MAGER'S INSTRUCTIONAL OBJECTIVES

Although by the 1960s the use of instructional objectives was widespread, there were still no guidelines on how to write good objectives. Teachers used many different styles in preparing objectives, some which worked better than others. Robert Mager (1962) published a book that provided us with a systematic approach to preparing objectives. Mager's technique was strongly influenced by the behavioral approach to teaching that was very popular at the time. Although education has shifted from a behavioral orientation to a cognitive orientation, many teachers still find Mager's approach very useful.

Mager argued that every well-prepared objective required three components. The first component is an *action verb.* We want our students to do something to demonstrate to us that they have met an objective. Therefore, requiring the students to *remember* the names of all five Great Lakes is inadequate. How can we tell that they remember the names? Instead, we want the students to do something to demonstrate to us that they remember the names of all five lakes. We could ask them to *recite* or *list* the names of all five Great Lakes. Avoid verbs such as *remember, know,* or *learn* and instead insist on action verbs, those that will actually require students to do something that can be observed so we know that they have achieved the objective.

The second component of an instructional objective is a *criterion.* As teachers, we need to decide how well the students have to do in order to have mastered the objective. In some cases we will only be satisfied with a perfect response. In the case of the names of the Great Lakes, I expect that the students must be able to name all five lakes. Four out of five would not suffice. However, if you were teaching your 8th-grade class a new math algorithm, you would want to make certain that they were proficient with it before you sent them off with homework. Therefore, you give them 10 practice problems in which they would apply the algorithm. How well would they have to perform before you could feel confident that they had mastered the new algorithm? Typically, in math and similar fields we are satisfied if students complete between 70% and 80% of the items correctly, to allow for computational errors which can occur even if the algorithm is applied correctly.

The third component of an instructional objective is *conditions of assessment*. These conditions spell out when and how we will ask the students to demonstrate that they have mastered the objective. Will we do this assessment at the end of the class? Will students be expected to rely on memory or will they be able to use their books or notes? Will they be allowed to use a calculator? Will there be a time limit?

Mager argued that frequently all three components could be written into a single sentence. Let's go back to the example of Sally Rodgers teaching her students about the Great Lakes. One of her first interests might be that the students will be able to name all five Great Lakes. Therefore, she might write the following objective: "At the end of the lesson the students will be able to list the names of all five Great Lakes from memory within 30 seconds." This objective contains all three of Mager's components. It has an action verb ("list"), a criterion ("the names of all five"), and conditions of assessment ("At the end of the lesson," "from memory," and "within 30 seconds.")

Mager's approach became very popular both because of its simplicity and its effectiveness. His book was written as a programmed instruction text. Students could work on it at their own pace, completing exercises, and within a few days could be proficient at preparing good instructional objectives. Many colleges made the book required reading for all for their education majors. There are likely to be hundreds of thousands of teachers working today who were schooled in this approach.

NORMAN GRONLUND'S INSTRUCTIONAL OBJECTIVES

Not all educators have been enamored with Mager's approach. Norman Gronlund (2004) argues that Mager's approach is more appropriate for lower-level objectives, such as knowledge and comprehension, but falls short with higher-level learning involving problem solving, thinking skills, and performance skills. He differentiates between training and higher-level learning. With training we do frequently want to focus on very specific learning outcomes. However, with higher-level learning we need to frequently focus on broader outcomes.

Gronlund recommends that instructional objectives be written at two levels. First, the teacher should develop a general instructional objective. For example, in Mr. Jackson's Problems of Democracy class he could set as a general objective that the students will "comprehend the characteristics of the three branches of government." That then needs to be followed with a series of specific learning outcomes. Examples could include the following:

- Define in own words the role of each branch.
- Describe examples of checks and balances.
- List departments within the executive branch.

Gronlund (2004) describes how to write objectives in both the cognitive and affective domains, and what he calls performance skills. He also stresses how to translate content standards (which were described earlier in this chapter) into objectives. Finally, he stresses how to use instructional objectives to design assessment, a topic we will cover later in this chapter.

ROBERT GAGNÉ'S LEARNING OUTCOMES

Robert Gagné had an important influence on instructional design. He attempted to integrate instructional design with modern theories of learning (Gagné, 1984, 1985; Gagné, Briggs, & Wager, 1992). He also developed a system of writing instructional objectives that integrates Bloom's three domains with Mager's components (an action verb, a criterion, and conditions of assessment). However, he developed his own organizational system consistent with his theory of learning. In addition, for each performance category he recommends a specific action verb, or what he called a capability verb. See Figure 3.2.

Gagné's Categories

Let's take a few minutes and describe Gagné's system. Gagné broke his objectives down into five categories. The first category is *verbal information* which includes naming, listing, recognizing, and recalling. It is the same as Bloom's knowledge level. The next category, *intellectual skills*, encompasses all five of Bloom's higher-level cognitive skills, but is organized differently. *Discrimination* involves being able to determine whether two objects are the same or different. *Concrete concepts* involve identifying objects as belonging to a certain concrete concept (for example, showing a student a variety of geometric shapes and asking the student to identify which are squares). *Defined concepts* involve concepts at an abstract level. In this case the student should be able to recognize that swimming, reading, and watching a DVD are all leisure activities. Rules have to do with relationships between concepts. For example, in high school biology, students learn about mammals and later in the year they learn about important organs, such as the brain and the heart. The recognition that all mammals have four-chamber hearts involves use of a rule. *Higher-order rules* involve the complex relationships that are frequently required for problem solving. For example, many years ago I was attempting to put a new starter into my car. However, I could not loosen one bolt on the old starter to remove it even though I had a long-handled socket wrench. I simply could not get enough leverage. Several weeks earlier, when trying to remove a large rock from my garden, I placed a six-foot pipe over the pry bar I was using and moved the rock easily.

Learning Outcomes	Capability Verbs
Verbal Information	states
Intellectual Skills	
Discriminates	discriminates
Concrete Concepts	identifies
Defined Concepts	classifies
Rules	demonstrates
Higher-Order Rules	generates
Cognitive Strategies	adopts
Motor Skills	executes
Attitudes	chooses

Figure 3.2 Gagné's classification of learning outcomes.

After several hours of not being able to free the frozen bolt on the car, I spotted the pipe in the corner of the garage. I realized that I could slide it over the wrench extending its handle. I soon had the bolt free. This was an application of a higher-order rule.

Additional Categories

There are three additional categories of learning outcomes. *Cognitive strategies* involve the recognition that a certain strategy will work best for a certain type of learning situation. For example, a student recognizes that if she wants to remember the taxonomic structure used in biology (kingdom, phylum, class, order, family, genus, and species) it would help to use some mnemonic device (memory strategy). *Motor skills* cover all learning involving movement and matches Bloom's psychomotor domain. Finally, *attitudes* involve Bloom's affective domain.

Components of Objectives

Gagné recommended that each objective contain five components. Those components include the situation, a capability verb, an object, an action, and any special conditions. The *situation* is the context in which the student must use the skill. The *capability verbs* are those listed in Figure 3.2. The *object* is the substance of the objective. The *action* is how the capability will be demonstrated. *Special conditions* are optional, but may include a criterion. Here is an example of an objective that I wrote. "While reviewing the correlation exercise in class, the students will be able to demonstrate the use of the computational formula for correlation by completing the problem which was started on the chalk board, without the aid of their notes." The first phrase, "while reviewing the correlation exercise in class," is the situation. The capability verb is "demonstrates." The object is the "computational formula for correlation." The action is "completing the problem." Finally, the special condition is "without the aid of their notes."

USING OBJECTIVES

As you can see, there are a variety of ways to write objectives, even more than I have described. Although each approach may appear cumbersome at first, with practice teachers can become quite adept at using any of them. Now the next logical question is, "How can teachers use objectives?"

The most common use of objectives is in lesson planning, which is why objectives were established in the first place. Although there are numerous approaches to preparing lesson plans, many of those approaches use some types of objective. A second use of objectives is in the development of tests. Let's spend some time discussing how we use objectives to design tests.

When you plan a unit and begin to teach it, you need to start to plan how you are going to assess the students at the end of the unit to measure how well the students have learned or mastered the material. Let's say that you decide that a classroom test is the most appropriate assessment device. How do you decide what to cover on the test? One of the most logical approaches to choosing what to cover on the test is to use the objectives that you prepared. If the unit is sufficiently brief, perhaps with a maximum of 25 to 50 objectives, you might decide to use a criterion-referenced test. In that case you simply develop an appropriate test item to measure each objective. Even if you have too many objectives to use a criterion-referenced test, you can still use the objectives to design the test. If you have 75 objectives in the unit, though, a test covering each would simply be too long for the time you have available to administer the test. In that case you may decide to use 40 items. You could randomly select 40 objectives to cover on the test and develop an appropriate test item for each selected objective. You would then interpret the test scores from a norm-referenced perspective.

A second common approach is to use a *Table of Specifications*. To do that you will first have to separate the objectives by topic. So, although you may have had 30 objectives for a chapter, you might be able to sort them into five topic categories. Then you will need to use a taxonomy; in this case I used Bloom's *Taxonomy of Cognitive Objectives*. You look at each topic, and the objectives it contains, and try to match the cognitive category to the objective. For example, if an objective was taught at the comprehension level, then it should be tested at the comprehension level. In Figure 3.3, I have included a Table of Specifications for a chapter that contained five general topics.

The taxonomy is listed down the left column and the topics are shown across the top. The numbers in each box represent the number of items for each topic at each level. Most of the teaching was at the knowledge, comprehension, and application levels, with one objective from each topic at the analysis level. Therefore, you would develop a Table of Specifications to match that. The test would have 35 items measuring the various objectives at the appropriate cognitive level. Since this chapter did not involve either synthesis or evaluation, there are no questions at those levels. Many standardized tests are built from a Table of Specifications or a similar blueprint.

These two approaches represent only two of a number of ways to design a test or other assessment device. The major advantage of these two approaches is that they assure that the test will accurately reflect the material that was taught. This is especially important when we consider content-related evidence of validity, which we will cover in Chapter 5.

SUMMARY

In this chapter we discussed standards, goals, and objectives. Curriculum standards are frequently set by each state from guidelines that have been developed by national professional teacher organizations. Those standards are passed on to the classroom teacher through the local school system. Using those standards as guides, teachers then plan their daily lessons, frequently using goals and objectives. Planning which incorporates the use of goals and objectives has been popular in the United States since the early 1950s. Bloom, Mager, Gronlund, and Gagné each developed their own system to help teachers prepare objectives.

Objectives can be used when planning a classroom assessment. One approach

Objective	Topic 1	Topic 2	Topic 3	Topic 4	Topic 5
Knowledge	2	3	2	2	3
Comprehension	2	2	2	2	2
Application	2	1	2	1	2
Analysis	1	1	1	1	1
Synthesis	0	0	0	0	0
Evaluation	0	0	0	0	0

Figure 3.3 A Table of Specifications.

involves matching each objective to a test item. Another method involves using a Table of Specifications.

EXERCISES

1. Using Bloom's *Taxonomy of Cognitive Objectives*, to which level do each of the following statements apply?

   a. The students will memorize multiplication facts through drill and practice.
   b. The students will follow the scientific method to perform a science experiment.
   c. The students will read a short story and identify the literary elements.
   d. The students will be asked to write a summary of the book they read that week.
   e. The students will decide if a math word problem is good or bad by noting if there is too much, too little, or the right amount of information.
   f. The students will do interviews, collect photographs, and gather information to complete a biography on a family member.

2. Using Gagné's methods, for each of the following, match the learning outcome with the capability verb.

1. Verbal information	A. Adopts
2. Motor skills	B. Identifies
3. Rules	C. States
4. Concrete concepts	D. Chooses
5. Attitudes	E. Discriminates
6. Discrimination	F. Generates
7. Higher order rules	G. Classifies
8. Cognitive strategies	H. Executes
9. Defined concepts	I. Demonstrates

3. For each of the following objectives, label the three components according to Robert Mager's approach.

   a. At the end of the unit the students will be able to complete 100 multiplication facts without the use of a calculator within three minutes.
   b. At the end of the week the students will be able to accurately spell their 20 spelling words from memory.
   c. The students will be able to list all 50 states and capitals without any references within 15 minutes.

4. Write an objective for learning the names of the Great Lakes using each of the different approaches.

   a. Bloom / Mager
   b. Gagné
   c. Gronlund

SPOTLIGHT ON THE CLASSROOM

Ms. D'Austeri is a 3rd-grade teacher at Nicely Elementary in Greenville, Georgia. She is currently teaching a unit on *Charlotte's Web*, by E.B. White. Her unit consists of many lessons and activities in many subject areas.

In reading class, the children are writing short summaries after they read each chapter. They have a quiz each Friday on vocabulary from the book. The children are creating a script for the dialog from the book and will perform a readers' theater presentation.

In math class, the students will be working with multiplication word problems that relate to the story. Not only will the students be solving word problems, they will be evaluating them and creating their own. Students will be asked to determine whether given word problems have too much or too little information. They will write their own word problems and share them with the class.

During art, the students will create a diorama of a scene from the book. The students will write a paragraph about the scene and their creation.

In science class, the students are learning about farm animals. They will have a test on the chapter about farm animals at the end of the unit.

Discuss the objectives used is this unit. Identify each objective using Bloom's Taxonomy.

4

RELIABILITY

INTRODUCTION

One of the most important concepts in measurement is reliability. Reliability indicates whether a measurement device can measure the same characteristic over and over again and get the same results. In this chapter we will be looking at a theoretical model of reliability, at different methods that we use to estimate it, and what we can do in our classrooms to improve the reliability of our tests.

WHAT IS RELIABILITY?

Whenever we use a measurement device, whether it is a yardstick to measure a piece of lumber to be used to construct a table or a classroom test to measure students' knowledge of history, we need to use instruments that will give us consistent results. We should be able to measure the same object or characteristic over and over again and always get the same result. If my bathroom scale says that I weigh 165 pounds, I should be able to step off it and back on many times and it should read 165 pounds each time. The best single-word synonym for reliability is "consistency."

Before we discuss educational measures such as classroom tests, it might be better to start with a more concrete example from carpentry. I consider myself an amateur carpenter. Over the years I have built a number of objects for our house. I once built a work table for our garage. Although I thought that I was measuring each piece carefully, one table leg ended up being about one half of an inch shorter than the other three legs. I had to glue a small piece of wood to the short leg so that the table would not wobble because, obviously, I had not been consistent when measuring each piece of wood.

When carpenters measure wood to make cuts, they can use a variety of devices including 6-inch rulers, 1-foot rulers, yard sticks, and steel tape measures. If I wanted to cut a piece of wood exactly 43⅝ inches long, and I needed to do this a number of times, which instrument would give me the most consistent results? If you picked the steel tape measure, you were correct. With practice a carpenter can be very consistent with a tape measure. It is a reliable measurement device. Clearly, good carpenters want to use measurement tools that will give the most consistent results, tools that are reliable. So it is with classroom teachers.

Theoretical Model of Reliability

Classical measurement theory uses the concept of variance to explain reliability. You might recall from Part II Chapter 21 that the variance is the square of the standard deviation. Like the standard deviation, the variance is a measure of the spread of the scores. However, for practical purposes, it is typically easier to understand the standard deviation because it exists in the original scale that was used for the test scores. The variance, on the other hand, uses a squared scale and is more difficult to interpret. For example, let's say that on a 40-item test my students from two sections of the same class had scores from a low of 22 to a high of 37 (see Figure 4.1). It turns out that the mean is 29.5 and the standard deviation is 3.16. The standard deviation (3.16) is a number that is easy to understand: It means that most (about ⅔) of the students scored within about three points of the mean (49 out of 64 students had scores between 26 and 33). However, the variance would be 10.00 (3.16²), not directly related to the original 40-point test scale, and therefore, more difficult to understand. In most situations we cannot directly interpret the variance. The variance of 10 is not related to the original 40-point test scale. However, variances do have one advantage over standard deviations; variances are additive, whereas standard deviations are not. This addition property of the variance makes it more useful to psychometricians, as the next section will demonstrate.

In the 40-item test, the students had different scores. They did not all earn the same

Score	F		
40	0		
39	0		
38	0		
37	1		
36	2		
35	2		
34	3	Mean	$\mu_x = 29.5$
33	4		
32	6	Standard Deviation	$\sigma_x = 3.16$
31	7		
30	8	Variance	$\sigma_x^2 = 10.0$
29	8		
28	7		
27	5		
26	4		
25	3		
24	2		
23	1		
22	1		
21	0		
N = 64			

Figure 4.1 Exam scores for 64 students on a 40-item exam.

score, so we can say that there was variation from student to student. The students' scores are called the *observed scores*, since these are the scores we observe. Psychometricians point out that the variation in observed scores comes from two sources: the variation we would expect in the students' true scores, and measurement error (Linn & Gronlund, 1995). The relationship can be described with the following formula (Equation 4.1).

$$Variance_{Observed} = Variance_{True} + Variance_{Error} \qquad (4.1)$$

This reads, "The observed-score variance is the sum of the true-score variance and the error variance."

Definition
Observed scores—scores that the students actually obtain.

True Scores

True scores are the scores that students should obtain if everything worked perfectly. As you will see in the next section, test scores are not typically true measures of students' knowledge. For example, if some omnipotent being were able to look down at my test, then take a look at Tad and determine the score Tad should obtain based on his knowledge and level of preparation, that would be Tad's true score. Actually, psycho-metricians consider the true score to be the mean of all the scores you would get if you could take the same test an infinite number of times. We do expect variation in true scores because of variations among students. Not all students will be equally know-ledgeable and/or equally prepared for any particular exam.

Definition
True scores—scores that students should get if the measurement device worked perfectly.

Error Variance

Error variance, also known as *measurement error*, is anything that causes a student's observed score to differ from his or her true score. Theoretically, measurement error is positive as often as it is negative; it can either help us (getting a better score than we should) or hurt us (getting a lower score than we should). We usually think about measurement error as coming from three sources: subject effects, test effects, and environmental effects.

Definition
Error variance, also known as **measurement error**, is anything that causes a student's observed score to differ from his or her true score.

Subject effects are all the sources of error related to the individual—any personal issues that cause the person to score other than what he or she should have scored. These can include, among others, illness, medication, excessive sleepiness, anxiety, personal pre-occupations, and luck. It is difficult to concentrate and perform well when you are ill. You tend to be preoccupied with those rumblings in your abdomen, the throbbing in your head, the throat that is on fire, and so on. Some students take medications to fight those temporary illnesses or to help control chronic health conditions, but are often unaware of the side effects of the medications. Any medication that is labeled, "may make you drowsy," also has the tendency to reduce your cognitive abilities. Lack of sleep also has a negative impact on one's cognitive skills. In elementary school and middle school you will see a few students who are sleep deprived. However, in high school sleep deprivation is almost epidemic. Many adolescents work after school, participate in activities and clubs, stay up late watching TV, text messaging, or are on the internet and, therefore, come to school with an inadequate amount of sleep. Anxiety also has a negative effect on test performance. High levels of anxiety reduce the ability to concentrate and to recall material from long-term memory. In addition, personal problems can have a negative impact on test performance. It is hard to concentrate on a test if you have just finished having a confrontation with your friends or family members and are still thinking about it during the test. Finally, luck (guessing on a test) can affect your performance—sometimes to your benefit, other times to your detriment.

Before we leave subject effects, we need to consider students with disabilities. Various types of disability can interfere with students' performance on a test. Even though many such students know the material and are well prepared, they frequently have difficulty with tests because of their disability. These also represent subject effects that contribute to measurement error. We, as teachers, are expected to accommodate these students and adjust our tests to meet their needs. As you become more used to having students who happen to have disabilities in your classrooms, you will become better at making appropriate accommodations.

> **Definition**
>
> **Subject effects** are all the sources of error related to the individual; any personal issues that cause the person to score other than what he or she should score.

Test effects are the various issues related to the test itself that cause the student to score other than he or she should. These can include, among others, ambiguous directions, confusing items, printing or clerical errors, non-objective scoring, and inadequate or inappropriate coverage of the material. Have you ever taken a test where you did not understand the directions and did not do what the teacher intended? Fortunately, in my experience, this does not happen often, but when it does, it can be disastrous to those students who did not understand the directions. Confusing items show up on many tests. Sometimes teachers will use a word or phrase in a test item that to many of the students has a meaning different from that intended by the teacher. It is important to carefully proofread your tests to eliminate clerical errors or test items that are difficult to read. Today's computers, with spell-checkers and laser printers, have reduced many, but not all, of these problems. We will discuss objectivity in scoring later when we talk about the different types of item format. However, you might imagine that when an instructor is not consistent in scoring essay questions, measurement error increases. Finally, a reliable test needs to evenly and fairly include all of the material that the test was intended to cover. Tests that do not do that affect students in an unpredictable fashion, and reduce reliability. We will discuss this more in the next chapter under the heading, Content-Related Evidence of Validity.

> **Definition**
>
> **Test effects** are the various issues related to the test itself that cause the student to score other than he or she should.

Environmental effects are all the sources of error as a result of the testing environment. These can include, among others, poor lighting, environmental noises, uncomfortable room temperatures, crowding, and too little time. Perhaps you have attempted to take a test in a room where the lighting was inadequate or glaring. This can make the test difficult to read and can interfere with your concentration. Have you ever tried to take a test in a room next to the one where the band is practicing or when the maintenance crew is cutting the lawn? Many students require a quiet place in order to concentrate and perform well on a test. In addition, it is difficult to concentrate when a classroom is either too warm or too cold. Fortunately, more and more schools are built today with better heating, air conditioning, and ventilation systems. Having desks or work spaces too close together can be an additional problem. Students need to be able to spread out their work to perform well without having to worry that others are copying from their tests. Finally, time can affect test scores. The vast majority of classroom tests should be power tests. A power test is one that students should be able to complete in the time available. However, frequently teachers make tests that are too long for the time allowed, often unintentionally, but sometimes because they mistakenly believe that classroom tests should be timed (a fairly common misconception among teachers). When students are unable to complete the test, that adds to error variance.[1]

> **Definition**
>
> **Environmental effects** are all the sources of error as a result of the testing environment.

We should once again consider students who happen to have disabilities before we leave test effects and environmental effects. There are test and environmental issues that may not have an impact on students without disabilities, but do affect students with disabilities. Students with visual impairments and attention deficit hyperactivity disorder (ADHD) can be affected by print that is too small or too light, answer sheets that are difficult to use, noise, distractions, and many other common factors. All of these problems can increase error variance for students with disabilities.

COMPUTING RELIABILITY

Theoretically, reliability is the proportion of observed-score variance that can be accounted for by the true-score variance. Remember, observed-score variance is the sum of the variance as a result of differences in true scores plus error variance (Equation 4.2).

$$Variance_{Observed} = Variance_{True} + Variance_{Error} \qquad (4.2)$$

Reliability is expressed as Equation 4.3.

$$Reliability = \frac{Variance_{True}}{Variance_{Observed}} \qquad (4.3)$$

Let us use the example that we started with earlier in this chapter to show you how this works. In that example, my classroom test had an observed score variance of 10.00. Let's say that we can break that observed-score variance into a true-score variance of 7 and an error variance of 3 (Equation 4.4).

$$10 = 7 + 3 \qquad (4.4)$$

If we plug these numbers into the reliability formula we get (Equation 4.5)

$$Reliability = \frac{7}{10} = .70 \qquad (4.5)$$

Here the reliability is .70. The way we interpret this is that 70% of the variation in observed scores is the result of variation in true scores. This is variation we would expect because of differences among students in their knowledge and level of preparation. Of course, this also means that the remaining 30% of the variation in observed scores is the result of measurement error.

Reliabilities can extend from 0 (zero), where all of the variation in observed scores is the result of measurement error, to a high of 1.00 (where there is no measurement error and all the variation in observed scores comes directly from variation in true scores). At times, physical scientists can develop instruments in their laboratories that show reliabilities of .99 or higher. However, when measuring human psychological characteristics, such as our knowledge or ability, it is extremely difficult to develop tests with reliabilities above .90. In fact, the typical classroom test has a reliability of about .70. It is often difficult to develop classroom tests with very high reliabilities. Therefore, measurement error is, at times, a serious problem in classroom testing.

RELIABILITY AND VALIDITY

Although we will not cover validity until the next chapter, validity essentially has to do with whether or not a test is actually measuring what it is intended to measure. Validity primarily has to do with true scores. Reliability affects validity. The formal way of describing this relationship is that reliability is a necessary, but not sufficient condition, for validity. In other words, a test can be valid only if it is reliable. Essentially, reliability sets an upper limit for validity. If a test is not reliable, there is a great deal of measurement error. Observed test scores do not relate well to the characteristic being measured and validity will be low. If a test is highly reliable (little measurement error), then the test has the potential to be highly valid since most of the variability in test scores is coming from variability in true scores. If the test has only moderate reliability (moderate measurement error), then the test can, at best, be only moderately valid; measurement error is playing a larger role in the variability of test scores. Finally, if a test has low reliability (a great deal of measurement error), then the test can only display low validity. Reliability is necessary for validity.

However, reliability does not assure validity. You can develop a test that is quite reliable, but with little validity because you are essentially measuring the wrong characteristic. Here is an amusing anecdote that I use in my classes. Let's say that it is spring finals week and I inadvisably take a shower during a thunderstorm before leaving for work. Lightning strikes near my house, then travels through the plumbing system, and gives me quite a jolt in the shower. I survive physically but, as a result of the electrical shock to my brain, my judgment is severely impaired. Later that day I go into my class where I am expected to give the final examination. However, I report to my students that I had a very enlightening experience earlier in the day. I recognized that I was being silly in giving them a final examination. I say, "I realized this morning that the amount that you learned in my class is, in reality, related to the size of your brains. The best way to measure brain size in living humans is by measuring your head circumferences. Therefore, instead of giving a final exam, I will simply measure each of your heads. Those with the largest heads will get As; those with somewhat smaller heads will get Bs; and so on." Although I can measure head size reliably using a new plastic tape measure, only those students with very large heads think that it is a valid way to give out grades in the class. Even though I can measure each student's head size quite accurately (and therefore, reliably), it is not a valid way to evaluate how much each student has learned.

ESTIMATING RELIABILITY

When we discussed the theoretical view of reliability, it may have occurred to you that we cannot actually measure reliability from that perspective. We can compute observed-score variance directly from the test scores. However, we cannot directly calculate true-score variance. We have no way of actually measuring true scores; they are purely theoretical. Only, some omnipotent deity would be able to reveal true scores to us.

Although we cannot calculate actual reliabilities, over the years psychometricians have developed a number of techniques that allow us to do a very good job of estimating reliability. You might recall that reliability means consistency. However, as Popham (2005) points out, there are at least three ways to look at consistency. One way to look at reliability is consistency over time. If the same person took a test over and over again, would that person achieve about the same score each time? This is what Popham (2005) refers to as *stability*, which is important for many tests, especially those that are designed to measure relatively stable traits, such as intelligence. Another way to look at consistency is with *alternate forms* (Popham, 2005). There are times when we want two or more equivalent forms of the same test. Will students obtain the same scores regardless of which form of the test they took? Still another way to look at consistency looks at the particular items on the test. Are all of the items measuring the same single skill? This is what Popham (2005) refers to as *internal consistency*. This is important for many classroom tests that are designed to measure a single set of skills. A good example might be a mathematics test measuring addition with two-digit numbers. Some of the methods that estimate reliability focus on stability, others focus on alternate forms, and others focus on internal consistency.

Definitions

If a test score remains consistent over time this is referred to as **stability**.

If students perform equally as well on various forms of the same test, the test is displaying **alternate form** reliability.

If the various items on a test are all measuring the same skill, the test is displaying **internal consistency** reliability.

Test–Retest Reliability

If you are primarily concerned about a test's stability over time, then administering the same test to the same group of students at two different times would appear to be the way to go. We simply compute a correlation between the scores from two testing situations and we have an estimate of test–retest reliability. This procedure is most appropriate for tests that measure stable traits, such as intelligence.

However, there are two major drawbacks with this technique. The first has to do with memory. Unless the tests are separated by a substantial amount of time (let's say a year or more), those taking the test the second time may remember how they answered the items the first time they took it and simply repeat the same answers. In addition, if they found some items especially interesting or puzzling the first time they took the test, they may have explored ways to find the answers between the two test administrations. They may have looked up the answers in the book or discussed them with other students. The second drawback is the lack of stability of human characteristics over time. Most psychological traits, such as personality characteristics, are not extremely stable over time. If the test–retest reliability coefficient is not acceptably high, we will not be able to tell if the differences in scores are because of the low reliability of the test or individual changes in the psychological characteristic. We can reduce the stability of the characteristic-over-time issue by administering the second test soon after the first administration. However, doing so increases the memory problem—the likelihood that the students simply remember how they answered the questions the last time they took the test and answer them in the same way.

Test–retest reliability estimates are more appropriate for some testing situations than they are for others. For example, in spite of limitations, authors and publishers of tests designed to measure personality traits are generally expected to provide evidence of test–retest reliability. However, test–retest reliability estimates are likely to be inappropriate for most classroom tests. Many classroom skills that we teach are developmental. We expect the skills to improve over time. In reality, a skill that was taught and tested in October is often practiced and used by the students in developing sub-sequent skills. If they were given the October test again in December, they would be likely to obtain even higher scores. Unfortunately, other skills—those that are more isolated, taught once and then not used often—are frequently partially forgotten over time. Therefore, if students were retested on those skills two months after the skills were taught, their test scores would be significantly lower.

Alternate Form Reliability

At times it may be necessary and appropriate to have two or more forms of the same test. A number of standardized tests are designed so that individuals might take the test several times over a relatively short period. In addition, many secondary education teachers have multiple sections of the same course each semester. At times they would like to have alternate forms of the same test so that students who take the test later in the day do not inappropriately benefit from discussions over lunch with students who took the same test that morning. When we use alternate forms of the same test, we would like to be able to demonstrate that if a student obtained a certain score on one form of the test then he or she would obtain a very similar score on any other form of the test.

How do we demonstrate alternate form reliability? The best way to measure it is to start with a list of objectives that will be covered by the test. You would then develop two or more (depending on the number of forms of the test) similar items measuring each objective. Next, you randomly place one item from each set of items onto one form of the test. Finally, you would choose a set of students and administer each student two forms of the test. If the test is brief the students can complete both forms the same day. If the test is longer the students could take the tests on successive days. Finally, you need to compute the correlation to obtain the alternate form reliability estimate.

Although my description of alternate forms may sound relatively simple, in reality the technique involves some complexities. Alternate forms of tests are used more frequently in the standardized testing industry than in the regular classroom. Most classroom teachers simply do not have sufficient time in their busy schedules to develop two or more forms of every test they give their students. They certainly do not have time to check every alternate form test for reliability. In addition, although we may have a relatively high alternate form reliability coefficient, high reliability does not guarantee that alternate forms of the test are equally difficult. There are a number of techniques for equating test difficulty, most often using item-response theory. However, that is well beyond the scope of this text.

Internal Consistency Reliability

The third way of estimating reliability is with internal consistency: Is each item on the test essentially measuring the same general skill? This approach has an advantage over the other two approaches in that it requires only one administration of the test. Although this approach is appropriate for many standardized tests, it is even more appropriate for the majority of classroom tests. There are basically two ways to measure internal consistency reliability. You can use either *split-half reliability* or a variety of *internal consistency formulas* such as *KR-20*.

Split-half Reliability

Split-half reliability resembles alternate form reliability in that you separate the test into halves and then compare each half. For example, let's say that we have a 50-item test. The most common approach is to split the test into two tests by separating the odd-numbered and even-numbered items.[2] First, compute the score that each student obtained on the 25 odd-numbered items (items 1, 3, 5, 7, . . ., 49). Then, compute the score that each student obtained on the 25 even-numbered items (items 2, 4, 6, 8, . . ., 50). Now you have two scores for each student. Next, you compute the correlation between the two sets of scores (see Part II, Chapter 22 for how to compute correlations). However, you are not yet finished.

Reliability is directly related to the length of the test and the number of items. The more items there are on a test, the higher the reliability that you can expect (assuming that the additional items are of the same quality as were the original items). In addition, the relationship between test length and reliability is quite predictable. Once you have computed the correlation between the two 25-item tests, you have an estimate of the reliability of a 25-item test. In reality, you have a 50-item test. Therefore, you then need to use the *Spearman-Brown Prophecy Formula*[3] to estimate what the reliability is for the 50-item test. The formula looks like this (Equation 4.6).

$$Rel_{new} = \frac{n \times Rel_{old}}{1 + Rel_{old}} \tag{4.6}$$

The Rel_{new} is the reliability that we are trying to estimate. The Rel_{old} is the reliability that we started with. In this case it is the correlation between the two 25-item parts of the test. The n is the size difference between the two tests. Since we want to estimate the reliability of the full 50-item test, and it is twice as large as the 25-item test, $n = 2$.

> **Definitions**
> Rel_{new} = reliability that we are trying to estimate.
> Rel_{old} = reliability that we started with.
> n = the size of the difference between the two tests. (In this case the 50-item test is twice as large as the 25-item test and $n = 2$.)

Let's try an example. If we computed the correlation between the 25-item halves of the test and found that it was .60, we can calculate the split-half reliability for the 50-item test by plugging the values into the formula (Equation 4.7).

$$Rel_{new} = \frac{2 \times .60}{1 + .60} = \frac{1.20}{1.60} = .75 \tag{4.7}$$

The split-half estimate of reliability is .75 for the 50-item test.

Internal Consistency Formulas

The second approach to estimating internal consistency is to use one of the appropriate internal consistency formulas. Essentially, these formulas look for consistency between how students performed on each item and on the test as a whole. For example, we expect that students who have high test scores will do better on the more difficult items than students with low test scores. The two most frequently used formulas are *KR-20* (Kuder & Richardson, 1937) and Cronbach's coefficient α (Cronbach, 1951).[4]

The *KR-20* can be used whenever test items can be scored dichotomously (e.g. either right or wrong). The formula is shown below (Equation 4.8).

$$KR\text{-}20 = \frac{k}{k-1}\left(1.00 - \frac{\Sigma\, p \times q}{\sigma_x^2}\right) \tag{4.8}$$

(Remember, the symbol Σ is the summation operator.) The k represents the number of items on the test. The p represents the proportion of students who had an item correct, whereas the q represents the proportion of students who had the item wrong. Of course, σ_x^2 is the variance of the test scores.

Definitions

k = the number of items on the test.
p = the proportion of students who had an item correct.
q = the proportion of students who had the item wrong.
σ_x^2 = the variance on the test (pronounced sigma squared).

For each item, if you multiply the p (the proportion of students who had the item correct) times the q (the proportion of students who had the item wrong), you get the item variance. You then add up all of the item variances. *KR-20* essentially compares the total of the item variances to the total variance on the test. With a highly reliable test, the sum of the item variances will be much smaller than the total test variance. On a reliable test, most of the variation in test scores will be as a result of differences between students, not because of irregularities in the test items.

KR-20 is just one of a number of formulas developed by Kuder and Richardson (1937) to be used in specific settings. Lee J. Cronbach (1951) developed a general version of the formula which can be used with any test (not just those with items that can be scored dichotomously). It is referred to as *Cronbach's coefficient alpha* and is represented by the following formula (Equation 4.9).

$$\alpha = \frac{k}{k-1}\left(1.00 - \frac{\Sigma\, \sigma_{item}^2}{\sigma_x^2}\right) \tag{4.9}$$

Definitions

σ_{item}^2 = the variance on each item.
σ_x^2 = the total variance on the test.

Again, this compares the sum of the item variances with the total test variance.

These formulas are rather laborious to compute by hand. Thankfully, most computer programs that score tests will compute them for you.

Limitations of internal consistency estimates Internal consistency estimates of reliability do have some limitations. They work best if all of the items on a test are measuring the same skill. Let's say that you were giving a test made up of 50 arithmetic items involving the addition of two two-digit numbers. Each item is essentially measuring the same skill. Such a test could display very high internal consistency. However, if a test is rather broad and is measuring a variety of skills, then internal consistency measures will tend to underestimate reliability. For example, in my college courses, my exams typically cover three or more chapters which each include many topics. Some students understand some topics better than other topics. The tests are measuring many skills, not one uniform skill. Internal consistency measures will tend to underestimate the reliability of such tests.

INTERPRETING RELIABILITIES

When is a test reliable enough? How do we know if a reliability estimate is high enough to consider the test acceptably reliable? Ideally, all tests should have reliabilities close to 1.00. However, as we said earlier, human psychological characteristics and day-to-day testing situations are affected by so many variables that we rarely achieve such a goal.

In general, when looking at standardized tests, we expect to see alternate form or internal consistency measures of reliability at about .90 or higher for the full tests. Many standardized tests also have subscales, different skills that the test measures with some of the items from the full test. Since those subscales are based on only part of the test (fewer items than the full test), we expect reliabilities on the subtests to be somewhat

Method	Type of Reliability	Procedure
Test–retest	Stability over time	Give a group the test and repeat several months later.
Alternate form	Alternate forms	Develop two parallel forms of the same test. Give each test to the same group.
Split-half	Internal consistency	Give the test to a group. Divide the items into odd and even. Correlate the scores for each half test.
KR-20 and Cronbach's α	Internal consistency	Give the test to a group. Compute the *KR*-20 reliability or Cronbach's α.

Figure 4.2 Comparison of methods for estimating reliability.

lower (perhaps .70 to .80). When test–retest reliabilities are reported for standardized tests, as long as the tests were administered within a few months of one another, reliabilities of about .80 are typical and acceptable.

As mentioned earlier, the situation is quite different with classroom tests. Classroom teachers typically have a limited amount of time to develop tests, and do not typically have as much training in test development as those who develop standardized tests. Therefore, the typical classroom test (taking about 50 minutes) can be expected to display an internal consistency reliability of between .60 and .80. This means that, on average, with the typical classroom test, between 20% and 40% of the variation in the students' scores is a result of measurement error.

What are the implications of using a test with moderate to low reliability? First, you need to recognize that you should not be making important decisions about students based on a single test with questionable reliability (and validity). You should use multiple ways to measure students' mastery of the course material or skills. Even if each measurement technique only possesses moderate reliability, if they each give similar results, then we can be more confident that the decisions that we are making are based on good information. However, if the various tests give conflicting results, you need to exercise much more caution in making decisions. Any decision that you make could be based on inaccurate information and you could be making the wrong decision. The second implication extends from the first. Tests are not by themselves magical. They can rarely give you more information than that which is already available to the astute observer. If a test result conflicts with your personal observations of a student, there is little reason to assume that the test is necessarily right and you were wrong. As an experienced teacher, your personal observations will often be as accurate, or more accurate, than the test results. Tests can be very useful in helping you make educational decisions, but should not be considered infallible.

IMPROVING TEST RELIABILITY

It should to clear to you now, based on what you've read in this chapter, that teachers would like to use tests that maximize reliability. When choosing or preparing tests, you want to keep reliability in mind. You may recall from earlier in the chapter that the sources of measurement error typically can be broken down into subject effects, test effects, and environmental effects. Let's look at improving test reliability from each of these three perspectives.

Reducing Subject Effects

You may recall that subject effects include, among others, illness, medication, excessive sleepiness, anxiety, personal preoccupations, and luck. Although we are unable to control many of these factors, we, as teachers, can influence others.

Illness, Medications, and Personal Preoccupations

You are not able to directly control many subject effects such as illness, medications, or personal preoccupations. However, you can be sensitive to students who are taking tests while ill or who are under the influence of medications that reduce their cognitive abilities. You also need to be aware that many events in your students' lives distract them. You can't be aware of all the personal issues that they deal with from day to day, but you can be aware of holidays and major school events. Young children are frequently quite preoccupied prior to holidays. Even minor holidays such as Halloween, which are fairly innocuous to most adults, can result in a high level of preoccupation in children. In high school, many students are equally preoccupied by events such as the big game or the prom. If possible, it is best not to schedule tests just prior to or following one of these events.

Anxiety

Many students suffer from excessive anxiety and especially test anxiety, and there are things teachers can do to reduce anxiety. Oftentimes, what we call test anxiety would be better called performance anxiety. Students are fearful of performing poorly because of all of the both real and imagined negative consequences. As teachers, you can help to reduce anxiety by avoiding stressing the negative consequences of poor test performance. You should put more emphasis on the importance of learning the material and how it can be useful than on the importance of good test performance. Keeping test grades confidential can also help. Pointing out in class which students scored well may motivate those best performing students, but can have a negative impact on most of the other students who performed less well. You can also lower anxiety levels by making sure that students have plenty of time to complete tests. Time pressure will surely raise the anxiety level of those students prone to performance anxiety.

Reducing Test Effects

You may recall that test effects can include, among others, ambiguous directions, confusing items, printing and clerical errors, non-objective scoring, and inadequate or inappropriate coverage of the material. There are a number of things you can do to reduce measurement error related to test effects, and several chapters in this text address that issue. Therefore, we will discuss only a few here.

Unclear Test Directions

Test directions need to be clear and concise. What may seem perfectly clear to you, an adult, might be confusing to an 8-year-old. If you need to use some unusual testing format, it is helpful to have the students take a practice test a day or two before the real test is administered to help them become familiar with the new format. It also helps to read the directions aloud to students. Younger students, especially, may have problems taking a test simply because they have trouble reading the directions. If it is a math test, for example, it should measure math skills, not reading skills.

Confusing Items

Confusing items contribute to measurement error as well. This is an issue that we will deal with repeatedly throughout the text. Items need to be written as clearly, simply, and concisely as possible. Any student who is well prepared should be able to read the item, immediately be able to determine the knowledge or information that is required, and answer the question. With practice, teachers can learn to write good test items.

Printing and Clerical Errors

Printing and clerical errors are relatively easy to avoid, or at least reduce. Sometimes, in an attempt to save paper, teachers tend to cram too many test items onto a single page.

Unfortunately, this can, at times, make the test difficult to read. This can be especially true for students with learning disabilities. I once heard the advice, "leave plenty of white space." Well-spaced items are easier to read. We are fortunate that we live in a time with laser printers and high-quality copiers. Most tests today have a very professional appearance and are easy to read. This was not always the case.

Today's spell-checkers and grammar-checkers can also help reduce clerical errors, but do not catch everything. Nothing can replace a careful proofreading. In fact, it is often helpful to have someone else proofread the test, since we tend to see what we expect to see and frequently miss some of our own errors.

Objectivity in Scoring

Objectivity in scoring has to do with how consistently an item can be scored. If an item requires a single correct answer and any other answer would be incorrect, then it can be scored consistently and would be considered highly objective. However, on an open-ended question, where students could provide a variety of reasonable answers, the instructor frequently has to use personal judgment about whether an answer is correct. Because subjectivity is involved, scoring is frequently less consistent. These types of items are then considered non-objective and contribute to more measurement error.

Sampling Errors

Finally, inadequate or inappropriate sampling of items contributes to measurement error. You might recall from earlier in the text that we discussed using samples to make estimates about a population. A good sample is representative of the entire population. Any measurement that we take from a representative sample should be a good estimate about that measure for the entire population. An example would be using the sample mean to estimate the population mean. This is analogous to tests. A test is made up of a sample of items that represents the population of material that the test was intended to cover. A good test has a representative sample of items and should do a good job of estimating the students' true scores, their knowledge of the material. However, a test that does not have a true representative sample of the items will measure the skills inconsistently, and will contribute to measurement error. This same issue affects content-related evidence of validity and will be discussed in more detail in the next chapter.

Reducing Environmental Effects

You may recall that environmental effects include, among others, poor lighting, environmental noises, uncomfortable room temperatures, crowding, and too little time. At times you only have limited control over these environmental effects. However, as much as possible you need to have your students take tests in rooms that are comfortable, quiet, uncrowded, and well lit. Distractions can have an even greater negative impact on students who happen to have disabilities. You also need to make sure that your tests are not too long for the time in which the students have to take them. Tests of knowledge work best as power tests rather than speeded tests. At least 80% of the students should be able to complete the test in the time available. I personally prefer that to be closer to 100% of the students.

As you can see, although you cannot eliminate all sources of measurement error, there are a number of steps you can take to increase the reliability of your classroom tests.

SOME FINAL COMMENTS ABOUT RELIABILITY

Psychometricians have come to understand that reliability and validity are not actually intrinsic characteristics of tests and other measurement devices. Rather, the reliability and validity of a device is dependent on how it is being used and the students whose skills are being measured. Therefore, a test that is being used on one set of students in one setting may display fairly high reliability and validity, yet when used with other students in another setting may display lower reliability and validity. Many tests work best when used solely as the test was intended to be used. However, when used with different populations or in settings where it was not designed to be used, it may display lower reliability and validity. Rather than discussing reliability and validity as intrinsic characteristics of a test, we now talk about gathering evidence of reliability and validity.

SUMMARY

Reliability is one of the most important characteristics of measurement. Will the device you use (frequently a test) consistently measure the characteristic that you want to measure (e.g. students' knowledge)? Theoretically, we describe observed scores as consisting of both true scores and measurement error. Reliability is the proportion of observed-score variance that can be accounted for by true-score variance (the amount of variation you should see among students). Reliability is reduced by measurement error.

There are a variety of ways of estimating reliability. Test–retest reliability is the primary way to look at the stability of test scores over time. If you can develop two or more forms of a test that each measures the same characteristic similarly, you have alternate form reliability. If the various items on a test are all measuring the same characteristic, you have internal consistency reliability. Two internal consistency measures include split-half reliability and internal consistency formulas such as *KR*-20.

Although you cannot control all sources of measurement error, there are various things that you, as teachers, can do to make your tests more reliable. You can reduce subject effects, test effects, and environmental effects that reduce the reliability of classroom tests.

EXERCISES

1. Lee Chen gave his class a 40-item test. He then performed a split-half reliability by computing the score each student had on the odd-numbered items and the score each student had on the even-numbered items. The odd-even correlation turned out to be .68. Using the Spearman-Brown Prophesy Formula, compute the split-half reliability for Mr. Chen. (Hint: Remember that the full test is twice as long as each half test.)

2. Sarah Parker gave her students a 50-item grammar test. She wants to compute the internal consistency reliability using Cronbach's coefficient α. She computed each item variance and found that the sum of the item variances was 4.40. She also computed the variance for the test scores and found that it was 16.24. Calculate Cronbach's coefficient α for her.

3. Inez Delgado gave her 4th-grade class a unit math test. She computed the variance on the scores (obtained scores) and found that it was 15.5. She also was able to determine that the error variance was 5.3. What was the reliability of her test?

4. For which types of tests would it be the most appropriate to use test–retest reliability, alternate form reliability, and internal consistency reliability? Develop two examples for each.

5. From your experiences as a student, see if you can recall and list at least three examples of each of the following sources of measurement error. How would you have corrected those problems?

   a. Subject effects
   b. Test effects
   c. Environmental effects

6. Sandra Brown has a reading disability and is in the 3rd grade. What types of testing accommodations should her teacher provide to improve the reliability of her test scores?

SPOTLIGHT ON THE CLASSROOM

Sarah Bruckner is a 5th-grade teacher at Grand Junction Elementary School and has only been teaching for three years. She has been pleased to notice that each year her lessons seem to go better than they did the year before and her ability to manage the classroom has steadily improved. This year she wants to focus on improving her classroom tests.

As a first-year teacher she relied exclusively on the tests that were provided in the teacher's edition of her textbooks, but felt that many of those tests were unsatisfactory. Last year, she self-designed about one half of the tests she gave her class but felt that her students scored inconsistently on those tests. Students who scored well on one test often scored poorly on the next one. She now thinks that last year she tried to introduce too many innovative testing formats that frequently confused her students. She had even tried testing in small cooperative groups where students could discuss the questions with one another before providing an answer.

In social studies, she just spent the last four weeks covering the European explorers of the 13th, 14th, and 15th centuries. She is planning to give a test and would primarily like the students to be able to connect each explorer with the area that he explored. How should Ms. Bruckner design a social studies test for this unit? What steps should she take to develop and administer a test that will assure that the test will be reliable?

NOTES

1. Frequently time issues are labeled as test effects, rather than environmental effects.
2. Another approach would be to compare the first 25 items to the last 25 items. However, the odd/even split is used to avoid problems related to issues like fatigue, where students tire and perform less well on the later question, or if students do not complete the test, leaving the last items blank.
3. This abbreviated form of the Spearman-Brown Prophesy formula works well with computing split-half reliabilities. Another form of the formula can be used in other situations where you would like to predict reliabilities for longer or shorter tests.
4. This is pronounced "Cronbach's coefficient alpha."

5

VALIDITY

INTRODUCTION

Now that we've discussed reliability—consistency within a test—we need to discuss validity: Does a test actually measure what we think it is measuring? Although validity is one of the most important concepts in the field of measurement, there is no one single way to look at it. Instead, we must examine validity from several different perspectives. One perspective is content-related evidence of validity. How well does the test match the content that was taught? A second perspective is criterion-related evidence of validity. Frequently we use a test as a short cut to measure a skill or talent that could be measured in some other way. How well does the test relate to the alternative way to measure the skill or talent? A third perspective is construct-related evidence of validity. Does the test actually measure what the applicable theory says the test should measure? Finally, we will examine the relationship between reliability and validity.

PERSPECTIVES ON VALIDITY

The most important characteristic of a test is validity. Does the test actually measure what it is supposed to measure? When I was in graduate school, I developed a reputation as an effective consultant and worked on several funded research projects and, in addition, gave assistance to other doctoral candidates. One thing that I saw with some frequency was that, when graduate students were devising the research for their doctoral theses, they often ran into problems in designing the instruments they planned to use to gather their data. They would frequently come to me with instruments (tests) that others had recommended. The first two questions that I learned to ask were, "What behavior do you want to measure?" and, "Will this instrument actually measure that behavior?" Of course, I was asking the validity question. In many instances, novice researchers had chosen an instrument without really considering the issue of validity. This also happens in the classroom. Many times, teachers give tests that are available, thinking that the tests will measure what they want them to measure without closely examining the tests themselves.

Although validity sounds like a straightforward concept, it is actually somewhat complex. In fact, it is a purely theoretical concept since there is no way that we can actually demonstrate that our instruments are truly valid. As a result, the best that we can do is to seek good evidence of validity. As you will see, there are, at least, three ways to look at validity. We frequently talk about *content-related* evidence of validity, *criterion-related* evidence of validity, and *construct-related* evidence of validity. In addition, within two of those categories there are two or more subtypes.

Content-Related Evidence of Validity

One way to look at validity is to use the content-related approach. We will be examining content-related evidence of validity as a general concept. We will also look at three specifics types of content-related evidence of validity: *instructional validity, curricular validity*, and *face validity*.

Instructional Validity

Let's begin with a general discussion of content-related evidence of validity. For example, Marion Jenkins teaches her high school biology class a unit on vascular plants. As she prepares the unit test, she is very careful to make certain that the test accurately reflects what she has taught. Since she spent about 50% of the time covering angiosperms, she wants to make certain that about 50% of the test covers that topic. She also makes certain that the individual test items match the material that she covered in class. She wants her test to mirror what she taught. Ms. Jenkins is designing a test that will display content-related evidence of validity.

Definition

Content-related evidence of validity refers to the match between the test items and the content that was taught.

There is a theory in measurement known as the Domain Sampling Model. Essentially, the domain (the material that has been covered) is represented by the oval. In this case, it could include all of the material that Ms. Jenkins included on vascular plants. The small circles within the oval represent items on Ms. Jenkins' test (see Figure 5.1). A good test should sample material evenly from throughout the domain. Such a test would be said to display high content-related evidence of validity.

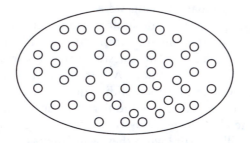

Figure 5.1 Domain Sampling Model—Ms. Jenkins' biology test.

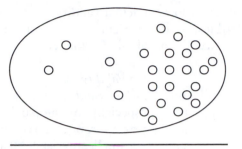

Figure 5.2 Mr. Petrie's math test.

Now let's look at another example. Mr. Petri teaches 8th-grade math. He is giving a test that is expected to cover three chapters. However, the majority of the test items actually come from the third chapter. Only a few of the items come from the first two chapters. In this case there is not a very good match between the material that was taught and the test items (see Figure 5.2). As you can see, this test does not display very good content validity.

For another example, let's consider Mr. Astro who teaches earth and space science. He is also giving a test on a three-chapter unit. There are a number of items from each chapter on the test. However, there are also several items on the test from material that was never taught (see Figure 5.3). Even the most prepared students will not be able to answer these questions. These items that are beyond the domain also reduce the content validity of the test.

Curricular Validity

What we have been discussing so far is sometimes referred to as *instructional validity*. How well does the test match what was actually taught? However, at times we are interested in what is known as *curricular validity*. How well does the test match what the official curriculum guide says should be covered in the unit? Impara (2007) points out that this is now often referred to as alignment between tests and content standards. If the test does not cover the material in the official curriculum, it could have high

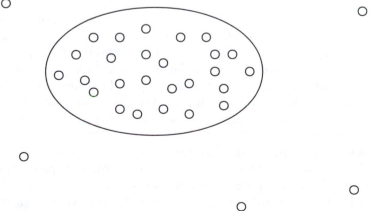

Figure 5.3 Mr. Astro's earth and space science test.

instructional validity but rather low curricular validity. On the other hand, if the school system supplies a standard test on the curriculum, that test could have good curricular validity but rather poor instructional validity for that class.

Face Validity

A third perspective is what is known as *face validity*. Here we are looking at whether the items on the test are appropriate, especially for the particular students taking the test. Do the items, on the surface, appear appropriate? For example, do items on an intelligence test appear to be measuring intellectual skills. Face validity can also be important in terms of the students taking a particular test. For example, I often teach an Introduction to Educational Psychology class to nursing students. Many nursing programs require such a course because nurses frequently find themselves teaching; patient education is an important part of nursing. I teach the same concepts to the nurses that I teach to the education majors. However, in that class I try to use more examples related to nursing since they seem more appropriate. On the tests, I also rewrite my questions so that they relate more to health care than to the classroom. By making the test items appear more appropriate for nurses, I am improving the face validity of the test.

Definitions

Instructional validity refers to the match between the items on the test and the material that was taught.

Curricular validity refers to the match between the items on the test and the official curriculum.

If the items on a test appear to be measuring the appropriate skills, and appear to be appropriate for the students taking the test, the test is said to have **face validity**.

Measuring Content-Related Evidence of Validity

Content-related evidence of validity is extremely important for classroom tests, although there is no way to estimate it mathematically. Typically, we ask a content expert to examine the material that was taught and compare it to the items on the test. In fact, a teacher can achieve good content-related evidence of validity by taking care in designing a test, which normally means following one of the procedures described in Chapter 3. Either the teacher develops test questions for each objective, or completes a Table of Specifications containing a chart with a taxonomy listed on one axis and content listed on the other. The teacher then decides, for example, how many knowledge-level questions will be asked on the first topic, and so on. Both procedures will assure good content-related evidence of validity.

Sometimes teachers believe that they can develop a content-valid test without a formal plan. If they are lucky they may be successful. However, they frequently get off track and end up with a test with limited content validity. It is like a carpenter trying to complete a building project without a plan. There is a good chance that, at some point, the carpenter will have to tear apart some of the work to make corrections so that the finished product will actually fit together.

Criterion-Related Evidence of Validity

We often use a test or other assessment device as a short cut to measure a skill that would otherwise take a longer time to measure. Let's say that you are teaching your 7th-grade students a variety of math skills. At some point, you will want to see how well they can perform those skills. If you give them problems to solve demonstrating all of the skills that were taught, it might take them several hours to be able to demonstrate all of those skills. Instead, you can develop a test that samples the skills that were taught and can be administered in 40 minutes. Hopefully, the briefer test will be as effective in measuring their skills as would the longer procedure. Essentially, you are using the test score as an estimate of how the students would do using all of the skills taught. In this case the longer procedure is the criterion and, hopefully, the shorter test demonstrates *criterion-related evidence of validity.*

If the shorter test has high criterion-related evidence of validity, then students who get high scores on the test would also get high scores on the longer procedure; those who get average scores on the test would get average scores on the longer procedure and, similarly, those who get low scores on the test would get low scores on the longer procedure. To establish criterion-related validity, you actually have to follow three steps. You give a test to a group of students. Next, each student is required to perform a series of tasks that also measure the same skill. Finally, you correlate the test scores with the scores that the students obtain with the alternative assessment. This correlation coefficient can be interpreted as a validity coefficient.

Definition

A test has **criterion-related evidence of validity** if the test scores correlate well with another method of measuring the same behavior or skill.

Concurrent Validity

Criterion-related evidence of validity comes in two forms, the first of which is known as *concurrent validity.* Concurrent validity is demonstrated when a test is correlated with another measure of the same behavior or skill that is taken at about the same time as the test is given. The test measures the student's current skill level. The example used previously demonstrated an example of concurrent validity.

Definition

A test has **concurrent validity** if it displays a positive correlation with another method of measuring the same behavior or skill given at about the same time.

For another example of concurrent validity, imagine that you are a driver's education teacher and that you have developed a paper-and-pencil test of driving skill. After you administer the written test to your students you also evaluate them on a driving course where they actually have to deal with simulated driving challenges. If the scores on the written driver's test correlate well with the scores that the students received in negotiating the driving course, then you have demonstrated evidence that your written test has concurrent validity.

Predictive Validity

The other type of criterion-related evidence of validity is known as *predictive validity*. We can sometimes use a test to predict future performance. Good examples of this include the SATs and the ACTs. These are the two most commonly used college entrance tests in the United States. Most selective colleges receive many more applications than they can accept each year. It is generally believed that the fairest way to select those students who will be admitted is to choose those students most likely to be successful. Both the SATs (Scholastic Aptitude Tests or Scholastic Assessment Tests) and the ACTs (American College Tests), which are typically taken while the student is still in high school, are designed to predict how well students will perform during their first year in college. These tests display a positive correlation with freshmen grade-point average. They have predictive validity because they are able to predict future performance.

Definition

A test is said to have **predictive validity** if it is positively correlated with some future behavior or skill.

Employment selection tests are another example of tests that are expected to have predictive validity. If an employer has one job opening and many applicants for that job, an employment selection test may be used. The test is designed to measure the skills that an individual needs to be successful at that job. Of course, the test is expected to have predictive validity. Those who score high on the test are expected to be more successful at that job than those who earn lower scores. The federal and state governments frequently use civil service exams to select the best individuals for government jobs. Civil service exams are expected to display predictive validity.

Intelligence tests are also expected to have predictive validity. When Alfred Binet developed the first intelligence test in France in the early 1900s, it was expected to be able to predict those children who would be successful in school and those who would struggle with the academic demands of the classroom. Since intelligence tests do predict future school performance, that is the primary reason for using them in schools.

With criterion-related evidence of validity we are correlating a test with some other measure. Therefore, the correlation coefficient is frequently interpreted as a validity coefficient. This is the only type of validity estimate that almost always results in a mathematical index of validity, although we sometimes use correlation with the next type of validity also.

Construct-Related Evidence of Validity

A third perspective on validity is known as construct-related evidence of validity. In this case the term "construct" is a synonym for theory or a psychological characteristic of interest. A measurement device is said to display *construct-related evidence of validity* if it measures what the appropriate theory says that it should be measuring or if we have evidence that it is measuring the psychological characteristic of interest. A good example is an intelligence test. Most intelligence theories essentially define intelligence as our ability to learn, remember, problem solve, and to adjust to changes in our environment. If we develop an intelligence test based on that definition it should measure a person's ability to learn, to remember, to solve problems, and to adjust to changes in the environment. Our intelligence test could be said to be displaying construct-related evidence of validity if we had evidence that it was measuring those skills. Many measurement devices that are designed to assess personality or ability are expected to display evidence of construct-related evidence of validity. Examples of such constructs would include reading comprehension and sociability.

Definition

A measurement device is said to display **construct-related evidence of validity** if it measures what the appropriate theory says that it should be measuring.

Sometimes, it is difficult to measure construct-related evidence of validity because you must have another way (besides the test) to measure the construct. Finding another way to measure the construct can require creativity. In other cases, we must rely on a number of ways to measure the construct. For example, if you develop a new intelligence test, you have to relate it to the way you define intelligence. If it is defined as the ability to solve problems, you would need to find other ways to measure problem-solving skills. You might actually need to have a group of people solve problems in a variety of contexts and then correlate their success in this with the scores they received on the intelligence test. A high correlation would provide evidence of construct-related validity. In other situations, it is easier to demonstrate construct-related evidence of validity. If there is already a test available that has a reputation for displaying construct-related evidence validity, then you only have to administer your test and the established test to the same group of people and correlate the test results. Since the Standford-Binet and Wechsler intelligence tests have such good reputations, most new intelligence tests are compared to them. A high correlation with one of those tests is often one source of adequate evidence of construct-related validity.

Generally, in order to establish construct-related evidence of validity, it is necessary to perform a number of validity studies. We are typically expected to provide evidence from a number of perspectives before others will concede that our measurement device displays construct-related evidence of validity.

Which Perspective is the Most Important?

When you are trying to evaluate the quality of any test, which type of validity is the most important? It depends on the type of test and its purpose. On personality and ability tests, such as intelligence tests, we expect the tests to relate to the theory. Therefore, evidence of construct-related validity is highly relevant. However, we also want the tests to have some other uses. Many of those types of test are also expected to predict future behavior. In those cases, evidence of criterion-related validity is also extremely important. However, with ability and personality tests, we normally do not worry very much about content-related evidence of validity.

College entrance tests, employment selection tests, or similar instruments are expected to display evidence of predictive validity. After all, that is what they were designed to do. It is also important, however, that the tests have face validity (a type of content-related evidence of validity). If the test is expected to select the most qualified nurse, then the test must include questions on activities and knowledge related to nursing. In reality, we can sometimes develop a test of this type that does not seem to ask the right questions, but which is still quite predictive. However, unless the test displays face validity, the developers of the test can expect questions, criticisms, and perhaps even law suits.

For classroom tests, content-related evidence of validity is critical. We want our classroom tests to reflect what we taught. Therefore, in the majority of cases instructional validity will be the most important. However, in more and more situations, teachers may be expected to show also that their tests have curricular validity (i.e. they match the official curriculum). Students, on the other hand, often focus on face validity. Does the test ask the right questions and do the questions seem appropriate for the students? Therefore, if teachers wish to avoid unnecessary criticism from their students and parents, then their tests should, in addition, have face validity. Although criterion-related evidence of validity and construct-related evidence of validity are less important for classroom tests, they are not irrelevant. When I give a test in my educational psychology class, I certainly want my tests to display content-related evidence of validity— to be highly related to what I taught. However, since I also want my tests to relate to how my students will use this knowledge and these skills in other settings, I expect criterion-related evidence of validity. Finally, since my tests measure a theoretical construct—knowledge of educational psychology—then construct-related evidence of validity is also necessary.

The various types of validity are all inter-related. Messick (1995) points out that what we usually think of as construct-related evidence of validity also contains aspects of both content-related evidence and criterion-related evidence of validity. He suggests that we look at validity as a complex, yet unified, concept related to the meaning of test scores.

RELIABILITY AND VALIDITY

Although I discussed the relationship between reliability and validity in the previous chapter, it is an important relationship and, thus, worth repeating briefly here. You may recall that reliability is concerned with the relationships among observed scores, true scores, and measurement error. Theoretically, any variation that we see in observed scores (the scores that students actually obtain) is the result of both variation in true scores (the scores the student should actually obtain) and measurement error. A test is reliable if the variation in observed scores is largely due to the variation in true scores— how students differ from one another in reality. If there is a large element of measurement error, then much of the variation in observed scores is due to "junk"—situations that cause students to score other than they should. In this case, the test is not reliable. If the test is measuring a lot of "junk," then it is not measuring what it should be measuring and it is not valid. Therefore, reliability is necessary for validity. Essentially, reliability sets an upper limit for validity. A test cannot be valid unless it is reliable, which is why we strive to develop tests that are reliable.

I should again point out, as I did in the previous chapter, that psychometricians used to think of both reliability and validity as inherent characteristics of a measurement device. However, in recent years, we have begun to recognize that reliability and validity are dependent on at least three characteristics: the measurement device, the group of individuals being measured, and the way the scores are interpreted and used. For example, a reading readiness test that is being used on kindergarten students to determine what pre-reading skills still need additional attention may be judged to display both reliability and validity. However, if the same test were used on a group of 2nd-grade students to evaluate their reading skills, it might be judged to display much lower levels of both reliability and validity.

SUMMARY

Validity is the most important characteristic of a measurement device. Does the test measure what it is supposed to measure? Validity can be viewed from several perspectives. If the items on a test match the material that was taught in class, the test is said to display content-related evidence of validity. If the test scores relate to how individuals perform on another instrument that measures the same skill, the test is displaying criterion-related evidence of validity. If the test measures that which the relevant theory says that it should measure, the test is displaying construct-related evidence of validity.

The different types of validity are not equally important for different measurement devices. Classroom tests should stress content-related evidence of validity. There should be a very close match between the items on the test and the material that was taught. Other types of tests should stress other types of validity dependent primarily on how the tests are intended to be used.

EXERCISES

Which type of validity is demonstrated by the following examples?

1. Choose from: *instructional validity*; *curricular validity*; face validity.

   a. At Miami University, it is only biology majors who are required to take a test on the proper steps and techniques of dissecting a frog.
   b. After covering a unit on the solar system, Mr. Sobotka creates a test using the notes that cover the material he taught his class.
   c. Miss Becker is a 4th-grade teacher at East Deer Elementary. She composes a science test based on material that is required in the district's curriculum.
   d. Ms. Falepaini teaches her 1st-grade class the names and locations of the 50 states. The students then take a test in which they have to label every state on a U.S. map.
   e. The University of Connecticut holds a summer math course for all football players. The professor, Dr. Walsh, relates his test questions to sports such as football.

2. Choose from: *criterion-related validity*; *construct-related validity*.

   a. A student scores 650 on the writing portion of the SATs. Based on this score, her Composition I professor expects her to do well in class during her freshman year.

b. Sarah, a 1st-grader, has currently been listed by her teacher as a possible candidate for ADHD. A school psychologist gives her a specific test to measure her classroom behavior.
c. In Mr. Roberts' 5th-grade science class, the students are required to list and explain the steps of the scientific method. Afterward, the students must use the scientific method while carrying out an actual experiment.

SPOTLIGHT ON THE CLASSROOM

Miss Green is interviewing for a 2nd-grade teaching position at Harrison Park Elementary School in Phoenix, Arizona for the next school year. The competition is very tight for this job. After months of searching, the school board has narrowed the applicants down to five individuals. They reviewed college grades, Praxis exam scores, and letters of recommendation. Now that the numbers are narrowed down, the board will look more closely at the student-teaching evaluations and prior teaching experience. This is the most important part of the hiring process. The board members feel that the way a teacher performs in front of a classroom is a better indicator than his or her test scores. The board is also requiring the five candidates to teach a 2nd-grade math and reading lesson in front of the board members and administrators. Although they are not 2nd-grade students, they would like to see each candidate's teaching skills and classroom presence. The board members and administrators each use an evaluation sheet to critique and make comments about the lessons. They also complete a rating scale for each candidate. Taking all of the information into consideration, the candidate who displays the most potential for becoming a successful 2nd-grade teacher will be hired.

Discuss the various techniques that the board members used in terms of validity.

Section II

CLASSROOM TESTING

This section consists of six chapters on classroom testing. Four of the chapters discuss the various test item formats found in most classroom tests. The other two chapters discuss how you can produce, administer, and analyze your tests. Chapter 6 will teach you about completion and short-answer items. You will learn about the characteristics of those items and how to prepare good items yourself. Chapter 7 will introduce you to various types of essay items and how to use them effectively in your classrooms. Chapter 8 will teach you about the characteristics of the multiple-choice format, including how to prepare effective multiple-choice items. You will also learn about when it is most appropriate to use those items. Chapter 9 will introduce you to true–false items and variations of the alternative-choice format. You will learn about the characteristics of this format and how to prepare good items. Chapter 10 discusses the processes that a teacher should go through to build an effective classroom test. Finally, Chapter 11 will teach you how to go about analyzing a test once you have given it to your students.

6

COMPLETION AND SHORT-ANSWER ITEMS

INTRODUCTION

In this chapter you will learn about completion and short-answer items, perhaps the most common test format used at all grade levels in school. We will discuss the advantages and limitations of the short-answer format. You will also learn about the attributes and characteristics of items written in that format. Finally, we will discuss how to prepare better short-answer items and practice critiquing items.

SHORT-ANSWER ITEMS

Completion and short-answer items require answers as brief as a single word or as long as a sentence. There are several forms of the short-answer question. One form, known as the *completion* item, is an incomplete sentence with a blank at the end that the student is expected to fill. An example of a completion item is shown below.

Example

The season of the year when the leaves change color and fall from the trees, and the days grow cooler, is known as _____.

If the item were rewritten as a question, it would be considered to be a *short-answer* item.

Example

What is the season of the year when the leaves change color and fall from the trees, and the days grow cooler?

In this case the student is typically expected to provide the answer in the space provided below the question. A third form of this format is known as *fill-in-the-blank*.

Example

_____ is the season of the year when the leaves change color and fall from the trees, and the days grow cooler.

With this version the blank can appear anywhere within the sentence. All three of these questions are essentially the same format and will be treated as such in this chapter.

Definitions

A **completion** item is an incomplete sentence with a blank at the end that the student is expected to fill.

A **short-answer** item is a question that requires an answer as short as one word or as long as a sentence.

A sentence with a missing word(s) is known as a **fill-in-the-blank** item.

Short-answer items (the generic term for this format) are used with various subjects, including mathematics and science. However, in those fields, students' answers are frequently not written in English, but often require mathematical or scientific notation. Here are a couple of examples.

Example

Jim needs to plant grass seed in his yard. The woman at the lawn and garden store told him that she would need to know the area that he wanted to cover so that she could tell him the correct amount of grass seed to buy. The spot Jim wants to plant is rectangular, 8 ft wide by 12 ft long. Find the area he needs to cover. Show your work.

Answer: $Area = l \times w = 12 \text{ ft} \times 8 \text{ ft} = 96 \text{ ft}^2$

Example

Show the chemical formula for sulfuric acid.

Answer: H_2SO_4

Short-answer items are very popular ways in which to write test items. They may, in fact, be the most common type of item used from kindergarten through college. They show up on tests, quizzes, and in many additional ways. When teachers verbally ask students questions in class, the questions are frequently phrased in this format.

ADVANTAGES AND LIMITATIONS OF SHORT-ANSWER ITEMS

Advantages

Since this item format is so popular, it must have several advantages. One of the primary advantages of the short-answer format is that items of this type are relatively easy to construct. Most short-answer items simply require the recall of information since they typically measure knowledge and comprehension. This allows the questions to be written in a rather simple, straightforward manner. It does not typically take much time for a teacher to prepare many of these items. In comparison, when attempting to measure higher-level learning, like analysis or synthesis, it may take considerably longer to prepare good questions.

A second advantage of the short-answer format is that these items are relatively easy to score. Often there is only a single word or phrase, or at least a limited number of words or phrases, that is the correct answer which makes the scoring plan easy to develop. For example, to answer the question I phrased earlier in the chapter, the only answers that would be acceptable would be "autumn" or "fall." Any other answers would be considered incorrect. These items can usually be scored quickly and efficiently.

A third advantage of the short-answer format is that these tests require the students to supply the answer. Sometimes educational psychologists differentiate between recognition and recall learning. With the multiple-choice format, the answer is supplied as one option and the student needs only to recognize that it is the correct answer. However, with the short-answer format, the student must be able to recall the answer from memory, which involves a deeper level of learning. Students must know the material at a deeper level to recall the correct answer for a short-answer item.

Since short-answer items require recall, rather than recognition, this leads to a fourth advantage of this format. With both multiple-choice and true–false items (both recognition items), students can sometimes get an answer correct merely by guessing, which tends to limit reliability. However, since guessing is much less likely to lead to a correct answer with recall items, tests using these items can theoretically achieve higher reliabilities.

A fifth advantage of the short-answer format is that a teacher can include many of these items on a test. You may recall from the chapters on reliability and validity that it is advantageous to have as many items as possible on a test, and since students can typically complete short-answer items rapidly, it is possible to include a large number of them on a test. In addition, since teachers can normally prepare them quickly, it does not take very long to prepare the required number of short-answer items.

Limitations

Unfortunately, there are a number of limitations associated with the short-answer format. Perhaps the primary disadvantage is that this format works best only with knowledge- and comprehension-level questions, which often simply require the recall of information. You might recall Bloom's *Taxonomy of Cognitive Objectives* that we discussed in Chapter 3. Of the six types of cognitive objective, short-answer items work best with knowledge-level and comprehension-level items. Application-level items can sometimes also be measured with this format. However, you simply cannot easily measure any higher-level cognitive skills—such as analysis, synthesis, and evaluation—with this format. Although we do often need to teach at the knowledge and comprehension levels, we also want to teach, and test in an appropriate manner, higher-level skills.

A second disadvantage of the short-answer format is that teachers who use it a great deal may find that they are measuring minutia. In many instructional units, there is a limited amount of important information that students need to memorize. Once teachers have exhausted all of the important details with short-answer questions, there is a tendency for them to start writing questions on less important material until the questions are essentially measuring relatively unimportant details.

A third disadvantage of this format is that many short-answer items can be somewhat ambiguous, allowing for a number of potentially correct answers. Consider this example from an elementary school science class.

Example

Excessive moisture in the atmosphere will result in _____ .

Perhaps the teacher expected the students to respond with the word "rain." However, other reasonable answers would include snow, sleet, hail, fog, high humidity, stickiness, dampness, and the growth of mildew. Can you think of any other possible answers? How does a teacher respond to one of these alternative answers? Some teachers have told me that they expect well-prepared students to know the answer that was expected and, therefore, mark any other answer as incorrect. Students who know the material well, or who are creative, can sometimes be penalized with that type of approach because they are more likely to imagine many possible correct alternatives. This type of "ambiguous" question leads to greater measurement error and, therefore, to lower reliability and validity.

ATTRIBUTES DESIRED IN SHORT-ANSWER ITEMS

Good short-answer items should display certain attributes or characteristics. Some of these attributes are rather general and, therefore, desirable in any type of item format. Other attributes will be specific to the short-answer format.

1. *The item should measure the skill or knowledge that it was designed to measure.* How well does the item match the objective that it was supposed to measure? Every item should be based either on an objective or on a Table of Specifications. As you may recall, this is how we develop tests with content-related evidence of validity. Sometimes, however, items just seem to miss the point or they are only tangentially related to the objective. You should try to measure the objective in as simple and straightforward a manner as possible. Later in the chapter, we will consider some examples of items that fail to meet this attribute.

2. *The item can be answered by a few words, a phrase, or a sentence.* Is this an item that is appropriate for a short-answer format? Once an item requires more than one sentence, it becomes a brief essay and should probably be treated as such.

3. *The reading level of the item is appropriate for the students.* It is important that a test

item measures a single skill only. If the item uses difficult vocabulary or a complex sentence structure, then it may also be measuring reading skills as well as the skill it is intended to measure. When more than one skill is measured with a single item, measurement error is increased. Therefore, test items should be written simply enough that even the poorer readers in the class should be able to read them without difficulty.

4. *The correct answer to this item will be a single or very limited set of responses.* Will you be able to develop a scoring plan that has a limited number of correct answers? You want to avoid questions that can be answered with a variety of responses. Ambiguous items require you to make a judgment call which affects the objectivity (reliability) of the scoring. They also make it more difficult for teachers' aides and others to score tests.

5. *The blank in the item represents a key word or phrase.* Sometimes teachers have been known to pull sentences out of the textbook and randomly substitute a blank for a word. If the word or phrase that is left out is not a key word or phrase, then the item is not really measuring the objective. It is simply measuring the student's ability to memorize the textbook word-for-word.

6. *The number of blanks in the question is sufficiently limited to avoid confusion.* When using the fill-in-the-blank version of the short-answer format, it is important to use only a limited number of blanks. The overuse of blanks can result in an ambiguous item. An example of such as ambiguous item is shown below.

Bad Example

The _____ cycle is affected by the _____ from the _____.

If you took several science classes, you could probably fill in those blanks with a variety of alternatives. The 6th-grade teacher in this case was teaching a science unit on weather and wanted the students to fill in "weather," "heat," and "sun." Did you give those responses? Probably not, because the item was too ambiguous.

There are times, however, when it is permissible to use multiple blanks. For example, if some concept had several defining characteristics, then it might be acceptable to use several blanks. Let's consider an example from 6th-grade mathematics.

Better Example

In order for an object to be a square it must be a _____, with _____, and _____.

The teacher was looking for "quadrilateral" with "all sides of equal length" and "all right angles." Although this example is better than the last one, it is still potentially problematic. The stem of the question needs to contain enough information for the student to know clearly what the teacher expects. With three blanks, there would be students who knew the material, but were still uncertain what the teacher wanted. Therefore, it might improve the item if one of the required characteristics was included in the stem of the question.

> **Even Better Example**
> In order for an object to be square it must be a quadrilateral, with _____, and _____.

7. *The items are worded somewhat differently than the material was worded in the text or in class.* As I mentioned earlier, it is not an uncommon practice for teachers to simply take an important sentence from the book and substitute a blank for an important word. Unfortunately, that practice encourages students to simply memorize the important material from the text or from class without necessarily understanding it. In addition, students can sometimes recall what needs to go into the blank because of ESP—not extra-sensory perception, but the *encoding specificity principle.* We sometimes can more easily recall something if it is presented exactly the way we first encountered it (when the material was encoded into memory), even if we don't understand it. Therefore, if you want to make certain that your students understand the material, your questions should be worded or phrased somewhat differently from how they were in the text or in class.

8. *For items requiring a numerical response, the unit of measurement should be specified.* My daughter once told me a story about her driver's license examination when she was a teenager. After taking the driving portion of the exam, the state trooper was expected to ask a series of verbal questions from the driver's manual. One question that he asked her was, "What is the maximum distance that you can park from the curb?" She responded, "One foot." He said, "No, it's 12 inches." I imagine that the trooper knew that 12 inches and one foot were equivalent but that he was simply not at his best after spending the afternoon administering drivers' tests to teenagers. You should avoid that confusion by specifying the unit of measurement that you want. By including the unit of measurement in the question, you are more likely to get the exact response that you want. An example is shown below.

> **Example**
> What is the maximum distance (in inches) that you can park from the curb?

9. *The blanks should be placed at, or near, the end of the question.* Students can move through a test more rapidly if the blanks are placed near the end of the question. Many times, when the blank is near the beginning of the question, students find that they need to read the question twice to understand it. Try to place blanks near the end of the question whenever possible. However, at times, this could lead to writing an awkward sentence, which can be potentially confusing. In those cases, put the blank earlier in the question, especially if time will not be a factor.

10. *Each blank should have the same physical length.* I have seen teachers use a short blank when the correct answer is a short word, a long blank when the correct answer is a

long word, and even four blanks when the correct answer is a four-word phrase. That procedure gives a clue to the test-wise student that other students do not always catch. In order to maintain reliability and validity, students should have to rely on the question itself, and not subtle clues, for the answer. Try to keep all of the blanks the same physical length. If you decide to use multiple blanks for multiple-word answers, tell the students that each blank should contain one word.

11. *The items should be designed to make scoring efficient.* If the students are expected to fill in the correct answers right on the blank, it means that the correct answers are all over the page, which results in inefficient scoring. When scoring the test the teacher has to skip all over the page. Not only is that a slow process, but it can also lead to errors as the teacher may sometimes fail to score an answer. It is often better to have the students complete the answers in the same place for each item, perhaps in the right margin, which will allow for more efficient scoring, as in the following example.

Example

The Portuguese man who explored the west coast of
Africa was ____(1)____ .   1. _____

____(2)____ conquered the Aztecs in Mexico.   2. _____

The man who traveled up the Mississippi River
and claimed it for France was ____(3)____ .   3. _____ [1]

With very young students this procedure might be confusing. In that case it is better to allow them to fill in the answers on the blanks within the questions. I imagine that by 4th grade this would no longer be necessary.

Attributes Desired in Short-Answer Items [2]

1. *The item should measure the skill or knowledge that it was designed to measure.*
2. *The item can be answered by a few words, a phrase, or a sentence.*
3. *The reading level for the item is appropriate for the students.*
4. *The correct answer to this item will be a single or a very limited set of responses.*
5. *The blank in the item represents a key word or phrase.*
6. *The number of blanks in the question is sufficiently limited to avoid confusion.*
7. *The items are worded somewhat differently than the material was worded in the text or in class.*
8. *For items requiring a numerical response, the unit of measurement should be specified.*
9. *The blanks should be placed at, or near, the end of the question.*
10. *Each blank should have the same physical length.*
11. *The items should be designed to make scoring efficient.*

EVALUATING SHORT-ANSWER ITEMS

Now that we have reviewed the various attributes of a good short-answer item, let us examine a number of items than contain some problems. In order to be able to appropriately evaluate each item, the objective that it is intended to measure and the intended grade level are provided for you.

Item 1

Objective: The students will be able to list all four New England colonies from memory.

Grade level: 7th-grade social studies

Item: Although originally founded in 1633, which New England colony was finally given a Royal Charter under John Winthrop, Jr. in 1662? (Answer: Connecticut)

What problems did you see in this item? As you were likely able to identify, perhaps the biggest problem with this item is that it does not address the objective. Although it is a question about a New England colony, it only has a tangential relationship to the objective. In addition, the item is too wordy; it contains too much information for a 7th-grader. The initial phrase is not essential for the item, so it should be omitted; it makes the item too long and may cause confusion.

Item 2

Objective: The students will be able to identify that nitrogen is the most abundant element in the Earth's atmosphere.

Grade level: 5th-grade general science

Item: _____ is the element most commonly found in the air that we breathe.

This item does measure the objective and is straightforward. What problem do you see with this item? If you said that it could be rewritten so that the blank occurred at the end of the sentence, you would be correct. That would help the student avoid having to read it twice.

Item 3

Objective: The students will be able to recall the details of the Battle of Saratoga during the Revolutionary War.

Grade level: High school American history

Item: General _____ lost the Battle of _____ in 1777 when the Americans captured _____ of his troops. (Answers: Burgoyne, Saratoga, 5,700)

This question violates many of the positive attributes of a good short-answer item. First, there are simply too many blanks. It could potentially refer to any battle won by the American troops in 1777, which makes the item too ambiguous. The physical length of the blanks varies from one to the other. The last blank could potentially be filled in correctly by other responses, such as "all," or "most." Do you think that this information is critical to the unit or would you consider it to be asking for trivia if students are expected to know that 5,700 troops were captured?

Item 4

Objective:	The students will be able to recognize an application of friction.
Grade level:	5th-grade general science
Item:	It may be easier to slide a piece of furniture over a smooth wooden floor than it would be to slide it over a carpet because of the effects of _____.

This item appears to possess all of the essential attributes of a good short-answer item. Did you know the answer?

SUMMARY

In this chapter we described short-answer items, which also include completion and fill-in-the-blank. We described the various advantages of the short-answer format. A primary advantage of this format is that the items are easy to construct. We described the disadvantages. A primary disadvantage is that this type of item is useful only with knowledge-level and comprehension-level material. We also described eleven attributes desired with this format, characteristics that you will want to use when preparing items of this type. Finally, you had the opportunity to critique several items.

EXERCISES

1. Write an appropriate completion item for the following objectives:

   a. The students will be able to identify the major countries that were involved in WWII.
   b. The students will be able to name how many rings Saturn has.
   c. The students will be able to change a percent to a decimal.

2. Write an appropriate short-answer item for the following objectives:

   a. The students will be able to identify the four steps of the writing process.
   b. The students will be able to recognize photosynthesis.
   c. The students will be able to identify what a thesaurus is used for.

3. Write an appropriate fill-in-the-blank item for the following objectives:

   a. The students will be able to identify what percentage of the Earth's surface is made up of water.
   b. The students will be able to recognize characteristics of a gas.
   c. The students will be able to name the 16th president of the United States.

SPOTLIGHT ON THE CLASSROOM

Mrs. Bacco is a 5th-grade teacher at East Green Elementary School. This year, her school bought new science books for all of the 5th-grade students. Mrs. Bacco loves the new book but does not like the tests that the book provides. Mrs. Bacco used the test items that came with the book for the first chapter test, but was disappointed with the results.

Many of the students scored lower on the test than on the quizzes that she had given. Several of the students are slow readers and were not able to finish the test in the allotted time. Two of the students, who had scored high grades on all of the quizzes, had very low scores on the unit test. She has decided to make her own tests to go along with the remaining chapters.

Mrs. Bacco feels that short-answer items would be most appropriate for her tests. She has decided to use all fill-in-the-blank questions because she thinks that they are the most effective way to get students to write correct answers. However, there are many things she must think about before writing the questions. What precautions must she take while writing the items? What are some of the advantages and disadvantages she will have by using short answer items?

NOTES

1. The answers are (1) Prince Henry, (2) Hernando Cortez, and (3) Robert LaSalle.
2. Some of these attributes are adapted from Oosterhof (2001).

7

ESSAY ITEMS

INTRODUCTION

In the previous chapter we discussed short-answer items. Another very common item format found on many tests is the essay format. Although it is not used very much in the early elementary grades, once students acquire the capacity to express themselves in writing, teachers tend to use essays with some frequency. The older the students are, the more often it is that they will see essay items on a test. By high school, essay items are used frequently.

Essays have several advantages. One of the most common reasons teachers use them is because they require students to express their ideas in writing. However, they also have limitations. For instance, they frequently require a significant amount of time to grade. In this chapter we will also discuss the attributes of good essay items and you will have the opportunity to practice critiquing such items. In addition, we will examine two types of essays, and scoring techniques.

ADVANTAGES AND LIMITATIONS OF THE ESSAY FORMAT

Advantages

The essay format is quite popular and has several advantages. It is especially useful, and, frequently, is the most direct method of measuring higher-level cognitive skills, such as application, analysis, synthesis, and evaluation. In order to demonstrate competence with higher-level skills, students typically have to produce more complex answers, often with supporting details and explanations. Essay questions allow students to demonstrate their competency with the subject matter and their ability to engage in critical thinking.

Another advantage of the essay format is that it requires students to express their ideas in writing, an important skill for older students. However, one must recognize that this advantage is accompanied by a couple of caution flags. First, as you might recall from the previous chapter, a test item should only be measuring one skill, such as knowledge of the subject matter. If you also plan to evaluate the students on their writing ability, that should be done separately. If you wish to evaluate both content and writing, the students should be given two separate scores: the first for the content of their answer, and the second for the quality of their writing. The two scores should not be combined, for to do so will lower the reliability and validity of the test scores. A second word of caution is also in order. Essay tests are not the best way to teach writing. Frequently, when writing an essay for a test, students are under pressure because of time limitations. They are often more focused on the content of their answers than on their writing, and often do not display their best writing skills. It is frequently better to teach writing skills in contexts where there is more time to focus on the writing. In addition, many believe that good writing requires the opportunity to plan, write, and then go back and rewrite. That is certainly what most professional writers do. Students rarely have time on an essay test to edit and revise their answers.

A third advantage of the essay format is that it requires students to construct an answer from memory rather than simply from a list of choices. This requires the students to know and understand the material at a deeper level. To write good essay answers, students must be able to present the material in an organized way. To do so, the material must be well organized in their memory. This allows the teacher to better assess their level of understanding.

A fourth advantage of the essay format is that essay tests typically do not take a great deal of time to construct. Although an individual essay item may take more time to construct than an individual short-answer item, if the test consists of only essay items, the full test will take much less time to construct. It certainly takes much less time to construct a five-item essay test than a 40-item short-answer test.

Limitations

As you might anticipate, the essay format has several limitations. Perhaps the greatest limitation is the amount of time it takes to score essay items. A teacher can easily spend 5 to 10 hours, or even longer, grading essay tests. If you give five essay questions each to a class of 25 students, it means that you have 125 essays to score. Even if you can score one essay question every three minutes, it will take over 6 hours to score the tests for that one class. If you follow one of the recommended procedures and read each essay twice, it will take even longer. Clearly, if you value your time, you need to use essays judiciously.

A second limitation is that essays are not suitable for all types of material. You can use essays to measure knowledge-level and comprehension-level learning, but it is simply not a very efficient way to measure those skills. Other item formats are more suitable in this case. Even higher-level learning is not always amenable to the essay format. For example, students can best demonstrate their knowledge of driving by actually driving a car. However, the essay format is relatively flexible and, with practice, can be adapted to many types of learning.

A third problem with the essay format is that it is dependent on a student's ability to communicate well in writing. Even if you do not grade the students' writing skills, poor writers simply may not be able to organize and communicate what they know about the subject. Many essays and papers are so poorly written that teachers are not able to tell whether the students actually understood the material. We see this frequently enough with native English speakers—students who grew up speaking nothing but English—but we see it even more frequently when grading essays from students who are still developing English skills as a second language. In addition, many students who happen to display a disability will also have difficulty communicating their ideas well in writing.

A fourth problem with essays is that they frequently result in tests that are limited in sampling the content. In Chapter 4 you learned that a reliable test does a good job of sampling from all parts of the domain—most of the material that was taught is covered on the test. You can achieve this best by using many items on the test. However, an essay test must, by its very nature, contain many fewer items, and it, therefore, samples much less of the domain. When domain sampling is limited, as it frequently is on an essay test, reliability and validity are commonly much lower than desired.

One other serious problem with essay tests is that they are much more difficult to score in a consistent manner. They are what we refer to as "non-objective tests." The scoring is much more dependent on the personal judgment of the teacher who is scoring the question. It is not unusual for two teachers to score the same answer and each assign it a different grade. Obviously, this lack of consistency in scoring lowers reliability and validity. Later in the chapter we will discuss how to score essay items in a more consistent way.

TYPES OF ESSAY ITEM

Essentially, we encounter two general types of essay question: the global essay and short-answer essay. *Global essays* (also known as extended-response essays) are rather broad questions that allow students to select what they want to write about from material that was taught. For example, perhaps you have just finished teaching a three-week unit on the Civil War in your high school American history class. You have 40 minutes in which to administer a test and decide to ask one general question. Although you probably would not write a question this way, you could ask something as broad as, "What were the most important aspects of the Civil War?" The students would have the entire 40 minutes in which to answer the question. The question is quite general and allows each student to choose what he or she thought were the most important aspects of the war. However, even the well-prepared students may be uncertain about what you expect them to include in the answer. As a result, many of the answers will be quite different from one another. As you will see later in the chapter, this type of question is difficult to score reliably.

The second type of essay question is the short-answer essay. A *short-answer essay* (also known as a restricted-response essay) is a question than can be answered in about 10 minutes with one good paragraph of about 100 words. This type of essay question is much more specific. A well-prepared student should be able to determine exactly what the teacher expects in the answer. In this case, you could construct a short-answer essay that is similar to the following example.

Example
Name and briefly describe (in 2 to 3 sentences each) four social/political conditions discussed in class that led to the Civil War.

> *Definitions*
>
> **Global essays** are rather broad questions that allow students to select what they want to write about from the material that was taught.
>
> **Short-answer essays** are questions than can be answered in about 10 minutes with one good paragraph of about 100 words.

Psychometricians overwhelmingly favor the short-answer essay item over the global essay for, at least, two reasons. The first reason is related to the Domain Sampling Model. Reliable tests sample as much of the material that was taught as possible. You can typically achieve greater reliability, therefore, by simply increasing the number of items. In doing so, you cover more of the material. With a global essay you can sometimes only ask one or two questions. However, if you use short-answer essays you can ask four or more questions in the same amount of time. This will almost always result in a test with greater reliability and content-related evidence of validity. The second issue has to do with how essays are scored. Although we will discuss scoring later, it is often much easier to score a short-answer essay more consistently than a global essay. Consistency in scoring will also affect reliability and validity. Short-answer essays are more reliable because they can often be scored more consistently.

SCORING ESSAY ITEMS

Scoring essay items can present a challenge to the classroom teacher. We will discuss how to score global essays and short-answer essays separately. We will then look at scoring procedures that should be used with both types of essay.

Global essays generally present the greatest scoring challenge for teachers. When you prepare any type of question, you also need to prepare a key or a scoring plan. You will need to decide which answers you will accept for full credit and which answers you will accept for partial credit. This process is relatively simple with objective test formats, such as short-answer, multiple-choice, and true and false. However, it can be quite challenging for essays, and especially global essays. If the question is open ended, as many global essay questions are, students can theoretically produce a large variety of acceptable answers. In such a case, it is impossible for a teacher to develop scoring plans that account for all possible acceptable answers. Teachers are, therefore, frequently forced to use a holistic scoring strategy.

Holistic Scoring

When using a holistic scoring strategy, you are looking at the answer as a whole, rather than scoring different parts of the essay separately. Essentially, you need to read each essay twice. During the first reading, you skim the answer so that you can place the essay into one of three piles: answers that appear to be very good, answers that appear to be acceptable, and, finally, those that appear to be less than acceptable. Once sorted, you then reread each pile of essays more carefully. For the very good answers, you must determine which deserve an A and which deserve a B. When reading the essays in the acceptable pile, you have to decide which should go into the B pile, which deserve a C, and perhaps a few that should be moved down to the D pile. Finally, as you read the less-than-acceptable answers, you would need to sort them into either the D or the F pile, but may, on occasion, move some up to the C pile.

As you might expect, holistic scoring is one of the least objective scoring techniques available. Since a teacher's judgment is required, consistency can be a serious problem. If you are concerned about consistency, there are two ways to check it. The first technique is to score the essays but not record the grades on the essays themselves. You might jot down the grades on a copy of the class roster, for example. Several days later repeat the entire process. You then can compare how you scored each essay on each of the two occasions. If there is a high correlation, then you can feel reasonably confident that you have been relatively consistent. The second technique involves recruiting a colleague. After you have scored the essays (without recording the grades on the essays) ask your colleague to also score each essay. You then can compare the scores. Again, if there is a high correlation, you can feel assured that you scored the essays consistently.

Normally, holistic scoring will be required any time when there are not a limited number of correct answers. If students could potentially provide a number of correct answers, or if the question encourages students to be creative, then holistic scoring is required.

Another technique that can sometimes be used with global essays is a rubric, or scoring plan. Rubrics are discussed in Chapter 13, Performance Assessments. Essentially, with a rubric you spell out the various characteristics that you expect to see in an excellent answer, a very good answer, an acceptable answer, a poor answer, and so on. Well-developed rubrics can allow you to score global essays more objectively.

Analytic Scoring

Short answer essays, on the other hand, can frequently be scored far more consistently. Teachers are often able to use an analytic scoring plan that is based on a point system. Let's return to the example of the question that I used earlier.

Example

Question: Name and briefly describe (in 2 to 3 sentences each) four social/political conditions discussed in class that led to the Civil War.

Let's say that in class you discussed five social/political conditions that led to the Civil War. If this item were worth a total of 20 points, you might award 2 points apiece for each condition that the students appropriately name and up to 3 points apiece for each condition that they accurately describe. You can even go further and describe what you will accept as a 1-point, a 2-point, and a 3-point description of each condition. Although such a scoring plan takes some time to develop, it does allow you to be much more consistent in scoring short-answer essays.

General Recommendations for Scoring Essay Answers

There are additional procedures that you can employ when grading either global or short-answer essays that will increase reliability. You should score your students' essay answers anonymously, without knowing whose test you are scoring. We do get to know our students fairly well and we often develop expectations about their typical level of preparation and their prior performance on tests. If you are aware of whose essay you are grading, you might let your expectations influence how you evaluate their answers, resulting in grades that are either too high or too low. You can achieve anonymous scoring (also known as "masked scoring") by having the students identify themselves only on a cover sheet. Before scoring the essays you turn over the cover sheet so that you cannot see the name.

A second procedure is to score each essay question independently. Have the students start each essay answer on a new page. After scoring Joe's answer to essay question number 1, turn the page over to his answer to question number 2, so you will not see the score you gave him on question 1 when you score his answer to question 2. If you know that he scored well on question 1, you might be influenced to give a higher score on question 2. In addition, score all the students' answers to question 1 before moving onto scoring answers to question 2. You will be more consistent in awarding points, especially partial credits points, since the scoring plan will be clearly in your mind.

The third procedure is to shuffle the students' papers after scoring an answer. The test papers, or booklets, should start in one pile. After scoring each question for each student, you turn the page to the next answer and put the test booklet into the finished pile. After you finish scoring all of the answers to question 1, shuffle the test booklets before you start scoring the answers to question 2. When scoring essays you sometimes change your criteria. Perhaps the question was more difficult than you intended and you start by giving the first few students low scores. After a while, however, you realize that perhaps you did not explain some points as clearly as you thought that you had. As a result, some of the later essay answers are scored more leniently. The students whose answers were at the bottom of the pile benefit from your growing leniency. At other times, you may become frustrated with the students' answers and start scoring later answers more harshly. You can avoid any student consistently benefiting or being harmed by your changing expectations by shuffling the test booklets.

When giving essay tests, many teachers will list a number of essay questions and require the students to choose several from that list. Perhaps there are five questions listed and students must choose three from the list. Although students tend to like this procedure, it is not recommended from a psychometric perspective. When students choose different questions to answer, they are not all actually taking the same test. Some items may be much more difficult than other items and, surprisingly, students do not always choose the easiest items. Comparing students' scores to one another then becomes more problematic. This tends to reduce both the reliability and the validity of the test. It is best to have all of the students answer the same questions.

ATTRIBUTES DESIRED IN ESSAY ITEMS

As was true with short-answer items, essay items should display certain attributes. Since psychometricians strongly favor the short-answer essay, the attributes that we will deal with will be specifically aimed at that type of essay item.

1. *The item should measure the skill or knowledge that it was designed to measure.* This very general attribute is expected from every item, no matter what format is used. How well does the item match the objective that it was designed to measure? Frequently, because essay questions are somewhat lengthy, it is easier to design a question that

matches the objective. However, this should not be taken for granted. If you lose sight of the objective (for example, by forgetting to review it before preparing the item), it is not difficult to get off track and design an item that does not measure what it was intended to measure.

2. *The item can be answered in about 10 minutes with one paragraph of about 100 words.* It takes some careful planning to make certain that a short-essay item is sufficiently limited in scope. As a new teacher, you may run into this problem more frequently than will more experienced teachers. With practice, you will be able to develop questions appropriate for this format.

3. *The reading level of this item is appropriate for the students.* Once again, the question should be testing the students' knowledge of the material, not their ability to read well. As I mentioned earlier, with the short-answer essay format the questions may be somewhat longer. This is desirable since it may take some additional explanation to make certain that the well-prepared students know what the teacher is looking for. However, you also need to make certain that you do not end up writing a question that presents a reading challenge to the less able readers in your class. Again, with experience, teachers get better at writing readable questions.

4. *The scoring plan is sufficiently complete and clear so that different teachers scoring the same essay would give it the same score.* There are really two issues here. First, the scoring plan needs to be complete. It must contain all of the possible correct answers—answers that experts in the field would consider to be correct. Second, it should be unambiguous. If you were to give the essay answers and the scoring plan to a colleague, that individual should give the same score to an answer that you gave. This is also a skill that develops with experience.

5. *The question is written in a sufficiently clear style so that well-prepared students will know exactly what is expected in their answers.* The question must be clear and unambiguous. The students need to know exactly what is expected. Although we generally prefer test questions to be as brief as possible, brevity in essay questions is not an essential issue. Clearly, superfluous material should be excluded. However, if it takes two or more sentences to clearly spell out what is expected in the answer, that is perfectly acceptable. In addition, you should identify how much the question is worth. If it is a 20-point question, that needs to be marked. Students need to be aware of how much a question is worth so that they can devote a sufficient amount of time to each answer.

Attributes Desired in Essay Items[1]

1. *The item should measure the skill or knowledge that it was designed to measure.*

2. *The item can be answered in about 10 minutes with one paragraph of about 100 words.*

3. *The reading level of the item is appropriate for the students.*

4. *The scoring plan is sufficiently complete and clear so that different teachers scoring the same essay would give it the same score.*

5. *The question is written in a sufficiently clear style so that well-prepared students will know exactly what is expected in their answers.*

EVALUATING ESSAY ITEMS

Now that we have reviewed the attributes desired in an essay item, let's look at several essay items. In order to fully evaluate the items, the objective is provided and a scoring plan is included when appropriate.

Item 1

Objective: The students will be able to recall the events that led to the Louisiana Purchase and their significance.
Grade level: High school American history
Item: Describe the details of the Louisiana Purchase.

As this item is currently written, it is simply too general. It is unclear whether the teacher wants the students to write about what was happening in the U. S. that led us to want to purchase New Orleans. Perhaps the teacher wants the students to describe the relationships among the United States, England, France, and Spain. Some students might think that the teacher wants a description of the negotiations between Robert Livingston, James Monroe, and Napoleon. As the question is currently written, well-prepared students could write an answer that would be the length of a research paper, or write an answer that was not what the teacher expected.

Item 2

Objective: The students will be able to name the parts of the respiratory system and describe the steps in respiration.
Grade level: 5th-grade science
Item: Describe the steps our body goes through when we breathe. As you describe each step be sure to name the parts of the respiratory system that are involved. (20 points)
Scoring plan: Students will earn 2 points each for appropriately naming the following parts of the respiratory system:
- nose
- nostrils
- mucus
- trachea
- bronchial tubes
- air sacs
- diaphragm

They will earn 2 points for describing each step:
- Diaphragm contracts allowing air to enter the respiratory system.
- Air passes through nose and nostrils and is warmed and moistened by mucus.
- Nostrils clean entering air.
- Air travels down trachea and bronchial tubes.
- Oxygen and carbon dioxide are exchanged in the air sacs.
- Diaphragm expands pushing air out of the respiratory system.

This appears to be a good essay item. However, most of a class of 5th-graders may not be able to answer it in about 10 minutes. If it took them a lot longer, I would suggest that you narrow the scope of the item.

While we are discussing this issue, it might be a good time to point out that you cannot always predict how well a particular test item will work. With experience, teachers learn how to prepare better essay items. However, on occasion, all teachers prepare items that are in some way problematic, often in ways that they had not anticipated. Most often, it is because some of the students interpreted the item to mean something that it was not intended to mean. Therefore, you need to realize that until you try an item, you will never be exactly sure how well it will work. It also means that you will have to be flexible in how you use the results of your tests.

Item 3

Objective: The students will be able to briefly describe how the themes of honesty and integrity affected the main character, Marty Preston, in the book, *Shiloh*.

Grade level: 5th-grade language arts

Item: In the book, *Shiloh*, Marty struggles with his need to lie to everyone to protect the dog, Shiloh. Briefly describe how Marty dealt with his lying.

This essay item addresses only part of the objective. Although the objective deals with both honesty and integrity, the item only deals with honesty. In addition, many 5th-grade students might not be able to recognize strictly on their own the role that honesty played in the story. Class discussion on the issue would be required.

SUMMARY

In this chapter we described two types of essay item. The global essay is a broad question and students frequently pick and choose which material to include in their answers. The short-answer essay requests specific information and can typically be answered by students with a one-paragraph answer. We then discussed the advantages and disadvantages of the essay format and when essay items can be used appropriately. We discussed how teachers should use different techniques to grade both global and short-answer essays. We discussed five attributes (characteristics) desired in essay items. Finally, we practiced evaluating several essay items.

EXERCISES

1. Write an appropriate global essay item for the following objectives:

   a. The students will be able to identify problems that occurred during the Great Depression.
   b. The students will be able to analyze a work by Walt Whitman.
   c. The students will be able to discuss different types of pollution and problems/concerns associated with each.

2. Write an appropriate short-answer essay item for the following objectives:

   a. The students will be able to discuss similarities and differences in the movie *The Outsiders* and the novel written by S. E. Hinton.
   b. The students will be able to identify ways we use fractions in our daily lives.
   c. The students will be able to identify inventors and inventions of the Industrial Revolution.

3. Select a topic that you have been studying and write one short-answer essay on the topic. Include the objective and the scoring plan for the answer.

SPOTLIGHT ON THE CLASSROOM

Mr. Garcia is a 9th-grade history teacher at Monte High School. He is thrilled because he just found out that he will be teaching the 9th-grade honors students for an advanced U.S. history course next year. However, he has a lot of work to do to develop the course.

Throughout the summer, he plans to revise some of his U.S. history tests from his regular classes so they more directly measure higher-level cognitive skills. He believes that including essay questions would be a fine addition for the honors students. Discuss some advantages and disadvantages of adding essay questions to his course. Why would using essay items be beneficial to Mr. Garcia's students? What should he do to be sure that the essay questions will be a reliable measure of the students' learning?

NOTE

1.   Some of these attributes are adapted from Oosterhof (2001).

8

MULTIPLE-CHOICE ITEMS

INTRODUCTION

So far we have discussed both the short-answer and essay item format. Another very popular item format is multiple choice. In this chapter, we will discuss both the advantages and the limitations of multiple-choice items. We will discuss the qualities desired in, and numerous variations of, the format. Finally, we will practice developing and critiquing multiple-choice items.

Multiple-choice items are popular among many teachers. Although used less frequently in the very early grades, by the later elementary grades they are used more often. By the time the students are in middle school, junior high, and senior high school, multiple-choice questions are used quite often. They are not the preferred format with some types of material (mathematics computations, for example) but, because of their flexibility, they can be used with a remarkably broad range of content (Downing, 2006). In addition, they possess some psychometric qualities that make them highly desirable with organizations that produce standardized tests. Standardized test developers rely heavily on the multiple-choice format.

ADVANTAGES AND LIMITATIONS OF MULTIPLE-CHOICE ITEMS

There are a number of advantages and disadvantages of using the multiple-choice format when developing test items.

Advantages

Better Sampling of Content

Multiple-choice items offer a number of advantages that sometimes make them more popular than other item formats. First, they often allow teachers to better sample the content domain. Compared to essay items, students can answer many more multiple-choice items in the same amount of time, which means that you can sample more content during a test. In addition, students can frequently answer multiple-choice items faster than they can answer short-answer items, which allows you to again have more items on a test. The multiple-choice format also allows us to ask questions on more types of material. As was mentioned in Chapter 6, the short-answer format is primarily limited to factual information—such as knowledge and comprehension—whereas the multiple-choice format is more flexible and can test higher-level learning. We will discuss this in more detail later in this section.

Easy to Score

A second advantage of the multiple choice format is that the items can be scored very quickly. For older students, you can use separate answer sheets, which are both fast and easy to score. If you have the option to use an answer sheet that can be scanned on a computer, it is even faster. Younger students should mark the answers in the test booklet to avoid confusion. Although this takes somewhat longer to score than does a separate answer sheet, it can still be scored very quickly.

More Objective Scoring

A third advantage of multiple-choice items is that they can be scored objectively. Once the scoring key is developed, the test can be scored consistently. The teacher's subjective judgment is called upon much less often. However, this does not mean that multiple-choice items are free from measurement error. Poorly written multiple-choice items are as much a source of measurement error as are poorly written items in any other format. We will also be discussing this in more detail later in the chapter.

Less Ambiguous

A fourth advantage of the multiple-choice format is that items can be better structured and are less ambiguous than short-answer items. Often, these two formats are quite similar. Frequently, a question that is suitable for the short-answer format can easily be converted into a multiple-choice format. However, sometimes an item written in the short-answer format can be rather ambiguous. Perhaps the teacher is looking for a particular response when a number of responses would actually answer the question. However, if the same item is converted into a multiple-choice format, the number of responses is limited with only one being correct. The ambiguity can thus be eliminated.

Can Test a Variety of Content

A fifth advantage of multiple-choice items is that they are flexible and can be used to test a variety of content material. A teacher who is skilled at preparing good multiple-choice items can prepare them to fit almost any content: science, social studies, language arts, and even math. However, unless there is a real need to do so, teachers should not use multiple-choice items to measure students' skills with processes like mathematical computations. Having students complete problems on paper and showing all of the steps is often a more direct way to measure their ability to apply math algorithms appropriately.

Can Test Higher-Level Learning

Critics of the multiple-choice format sometimes claim that it can only be used to measure knowledge-level cognitive objectives. That is simply not true! One of the strengths of this format is that it can be used to measure lower-level cognitive objectives, such as knowledge and comprehension, but can also be used to measure application, analysis, synthesis, and evaluation-level learning. Although it is relatively easy to develop multiple-choice items to measure the four lower-level cognitive objectives—knowledge through analysis—it does take training to learn to use it to measure synthesis and evaluation. It is a very flexible item format and can be a quite powerful measurement tool.

More Sensitive to Partial Knowledge

Finally, there is one additional advantage to the multiple-choice format. Since it is a recognition format (the correct answer is among the alternative answers), it is more sensitive to partial knowledge than are the other formats. If students know something about the content of the question, they have a better chance of getting the answer correct with multiple choice than with any other item format. In that sense, it makes the multiple-choice format more sensitive to learning. In some of the other formats, unless you know the material extremely well, you are less likely to get the item correct.

Limitations

Of course, the multiple-choice format is not without its limitations.

More Susceptible to Guessing

First, multiple-choice items are somewhat susceptible to guessing. If you have an item with four alternatives, A, B, C, and D, a student has a 25% chance of getting the item correct simply by guessing. Although students do not typically guess that often, the guessing factor does put some limits on the reliability of tests with multiple-choice items.

Indirectly Measures Higher-Level Objectives

A second limitation with multiple-choice items is that they provide only an indirect route to measuring higher-level cognitive objectives. Typically, when measuring synthesis and evaluation, the most direct route would be to have the students write out the answers. Using multiple-choice items to measure those skills is less direct. However, in reality, there are many phenomena in science that we measure only indirectly, and frequently do so quite well.

Construction of Items can be Time-Consuming

A third limitation of the multiple-choice format is that the items can be quite time-consuming to develop. It does not take much time to develop a poor multiple-choice item. However, it frequently takes quite a bit longer to develop a good item. A multiple-choice item consists of two parts: a stem and alternative answers. The stem should essentially present a complete problem. The alternative answers should consist of a correct alternative and several other alternatives that are plausible but clearly incorrect. The goal of the incorrect alternatives, sometimes known as foils or distractors, is to distract students who do not know the material well into choosing them as the correct answer. However, at the same time, well-prepared students should be able to identify them as clearly wrong. Writing a stem and the correct answer is the easy part. What frequently takes longer is developing several distractors that are plausible, but clearly incorrect. It is important to avoid distractors that are partially correct, since they have the potential to sometimes attract students who know the material. Therefore, this type of distractor reduces the reliability of the test. Preparing good distractors can be time-consuming.

Multiple-Choice Items are Inappropriate for Very Young Children

A fourth limitation of the multiple-choice format is that many of its forms (to be discussed later in the chapter) are inappropriate for very young children. Unless the items are very brief, providing a stem and several alternative answers can be confusing for young students, who are not yet proficient readers. If the questions are presented orally, students as early as 1st grade can sometimes handle them well. However, when presented in a written form, students can become more easily confused until about 4th or 5th grade.

Not Appropriate for All Material

A final limitation of the multiple-choice format is that it is not equally appropriate for all material. Clearly some material—such as factual knowledge in science and social studies—fits in well with the multiple-choice format. However, other material and skills—such as math computations, science problems, and analysis of literature—are often better measured with alternative item formats. As we will see later, good classroom testing involves flexibility. It is important to match the item format with the material if you want to use tests effectively to measure student learning.

ATTRIBUTES DESIRED IN MULTIPLE-CHOICE ITEMS

As was true for both the short-answer and the essay formats, there are a number of qualities that we look for in good multiple-choice items.

1. *The item should measure the skill or knowledge that it was designed to measure.* Of course, as is true for all test items, this is one of the most important characteristics of any test item. Is there a good match between the objective and the test item?

2. *The reading level of the item is appropriate for the students.* Once again, a test item should be measuring only one characteristic. It should not simultaneously measure the students' knowledge of content and their ability to read. Multiple-choice items can be especially challenging since students must be able to keep the question in mind while they are scanning the alternative answers. Complex sentence structures should be avoided whenever possible. Some of the other qualities on this list will also address issues related to the readability of multiple-choice items.

3. *The stem presents a clear and complete question.* The stem should present a complete question. After reading the stem, the well-prepared students should be able to provide the correct answer without looking at the alternatives. It is easy to prepare a stem that is simply too broad, and therefore too ambiguous.

Bad Example

Piaget was _____.

This item is simply too broad. It could be answered in a variety of ways. Here are some possible answers.

- a man.
- a Swiss psychologist.
- a child prodigy.
- a fellow who liked to ride his bicycle to work.
- a brand name for an expensive Swiss watch.

Here are some alternative stems. It really does not matter if the stem is in the form of a question or is reworded into an incomplete sentence, since either approach works well.

Better Examples

Who was the Swiss psychologist noted for his theory of cognitive development in children?

or

The Swiss psychologist noted for his theory of cognitive development in children was _____.

---

4. *The correct alternative is one with which experts in the field would agree.* Is the correct answer truly correct? It should go well beyond the teacher's opinion that the answer is correct. Other teachers and experts should also agree that the answer is correct. In some early elementary classes, topics are often taught in a simplistic manner. In trying to make the material simple enough for young students, some textbooks include material that is not exactly true. Oftentimes, the correct information is more complex. For example, in 1st grade, students are taught that we always subtract a smaller number from a larger number. It is not until later, when students learn to borrow, that they recognize that a large digit can be subtracted from a smaller digit. Students in higher grades are then taught that there are numbers smaller than zero (negative numbers). For another example, some elementary-school health books present current recommendations (for example, the nutrition pyramid) as if it were carved in stone. What is true about "good" nutrition changes every few years as we learn more about the needs of the human body.

5. *All of the distractors are plausible but clearly wrong.* Each distractor must, at least, seem like a plausible answer. For students who are not well prepared, each distractor should be viewed as possibly correct. We do not want students to be able to eliminate any distractors as simply implausible.

Bad Example

The 16th president of the United States was _____.

A. Ulysses S. Grant

B. Abraham Lincoln

C. James Buchanan

D. Madonna

It would be surprising to find a high school history student who would choose option D. Since most students could simply eliminate Madonna as a plausible option, even if they were uncertain of the correct answer, they would have an increased chance of getting the item correct simply by guessing.

The distractors should also be clearly wrong. It is also problematic to include a distractor that is partially correct. Even students who know the material relatively well can sometimes be confused by an answer that is partially correct. They see that part of the answer is correct and think that there are two or more possible correct answers.

Bad Example

Vascular plants have

A. true leaves and roots.

B. true roots and stems.

C. true stems and leaves.

D. true roots, stems, and leaves.

With this item the intended correct answer is D. However, alternatives A, B, and C, although incomplete, are also correct.

6. *Each of the alternatives should have similar content.* Some items contain three alternatives that are similar, and a fourth alternative that is very different. Most often, the teacher was only able to develop the correct answer and two similar distractors. Since one more distractor was needed, it had to come from a different perspective. Test-wise students will frequently recognize that they can simply ignore the obviously different alternative. This type of item also presents another dilemma for students. The three parallel distractors often represent one concept, whereas the odd distractor represents a different concept. This requires the students to evaluate two concepts and, therefore, consider the possibility that two answers are correct. Let's look at an example.

Bad Example

Which of the following is true of the relationship between the Earth and the Moon?

A. The average distance between the Earth and the Moon is about 265,000 km.

B. The average distance between the Earth and the Moon is about 385,000 km.

C. The average distance between the Earth and the Moon is about 505,000 km.

D. Although the Earth's core is primarily made of iron, the Moon's core is primarily made of nickel.

The correct answer is B. The first three alternatives deal with one concept, the distance between the Earth and the Moon. The last alternative deals with an entirely different concept, which, in this case, is also incorrect.

7. *Repetitive words should be avoided in the alternative answers.* We would like test items to be as brief as possible to reduce the time it takes students to read the items. You can often achieve that by moving repetitive words from the alternatives into the stem.

Bad Example

In a circle, what is the relationship between the radius and the diameter?

A. The radius is equal to ¼ of the diameter.

B. The radius is equal to ½ of the diameter.

C. The radius is equal to ¾ of the diameter.

D. The radius is equal to the diameter.

Better Example

In a circle, what is the relationship between the radius and the diameter? The radius is equal to

A. ¼ of the diameter.

B. ½ of the diameter.

C. ¾ of the diameter.

D. the diameter.

---

8. *The stem of the question should be as concise as possible.* Once again, our goal is to reduce the reading challenge for the students. Wordy questions with superfluous words or phrases present two problems. First, they simply take longer to read. Second, students have to be able to separate the important material in the question from the unimportant material. This makes the item more difficult and introduces a second skill into the question, which reduces the reliability of the test.

Bad Example

Since long essays are notoriously unreliable, they are not recommended by psychometricians who prefer brief essays. For a brief essay students are expected to be able to answer a question within about _____ minutes.

Better Example

For a brief essay, students are expected to be able to answer a question within about _____ minutes.

9. *Avoid using modifying words in the stem of the question that significantly alter the meaning of the question or statement.* The most troublesome modifiers are "least," "except," and "not." When they are used in a sentence, they frequently reverse the meaning of the same sentence without that word. If the students happen to miss that single word, they may misinterpret the question. Students frequently get these types of item wrong simply because they misread the question.

Bad Example
Which of the following is not a characteristic of mammals? They

A. are warm-blooded.
B. have vertebrae.
C. are all herbivores.
D. are primates.

There are times, however, when you simply cannot ask the question that you want to ask without using one of these potentially troublesome modifiers. If you must use one of them, the word(s) needs to be highlighted so that students are much more likely to read them.

Better Example
Which of the following is **not** a characteristic of mammals? They . . .

If at all possible, you should try to rewrite or reword the sentence.

Best Example
Which of the following is a characteristic of mammals? They . . .

---

10. *The grammar of each option agrees with the stem.* This is what students sometimes refer to as the "grammar give-aways." Sometimes the stem is an incomplete sentence, but not all of the alternatives agree grammatically with the stem. In that case, the students simply need to read the stem and each alternative as a complete sentence to select the one that is grammatically correct. In other cases one, or more, of the alternatives can be eliminated simply because they do not agree grammatically with the stem. These errors often involve subject/verb agreement or noun/pronoun agreement (one single and the other plural). However, there are other grammar give-aways, as are illustrated with the following example.

Bad Example
The African animal that has the greatest ability to leap great distances is a

A. antelope.

B. ostrich.

C. leopard.

D. impala.

This item can be improved with one addition.

Better Example

The African animal that has the greatest ability to leap great distances is a(n)

A. antelope.

B. ostrich.

C. leopard.

D. impala.

11. *Whenever possible, avoid options such as "all of the above" and "none of the above" in multiple-choice items.* Although there are times when it appears logical and reasonable to use either "all of the above" or "none of the above," research indicates that their use tends to lower the reliability of the test. In many cases, these alternatives simply "muddy the water." They make the items more confusing to the students. For example, if each of two or more alternatives contains any statement that may be true, many students will be inclined to go for "all of the above," even when that is not the correct alternative. In addition, if the correct alternative is even the slightest bit ambiguous, then some students will incorrectly go for "none of the above." When instructors use either of those alternatives very sporadically, students correctly guess that they are likely to be the correct answers. Although their use may sometimes improve an item, it appears that "all of the above" and "none of the above" generally do not help students demonstrate their knowledge as effectively as do items without those alternatives. Therefore, the best advice at the current time is to avoid those options.

12. *Whenever reasonable, the alternatives should be listed in a logical order.* Some questions call for a numerical response. In that case the most logical way to list the alternatives is in ascending numerical order.

Example

Each human cell contains _____ pairs of chromosomes.

A. 21

B. 23

C. 25

D. 27

In addition, there are other times when it appears logical to arrange the alternatives in some order. Frequently, however, there is no logical way to arrange the alternatives and some psychometricians have suggested that, in such a case, they should be arranged alphabetically. Since there does not appear to be any real advantage of alphabetical arrangements, I am not an advocate of that advice. However, if you have no other way to arrange alternatives, you could arrange them alphabetically.

What is perhaps more important is that the correct answer needs to appear in each spot roughly the same number of times. For example, if you have 40 four-choice (A, B, C, D) multiple-choice items, then the correct answer should be A about 25% of the time, B about 25% of the time, C about 25% of the time, and D about 25% of the time. This is sometimes referred to as "balancing the answer key." Some teachers tend to favor one answer slot over the others. If you use option C frequently and students do not know an answer, they would be wise to choose C. With a balanced answer key, students are less likely to be able to get answers correct by simply guessing on a test.

Attributes Desired in Multiple-Choice Items [1]

1. *The item should measure the skill or knowledge that it was designed to measure.*
2. *The reading level of the item is appropriate for the students.*
3. *The stem presents a clear and complete question.*
4. *The correct alternative is one with which experts in the field would agree.*
5. *All of the distractors are plausible but clearly wrong.*
6. *Each of the alternatives should have similar content.*
7. *Repetitive words should be avoided in the alternative answers.*
8. *The stem of the question should be as concise as possible.*
9. *Avoid using modifying words in the stem of the question that significantly alter the meaning of the question or statement.*
10. *The grammar of each option agrees with the stem.*
11. *Whenever possible, avoid options such as "all of the above" and "none of the above" in multiple-choice items.*
12. *Whenever reasonable, the alternatives should be listed in a logical order.*

EVALUATING MULTIPLE-CHOICE ITEMS

Several multiple-choice items are listed below. To make the critique more meaningful, the objective and the intended grade level are provided for each question.

Item 1

Objective: Students will be able to recognize that Jupiter is the largest planet in our solar system.

Grade level: High school earth and space science

Item: Which planet is the most massive?
                A. Jupiter
                B. Saturn
                C. Uranus

The first problem with this question is that it does not necessarily match the objective. Whereas the objective discusses the size of the planets, the question asks for the most massive planet. Although mass and size may be correlated, that is not always the case. Some gas giants may actually have less mass than some smaller planets with a metallic core. The term, massive, can have several meanings. It can refer to both size and to mass. This could be potentially confusing to a bright student with a good vocabulary. Actually, in this case this argument is rather moot since Jupiter has both the biggest diameter and the greatest mass. However, it is important, when writing questions, that you choose your words carefully.

   A second problem is that the question, as it is written, is not limited to our solar system. In the last number of years, astronomers have begun to identify planets outside our solar system. Although that could make this question ambiguous if it were a completion item, it is not as serious an issue as a multiple-choice item because all of the possible answers are planets from our solar system.

Item 2
Objective: Students will be able to name the two states that are largely desert.
Grade level: 7th-grade geography
Item: Which of the following states have the greatest proportion of their land
                area as deserts?
                A. California and Nevada
                B. Arizona and New Mexico
                C. Nevada and Utah
                D. Arizona and Utah
                E. Pennsylvania and Ohio

The correct answer is C, Nevada and Utah. Both states are about 90% desert. The main problem with this question is that alternatives A and D are each partially correct since they each include one of the two correct answers. In addition, since both California and Arizona each contain a substantial amount of desert, alternatives A and D would be attractive to even the knowledgeable student. Partially correct alternatives should be avoided. The other problem is with alternative E. Many students would know that neither Pennsylvania nor Ohio is a plausible choice for states that are largely desert.

Item 3
Objective: Students will be able to recall specific details about the life of Alexander
                the Great, including his family and his origins.
Grade level: 9th-grade world history
Item: Although in many ways Alexander the Great spread Greek ideas
                throughout his empire, he was actually originally from _____.

A. Canada
B. France
C. Rome
D. Macedonia

There are, at least, two problems with this item. First of all, the initial phrase in the stem about spreading Greek culture, although accurate, is not really necessary and makes the item more wordy than necessary. This type of extraneous material may actually confuse some students. The other problem is with two of the distractors. As far as I know, neither France nor Canada existed in 356 B.C. when Alexander was born. The new world was still largely unknown throughout Europe and Asia and modern-day France was then a part of Gaul. The knowledgeable student should be able to eliminate them as plausible alternatives. Remember, incorrect alternatives need to be plausible. By the way, Alexander was the King of Macedonia.

VARIOUS TYPES OF MULTIPLE-CHOICE ITEM

Although college students are fairly accustomed to seeing traditional multiple-choice items, there are also variations of the multiple-choice format.

Matching Items

Matching represents a variation of the multiple choice format. It is used fairly regularly in literature, social studies, and science classes, but is also used, on occasion, with almost any subject matter. Essentially, a set of parallel stems are listed on the left and a list of parallel alternatives are listed on the right. The stems might be the names of 10 explorers and the alternatives could be 10 or more places they were noted to explore. Matching tests can have variations in their directions. Some teachers make the items more difficult by having a certain number of stems and fewer or more alternatives. At times, some alternatives could be used more than once; whereas, at other times, there could be alternatives that are simply not used. Although matching is almost always limited to factual knowledge, it can be very effective as long as you follow the same guidelines used for multiple-choice items.

Range-of-Values Items

Sometimes multiple choice is used for mathematical computation items. Let's say that the correct answer is 1.732 (What is the square root of 3?). Typically, test developers include the correct answer and answers that students would obtain if they make the most common errors. However, if students obtain an answer that is not on the list, they then know that they have made an error. Some test developers use range-of-values alternatives. Alternatives to the question described previously might look like the ones listed below.

A. < 1.00
B. 1.00 to 1.50
C. 1.51 to 2.00
D. > 2.00

Since the correct answer is 1.732, C would be the correct alternative.

Ranking Options

Some test questions ask the students to rank some alternatives according to a criterion. For example, American history students could be asked the following question.

Example

Rank these four states according to the order in which they were admitted to the Union.[2]

A. Colorado

B. Iowa

C. Pennsylvania

D. Vermont

Although this format is not used very often in education, it is currently quite popular on some television quiz shows.

Interpretive Exercises

Perhaps one of the most sophisticated uses of the multiple-choice item format is interpretive exercises. With this technique teachers can measure higher-level cognitive objectives, such as application, analysis, synthesis, and evaluation. These items require two parts. First, you need the exercise material: a brief paragraph or two, a poem, a table, a chart, a photograph, or a similar item. Then you can prepare several test items that require the students to interpret the exercise material. This approach can be used to see how well students can read and interpret material presented in a chart or graph; to see how well they can comprehend and analyze a brief written passage; or to see if they can interpret a map or a diagram. This technique provides a way to measure higher-level skills in a variety of fields.

Here is an example which begins with an interpretive exercise.

Example

Most American colonies were founded by groups that were seeking religious freedom. Typically, the founders belonged to one of the less-favored churches in the country in which they lived. They decided that moving to the new world and founding their own colony would provide them with greater religious freedom than they currently experienced.

Once they received a charter and moved to the Americas, they had their work set out for them. They had to build log homes as quickly as possible. Although, they brought with them stores that would hopefully last many months, they had to establish ways to hunt and fish, plant fruits and vegetables, and trade with the Native Americans if they hoped to survive.

The colonists were also very interested in educating their children. Since they were typically very devout people, they built a simple church. Many times the church served as the local school when religious services were not being held. The colonists were simply modeling the, then prevalent, European model of educating

---

children through the churches. That model developed during the Protestant Reformation when Martin Luther introduced the idea that the common man should learn to read the Bible himself so that he could seek religious salvation. Therefore, those colonial religiously-based schools became the first education model for the northern American colonies.

Item:
Based on the previous passage, how would you characterize education in the northern colonies? It was designed to

A. produce children who would be able to return to Europe to obtain professional degrees.

B. teach basic literacy skills so that the children could meet their spiritual needs.

C. turn some of the boys into preachers.

D. turn children into productive adults who could meet the physical needs of their families.

NUMBER OF ALTERNATIVES

Multiple-choice items come in many forms with two, three, four, five, and occasionally more options. Is there an optimum number of alternatives? From a purely psychometric perspective, the more alternatives the better simply because with more alternatives the effect of guessing is reduced and reliability can be higher. With only two alternatives (A, B), a student has a 50% chance of getting the item correct simply by guessing. However, with five alternatives (A, B, C, D, E), a student's chance of getting the item correct simply by guessing is reduced to 20%.

However, there are other issues to consider. As the number of alternatives increases, the students must do more reading and consider more possible answers to a question at the same time. This makes items with more alternatives more cognitively challenging. In the very early grades, two to three alternatives are appropriate. However, in the later grades, students can typically handle four or more alternatives.

Another issue has to do with the difficulty of developing good multiple-choice items. Although I have been writing multiple-choice items for my college courses for over 25 years, I frequently find that developing an item with four alternatives is sufficiently challenging. When I have attempted to develop a fifth alternative, it frequently takes me much longer. It is a real challenge to develop good multiple-choice items with multiple incorrect alternatives. Remember, incorrect alternatives need to be clearly wrong, yet plausible. It is not too difficult to develop two to three plausible, but wrong alternatives. Frequently, however, as we try to develop additional incorrect alternatives, we sometimes develop alternatives that do not meet the required criteria. Some alternatives are partially correct, whereas others are simply implausible.

Researchers (Rodriguez, 2005) have found that when time is a factor, as it is on many standardized tests, three-option multiple-choice items are optimal. The primary advantage of three options over four or five options is that they involve less reading and can be completed faster. Test developers can include more items, in this case, which tends to improve both reliability and content validity. The positive effects of adding more items, with fewer alternative answers, more than offsets the negative effects of guessing.

SUMMARY

In this chapter we discussed the multiple-choice format, including its advantages and limitations. We discussed the attributes of good multiple-choice items. We practiced critiquing items, and examined the various ways that multiple-choice items can be used in the classroom. Finally, we looked at what should be considered an optimum number of alternatives.

EXERCISES

1. Write an appropriate *multiple-choice item* for the following objectives:

   a. The students will be able to identify the largest body of water on earth.
   b. The students will be able to use the Pythagorean Theorem to find the length of the missing side of a right triangle.
   c. The students will be able to identify an example of a metaphor.

2. Write an appropriate *matching item* for the following objectives:

   a. The students will be able to differentiate between animals that are predators and animals that are prey.
   b. The students will be able to match European countries with their current leaders.

3. Write an appropriate *ranking item* for the following objectives:

   a. The students will be able to rank animals and plants in the order they would appear in a food chain.
   b. The students will be able to list presidents in order of their U.S. presidency.

4. Write an appropriate *range-of-value item* for the following objective:

   a. The students will be able to find the average high temperature for Chicago, Illinois in the month of January.

SPOTLIGHT ON THE CLASSROOM

A group of teachers at Beyer Elementary School in Baltimore, Maryland have been asked to develop end-of-the-year exams for all of the 4th-grade students in the district. A major job for the teachers is to choose the type of questions to be used. This decision must be made before the first question is written.

The teachers were asked to formulate three different 4th-grade tests. One test covers basic science knowledge. It will test the content knowledge that Maryland educators feel the children should learn during the 4th-grade. Another test is designed to ask the students to summarize the plot of *The Indian in the Cupboard*. The third test is focused on mathematics. It will test the students' abilities with mathematic computations.

Which type of questions would be most appropriate for each of the three tests? What are some advantages and limitations to using each type? What criteria should the group use so that each of the tests is a reliable measure of student learning?

NOTES

1. Some of these attributes are adapted from Oosterhof (2001).
2. The correct order is Pennsylvania, Vermont, Iowa, and Colorado (C D B A).

9

TRUE–FALSE ITEMS (AND VARIATIONS)

INTRODUCTION

In this chapter we will examine the fourth type of item format, true–false items, which are sometimes also known as "alternative-choice" (Oosterhof, 2001) or "binary-choice" (Popham, 2005) items since they always appear with two possible answers. Although most of us have seen the true–false variation, there are several other variations that are used less commonly. In this chapter, we will discuss the advantages and limitations of the true–false format. For example, it is very popular because the items are relatively easy to develop. However, with only two alternatives, the effects of guessing could play a significant role in lowering the reliability of tests using this format. We will look at the characteristics of good true–false items and have several opportunities to critique items. Finally, we will look at a number of other variations of the true–false format.

ADVANTAGES AND LIMITATIONS OF TRUE–FALSE ITEMS

There are a number of advantages of using true–false items when preparing classroom tests, but there are also a number of limitations with this testing format. Therefore, be sure to consider them as you think about the testing formats you plan to use.

Advantages

Perhaps the greatest advantage of true–false items is that they are easy to construct. Teachers generally find that they can develop a large number of such items in a remarkably brief period of time: Most true–false items are short, concise sentences that do not take much time to develop, and most teachers find that they do not have to spend much time thinking about how to phrase them. Teachers are often able to develop one item after another rapidly without a great deal of thought.

A second advantage of true–false items is that a large number can be included in a test. Students can often answer as many as 100 true–false items in as little as 20 to 30 minutes. This means that many items can be placed in an examination or quiz and a great deal of content can be sampled. Of course, this leads to good content-related evidence of validity and helps increase reliability.

A third advantage of the true–false format is that items can be scored very quickly, and even more so if there is a separate answer sheet. Placing a key next to the students' lists of answers makes grading a very fast procedure. Teachers typically have to spend very little time scoring true–false items.

The last advantage of this format is that the answers can be scored objectively. Once the scoring key is developed, almost anyone—including a teaching assistant—can score the items accurately without the need to make judgment calls. After all, with only two possible answers, there is no need to interpret a student's response.

Limitations

Since true–false items are so easy to develop and so easy to score, you might suspect that those advantages come with some limitations. Your suspicions are well founded, as this format comes with several severe limitations.

The first limitation is that they are highly susceptible to guessing. Since the true–false item format and most of its variations offer two possible answers, a student could expect to get about 50% of the items correct simply by guessing. This results in what is known as a "floor" effect. Theoretically, on any test students should be able to earn meaningful scores from a low of 0% correct to a high of 100% correct. However, with true–false items, it is not really possible to interpret any scores below 50% as being correct; since students should perform that well even if they guessed at every item, then scores that low are essentially uninterpretable. Therefore, the possible range of interpretable test scores is somewhere between about 50% and 100% correct. This restriction in range of possible scores because of this artificial floor (the lowest meaningful score) tends to reduce both the reliability and validity of tests with true–false items.

However, this is actually the worst-case scenario. It is based on an assumption that students guess at most of the items, whereas, in reality, most students guess at relatively few items. In addition, on most classroom tests very few students actually achieve test scores lower than 50% to 60% correct. Therefore, the limitations imposed by the effects of guessing are not quite as significant as previously described. However, even with the best-case scenario (where students never make wild guesses) true–false items do have limited reliability and a number of psychometricians are wary about their use.

The second limitation is perhaps even more serious than the guessing issue. True–false questions can only be developed for materials for which there are two, and only two, possible outcomes: true or false, yes or no. Most issues, however, are not simply one thing or another (dichotomous). Frequently, there are many shades of gray, with many plausible answers or interpretations. Is this true? Well, it is true under most circumstances. For example, as a child we likely came to believe that all rocks will sink in water. However, pumice (a type of rock produced from a volcanic eruption) often contains so many air spaces that it has a density less than that of water and will float. In fact, the more we learn in any field, the more we realize that there are relatively few absolute truths. Anyone who has studied logic knows that unless a statement is true 100% of the time, then it is not actually true.

Did you ever argue with your teacher about a true–false item that you marked as false when the teacher insisted that the statement was true? In many instances, students are able to point out an exception to the statement, which would have made it false. In reality, relatively few statements are unambiguously true or false, which severely limits the use of the true–false item format.

There is another effect of this limitation. Since this format only works with matter that is clearly dichotomous, teachers frequently have to resort to developing test items that are essentially measuring trivial details. If you wish to develop 50 true–false items from a chapter or a unit, you are likely to be able to develop a dozen, or so, good items based on important material. However, once you have gone through all of the important material that is appropriate for the true–false format, you may find yourself developing additional items on trivial facts. Sometimes teachers simply take sentences out of the textbook and ask students if these are true. To make a statement false it is simply altered in a meaningful way. Here, we are simply measuring our students' memory of the material that they read. In many instances, it is difficult to develop a sufficient number of good true–false items based on important material.

The third limitation of true–false items is that they are primarily limited to testing factual knowledge. Although we can also use them to measure procedural knowledge (for example, the appropriate steps required to complete a chemistry experiment), we can only measure that knowledge indirectly.

Overall, in spite of the severe limitations of the true–false format and the poor reputation that it has among many teachers and psychometricians, it is still remarkably popular. It shows up on many tests. Each term I ask my college students if they have had any tests recently that used true–false items and most of their hands go up. It is also an efficient format with some types of material.

ATTRIBUTES OF GOOD TRUE–FALSE ITEMS

Like the other formats we have discussed, there are attributes that we look for in true–false items. Some of these attributes are common to all item formats; others are specific to the true–false format.

1. *The item measures the skill or knowledge that it was designed to measure.* Once again, we want a close match between the item and the objective it was intended to measure. Because many teachers tend to prepare true–false items rapidly, they occasionally prepare items without referring to their list of objectives or their Table of Specifications. Test items should be measuring important concepts.

2. *The reading level of the item is appropriate for the students.* Once again, we want the test items to measure the students' knowledge of the material and not their ability to read. By their very nature, true–false items need to be written in a very clear, concise manner. As items become longer, they frequently become much more difficult for students to evaluate. Longer statements also frequently contain multiple propositions that must be evaluated separately. We will address the multiple proposition issue again later in this section.

3. *The item is written so that one of the two options is unambiguously correct.* This is perhaps one of the more difficult issues in preparing good true–false items. Is the statement unambiguously true or false? As I mentioned earlier, most issues are not clearly right or wrong, which presents a challenge to a teacher who wants to prepare a true–false question. Oosterhof (2001) points out that you can take a potentially troublesome item and improve it by turning it into a comparison. Let's look at an example.

> **Bad Example**
>
> Kansas is considered a highly industrialized state.
> Answer: False

Although farming is still its biggest source of income, Kansas does have many industries. So, how do you answer the question? The statement can be improved through the use of comparison.

> **Better Example**
>
> In comparison to states like Pennsylvania and Delaware, Kansas is considered a highly industrialized state.
> Answer: False

After reading about the high level of industrialization in Pennsylvania and Delaware and the reliance on farming in Kansas, students should see this statement is clearly false.

When developing true–false items you must also look at the item from the perspective of your students. Young students do frequently look at the world as if most things are either black or white, true or false. So a statement that might not be considered true from the perspective of a physicist like Stephen Hawking, would still be considered true by all knowledgeable 5th-grade science students. Occasionally, you will find that some of your students have knowledge that is more sophisticated than you expected. If some of your students can see fallacies in your items, those items are likely to have to be deleted.

4. *The wrong answer must be plausible.* Sometimes a teacher can write a true–false item that appears to be reasonable. However, when you consider the incorrect alternative, you realize that no student who would think about it would ever make that choice. If the wrong alternative is simply not plausible, many students will get the item correct by default.

> **Bad Example**
>
> Since clouds are made up of small water particles, when we see clouds we can be relatively certain that it will rain.

5. *The statement represents a single proposition.* As mentioned earlier, true–false items need to be concise. As a statement becomes longer, it often begins to include two or more propositions. Let's look at an example.

> **Bad Example**
> When Pennsylvania ratified the U.S. Constitution in 1787 it became the second state to enter the Union.
> Answer: True

This question actually contains three separate propositions that each need to be verified before a student can answer the question. First, did Pennsylvania ratify the U.S. Constitution in 1787? (It did.) Second, was Pennsylvania the second state to enter the Union? (It was.) Third, did a state enter the Union by ratifying the constitution? (It did.) If any of those propositions were not true then the correct answer would be false.

Questions that contain more than a single proposition should be avoided. They frequently are measuring a student's ability to read carefully rather than the student's knowledge of the material. If the teacher is really interested in whether the students know that Pennsylvania was the second state to enter the Union, the question should look like this.

> **Better Example**
> Pennsylvania was the second state to enter the Union.

6. *The item is written in a simple and concise form.* By now you realize that true–false items should be written in as simple and concise a form as possible. First, we want to keep the reading level as simple as possible. Second, we want to avoid phrases and clauses that can add unintended propositions to the item. Third, we want to keep the item from being ambiguous. All of these factors tend to reduce the effectiveness of the item. We can frequently avoid those problems by keeping the item short and concise.

7. *Avoid using modifying words in the item that significantly alter the meaning of the item.* Words like "not" and "except" typically reverse the meaning of a sentence and present a reading challenge for many students. If the student reads through the item quickly and misses the important modifier, he or she is likely to misinterpret the item. Whenever it is reasonable to do so, these modifiers should be avoided. Especially, avoid using "not" in true–false items! However, if it becomes necessary to use one of these modifiers, they should be printed in bold type so that students are less likely to miss them and misinterpret the item.

> **Bad Example**
> During the Civil War, Maryland did not become a Confederate State.
> Answer: True

> **Better Example**
> During the Civil War Maryland became a Confederate State.
> Answer: False

8. *Avoid using modifiers with absolute meaning within the item.* Modifiers like "no," "never," "all," "always," and "every" are potentially problematic since they signify absolutes. Students frequently learn that there are few absolutes in the world and realize that most true–false items containing these absolute modifiers are false. Students are likely to choose false without even evaluating the content of the item. Although these modifiers can be used, they should be used judiciously.

9. *Avoid using modifiers that imply an indefinite degree within the item.* Words like "sometimes" and "often" are ambiguous. Does sometimes mean 5% of the time or does it mean 95% of the time. These modifiers frequently make statements too ambiguous. Remember, we want true–false items to be unambiguously true or false. These modifiers often simply "muddy the water," and should be avoided.

> **Bad Example**
> Most birds build their nests in trees.
> Answer: ?

There are many species of birds that build their nests in trees. There are also many species that build their nests in other places—such as on the ground, on ledges of cliffs and tall structures, in barns, and on occasion, on my outdoor lighting fixtures. There are even birds who don't build nests. A better example would be the following.

> **Better Example**
> One place where birds build their nests is in trees.
> Answer: True

> ### Attributes Desired in True–false Items [1]
> 1. *The item measures the skill or knowledge that it was designed to measure.*
> 2. *The reading level of the item is appropriate for the students.*
> 3. *The item is written so that one of the two options is unambiguously correct.*
> 4. *The wrong answer must be plausible.*
> 5. *The statement represents a single proposition.*
> 6. *The item is written in a simple and concise form.*
> 7. *Avoid using modifying words in the item that significantly alter the meaning of the item.*

8. *Avoid using modifiers with absolute meaning within the item.*
9. *Avoid using modifiers that imply an indefinite degree within the item.*

EVALUATING TRUE–FALSE ITEMS

Let's look at several true–false items and see if we can identify problems that exist within them. An objective for each item is included where that might prove helpful.

Item 1

Objective:	Students will be able to identify the significance of Christopher Columbus' voyages.
Grade level:	7th-grade history
Item:	Even though Christopher Columbus did not achieve his goal of finding a western route to China, his discoveries still were extremely significant for history.

This item presents several problems. First of all, the obvious answer is "true." The alternative answer, "false," is simply not plausible. Even 7th-graders should recognize that Columbus had a significant impact on history for no other reason than the fact that his name is so familiar. If he had failed, he would not be in the history books. This item also presents two propositions, rather than just one. Did Columbus fail to achieve his goal? Were his discoveries important for history? Therefore, this should be written without the initial clause. Finally, this subject is simply not very good for the true–false format. In reality, you would want students to know the ways in which Columbus had made an impact on the history of the Western world, not just that he had made an impact?

Item 2

Objective:	Students will be able to identify the characteristics of a rhombus.
Grade level:	5th-grade mathematics
Item:	A square is one type of rhombus.

This item is "true," and is not a bad item per se. However, it fails to address the objective. A rhombus is defined as a quadrilateral with all four sides of equal length. Therefore, all squares and some parallelograms fit the bill. However, recognizing that a square is also a rhombus does not guarantee that the student knows the characteristics of a rhombus.

Item 3

Objectives:	Students will be able to identify the conditions necessary for snow.
Grade level:	High school earth and space science
Item:	If the ground temperature is below 0° C then precipitation will always fall as snow.

If you live in the mountains where I do, you would know that the answer is "false." Sometimes there is a temperature inversion where the air in the upper atmosphere is warmer than it is at ground level. If the temperature in the upper atmosphere is above freezing, then precipitation will fall as rain. If it is below freezing at ground level, then the precipitation will freeze before hitting the ground as sleet, or freeze upon hitting the ground as freezing rain. In addition, test-wise students will typically choose "false" for this item simply because it contains the word "always." Finally, it fails to discuss all of the conditions necessary for snow; it discusses only one condition.

VARIATIONS IN THE TRUE–FALSE FORMAT

You have probably seen many examples of traditional true–false items. However, as I mentioned earlier in the chapter, over the years teachers have developed a number of variations in the traditional format. Some of those variations have been developed in response to criticisms of the traditional true–false format. Other variations have been developed to deal with specific types of content material. There are several true–false variations. Let's look at some of the more commonly used formats.

True–false with Correction

In an attempt to deal with some of the limitations of the true–false format, a number of teachers use a variation sometimes known as *true–false with correction*. If the statement is true, the student simply marks it as "true." However, if the statement is false, the student is expected to explain why it is false or rewrite the statement, in a substantial way, to make it true. In reality, this is a combination of the true–false format with the short-answer format. This reduces (but does not eliminate) the effects of guessing. It also reduces the effects of ambiguity in test items. For example, if the student thinks that the item, which was designed to be true, is somewhat ambiguous as written, the student can mark it as false and write an unambiguous alternative statement.

Although this approach reduces some of the problems associated with the traditional true–false format, it does have its own limitations. First, it can take considerably longer to score than would a traditional true–false format. In addition, it is less objective. The teacher must use a judgment call about the students' corrections. Overall, this variation is fairly popular, especially among high school teachers.

Embedded True–false Items

This variation of the true–false format is most often used in language arts. The students are presented with a paragraph where a number of words are underlined and numbered. They are then expected to make some judgment about each underlined word. For example, they might be expected to indicate if an underlined word is spelled correctly, or if it is a noun or some other part of speech, or if it contains a grammatical error.

Example

It was March and as Jim awoke[1] he looked out of his bedroom window to see if it had snowed again last night[2]. He was surprised that there were actually patches of green grass showing where yesterday the lawn[3] was completely covered with snow. It had actually stayed above freezing overnight and the snow was continuing to melt[4] slowly. He thought to himself that maybe Spring is not that far off. At that moment[5] he spotted a robin on the lawn, the first that he had seen that year. That made him even more hopeful that Spring would[6] soon begin and that he could once again be playing baseball.

Is the underlined word a noun?

1. yes   no
2. yes   no
3. yes   no
4. yes   no
5. yes   no
6. yes   no

This approach has some special strengths. For example, when it comes to parts of speech, words can often play several roles depending on the context. Some words (e.g. play) can be used as either a noun or a verb depending on how they are used in a sentence. This approach allows teachers to easily test the students' abilities to evaluate material within context—to determine how words are used within a sentence.

Sequential True–false Items

This variation can be used whenever there are sequential steps in problem solving. It is very useful in mathematics. Let's look at an example to see how it works.

Example

Here are a series of mathematical expressions. For those expressions 1 through 4, mark each as follows.

A. This expression is mathematically equivalent to the one just above it.

B. This expression is **not** mathematically equivalent to the one just above it.

$$(2X + 6)(2X - 8) = (X + 3)(X - 4)$$

1. $4X^2 - 4X - 48 = X^2 - X - 12$
2. $3X^2 - 36 = 0$
3. $X^2 = 12$
4. $X = 3$

Answers: 1-A, 2-B, 3-A, 4-B

Obviously, this type of item is complex and requires students to have had some training and practice prior to using it for testing. It probably should not be used until high school.

Checklists

A checklist is simply a list of standards that are used to evaluate some process or product. We frequently use them in a variety of ways in the classroom. For example, as you assign a term paper for the students in your class, you might provide them with a list of criteria. The list might look like this.

Example (*for term paper*)

_____ A cover sheet is included.

_____ The student used at least eight different sources.

_____ The student used APA style for reference citations.

_____ The paper is at least 1,500 words in length.

_____ There is a reference list that uses APA style appropriately.

When students turn in their papers you simply check to see that each criterion was met.

We can use checklists in many different ways in the classroom. Essentially, it is a list of criteria that you can check off for whatever you are evaluating. Later in the book we will discuss how we can use them to evaluate performance assessments or to evaluate portfolios. However, if you think about it, a checklist is simply a series of true–false items. Is this particular criterion present in the product that is being evaluated? For example, does Joe's term paper have an acceptable cover page? Did Jean's oral presentation start with an appropriate introduction?

These are just a few of the ways that true–false (or alternative-choice) formats can be used.

SUMMARY

The true–false format has many uses in the classroom and is relatively popular. One of its advantages is that true–false items are often easier to design than are items using other formats and are easier to score. However, true–false items are also limited by problems associated with guessing. In addition, only a limited amount of material is suitable for this format. In this chapter, we discussed nine characteristics of good true–false items and had some practice in evaluating items. Finally, we looked at some alternative approaches to the traditional true–false item.

EXERCISES

1. Write an appropriate *true–false item* for the following objectives:

   a. Students will be able to identify where the Andes Mountains are located.
   b. Students will be able to identify the artist who painted the Mona Lisa.
   c. Students will be able to identify characteristics of an obtuse triangle.

2. Write an appropriate "*with correction*" item for the following objectives:

   a. Students will be able to identify the state capital of Utah.
   b. Students will be able to identify the symbol for the element silver.

3. Write an appropriate *embedded item* for the following objective:

   a. Students will be able to identify spelling errors within a passage.
   b. Students will be able to name and describe all the steps of the water cycle.

4. Write an appropriate *sequential item* for the following objective:

   a. Students will be able to identify the correct order of operations (PEMDAS).

SPOTLIGHT ON THE CLASSROOM

Mr. Grubb is a veteran teacher at Harrison Park Elementary School in Longwood, Oregon. He has taught for 31 years. For the last 11 years, Mr. Grubb has taught 5th-grade science. The textbook he uses is based on basic geology. The students can usually cover one chapter in approximately a week and a half. After each chapter he gives the students a test. The tests always consist of 50 typical true–false questions. Mr. Grubb is very fond of this type of test. After the first few chapter tests, Mr. Grubb notices that some of the students who are getting high grades are not the same ones who get questions right when he discusses the chapters in class. He also notices that a few of the students who seem to be able to talk about the material during class, for some reason, get low grades on the tests. Mr. Grubb is puzzled by these revelations. Why do you think that this could be happening? What should Mr. Grubb do to find out what is wrong with his tests, if anything? Maybe, some of the students just study harder for the tests than do other students. That is a common practice, he thinks.

What other types of test question could Mr. Grubb use on his science tests?

NOTE

1.   Some of these attributes are adapted from Oosterhof (2001).

10

PRODUCING AND ADMINISTERING TESTS

INTRODUCTION

Now that you have learned how to prepare good short-answer, essay, multiple-choice, and true–false items, you need to learn how to plan, produce, and administer a classroom test. In this chapter we will discuss how a teacher goes about planning a test, choosing which item formats to use, deciding on the difficulty level of the items, and producing the test. We will also discuss how to set up an appropriate testing environment and how to administer a test.

DESIGNING A TEST

Many new teachers develop classroom tests without spending enough time planning what they want to do. With experience, they soon learn that planning is critical to developing high-quality tests. Teachers need to spell out the purpose of the test, the material that will be covered, the types of item that will be used, the difficulty level of the items, and the time that is available for the test—just to name a few of the steps that must be taken.

Defining the Purpose of the Test

You may recall from Chapter 2 that one of the first things a teacher must do in designing a test is to define the purpose of the test—decide how the test scores are going to be used. Is the test a formative assessment designed to let you know how the students are progressing in developing a particular skill? Or is the test a summative assessment given at the end of a chapter or unit to allow you to assign grades based on the students' performance?

Let's say, for sake of discussion, that you are developing a summative assessment, a unit test at the end of a three-chapter unit. The test scores will form a major part of the grades that the students will be assigned for the marking period, which means that the test will be covering a fairly large set of objectives. If the number of objectives is small enough, the test will be able to cover each objective and you can plan to use a criterion-referenced assessment—an assessment that covers all of the objectives from the content domain. However, if the number of objectives is too large, then you will have to sample the objectives on the test and use a norm-referenced interpretation—an assessment that samples objectives from the content domain.

Choosing the Types of Items to Use

You must choose the types of item format that you will use. Will the test be all short-answer items? Will the test contain items from several formats? This choice is based largely on the type of material that will be covered. If the objectives are primarily at the knowledge and comprehension level, then short answer, multiple choice, and true–false items are all appropriate. If there are higher-level cognitive objectives involved, then multiple choice or brief essays are more appropriate. Many classroom teachers tend to use two or more item formats on many of their tests. How many of your teachers did?

Choosing the Number of Items to be Used

Let's say that you have chosen to use only short-answer items. How many should you use? There are actually a number of issues to consider before you choose the number of items to use. One of the first issues must be time. If you are working with classes that last only 47 minutes, then you must be able to administer the test within 47 minutes. Those 47 minutes must also include time to take roll (if that is required) and deal with any other class business, pass out the testing materials, go over the instructions with the students, and collect the testing materials. If you like to review a test on the same day that it is administered, then you have to allow time for that, too. In this case, you may only be able to give the students 30 minutes to take the test.

Once you decide on a realistic time frame, you have to predict how many test items the students can complete in that time. Students can typically complete three to four simple short-answer items per minute if the items require one-word answers. More complex short-answer items can take about twice as long to answer. Computation items can take even longer, depending on the complexity of the computations. Similarly, students can answer three to four simple true–false items per minute. Multiple-choice items frequently take longer. Students can answer simply worded multiple-choice items at the rate of about two per minute, whereas more complex multiple-choice items can easily take a minute or longer to answer. Short essay items should take about 10 minutes to answer. These time estimates are only averages. Some students can take longer with certain types of item.

Choosing the Difficulty Level of the Items

What is the optimum level of difficulty for the items? This is also a complex and, sometimes, still debated issue. There are two primary issues here: The first has to do with the difference between speeded tests and power tests (discussed briefly in Chapter 4).

Speeded Tests vs. Power Tests

Speeded tests are tests with very specific time limits. They are designed to see how quickly students can perform certain simple tasks. With a speeded test there are more items on the test than most students can be expected to complete within the time limit. The items are simple so that students are expected to make few, if any, errors. The score is based on the number of items correctly completed. Speeded tests are most appropriate when measuring manual and clerical skills like typing. They are not appropriate when measuring most cognitive skills. Power tests, on the other hand, do not typically have time limits (although some time limits are necessitated by practical issues). Students are expected to complete all of the items. However, the items are more difficult. With power tests teachers are attempting to see how well the students can use the knowledge and skills that they have learned. In conclusion, speeded tests will typically involve many easy items, whereas power tests will involve fewer items that are moderately difficult.

Criterion-Referenced vs. Norm-Referenced Tests

The second issue has to do with criterion-referenced assessment versus norm-referenced assessment. With criterion-referenced assessment the item difficulty is not a very important issue. Items used in these tests can be anywhere from moderately difficult to fairly easy. A large number of students can earn high scores on a criterion-referenced test if the students are all competent with the skills being measured. Norm-referenced tests, however, are different in that they are designed to rank the students—to differentiate among the students who know the material well from the students who are less well prepared. This differentiation can only be accomplished if the test scores have a relatively large standard deviation—if the test scores are spread out. We want the students who are less prepared to obtain relatively low scores, the students who are moderately prepared to earn higher scores, and the students who are the most prepared to earn the highest scores. If the test items are too easy, most students will get high scores and the test will not differentiate well. If the test items are too difficult, most of the students will get low scores and the test, once again, will not differentiate well. We tend to get the largest standard deviation and the best differentiation when test items are moderately difficult (when about 45% to 85% of the students get the item correct, depending on the type of item). Therefore, we typically want more difficult items when we use a norm-referenced assessment.

Assuring Sufficient Accuracy

Most tests are used to help teachers make decisions about students. In order to make good decisions that are based on valid information, our tests must have a sufficient amount of accuracy. Because this is a somewhat complex issue it can best be demonstrated through an example. Let's say that a course is operated on a pass/fail system and, for simplicity, let's say that the grade in the course is based on one test only. In addition, let's say that a student must score 75% or above on the test to pass the course.

In such a situation four possibilities exist. Some students will be competent with the material and should pass the course, whereas other students will not be competent with the material and should not pass the course. The first possibility is that a student is competent with the material and gets a 75% or above on the test. The student passes the course and a correct decision has been made. The second possibility is that the student is not competent with the material and scores below 75% on the test. The student fails the course, and, again, a correct decision has been made. The third possibility is that the student is competent with the material but scores below 75% on the test. The student fails the course when he or she should have passed and a decision error has been made. This is sometimes referred to as a "false negative." The fourth possibility is that the student is not competent with the material but gets a 75% or above on the test. The student passes the course when he or she should have failed it and, again, a decision error has been made. This is sometimes referred to as a "false positive."

Overall, we would like all of our decisions to be correct decisions. We would like to avoid false positives and false negatives—misclassifications. However, there probably has not yet been a test invented that always makes correct decisions. Even with medical lab tests, it is not unusual to get these errors. Nevertheless, we can reduce these types of error with careful planning.

Why We Get Misclassifications

One reason why we get misclassifications is that we never know a student's *true* score—the score a student should receive with a perfect test. Because measurement error exists, students typically receive test scores a few points lower or higher than their true scores. For students whose true score is far from the cut-off score, misclassifications are rare. If a student's true score is 55%, it is very unlikely that he or she will obtain a test score above 75%. The student will probably get a failing grade and a correct decision will be made. On the other hand, if a student's true score is 95%, it is very unlikely that he or she will score below 75%. The student will probably get a passing grade and a correct decision will again be made. However, for students whose true scores are between 70% and 80%, close to the cut-off score of 75%, there is a much greater likelihood that they will score either too high or too low and a decision will be made in error. In such a situation, it might be possible for 30% (or more) of the students whose true score was within five points of the cut-off score to be misclassified.

How to Reduce Misclassifications

One way to reduce these misclassifications is to develop tests with greater reliability. With greater reliability, the difference between true scores and obtained scores is smaller. The simplest way to increase reliability is to have a large number of items on the test. When we have a test that will be used to make important decisions we want as many items on the test as we can possibly fit in. In that case, we can reduce the number of misclassifications.

When important decisions are to be made we want to use tests that are as accurate as possible, and frequently we want to use multiple tests. Let's use a medical example. Does an individual have type 2 diabetes? Recent research suggests that we can reduce many of the negative effects of diabetes if we begin treating it as early as possible. Since type 2 diabetes (also sometimes known as adult onset diabetes) can take 15 or more years to fully develop, we would like to pick it up as early as possible before there is sufficient damage to the patient's pancreas. Therefore, physicians will typically require their patients to have yearly blood tests. Part of those blood tests will be a check for blood glucose level. Let's say that our patient, George, has always had blood glucose levels within the acceptable range. However, this year the test score is five points above the acceptable level, indicating possible type 2 diabetes. Now, this test score could be an error. Perhaps George got up in the middle of the night before the test and had a glass of orange juice when he was supposed to fast. A cautious physician would not be likely to diagnose George as diabetic based solely on this one elevated test score. The physician could order other blood tests or simply have George repeat the test in a month or two. If those later tests fall within the normal range, the physician is likely to assume that the elevated blood test was an error, but will carefully monitor George's blood glucose level in the future. On the other hand, if the other tests confirm the first elevated test, then the physician is likely to diagnose George as having type 2 diabetes and will begin treating him.

The same applies to classroom tests. Because you are making important decisions about students, whenever possible, you should avoid making those decisions on the basis of a single test score. You should always try to obtain corroborating evidence to make certain that you have made the best decision that is possible. You should look at other tests and other indicators of the same skills. Decisions based on multiple test scores tend to be far more accurate than decisions made on a single test score.

PRODUCING A TEST

Now that you have planned the test, you have to prepare the items and produce the test. There are a number of issues to keep in mind when producing a test.

Preparing the Items

Generally, the most time-consuming part of developing a test is preparing the items. By using your list of objectives or your Table of Specifications, you can begin to write the items. Writing all of the test items yourself takes a great deal of time. Today, most textbooks come with a teacher's edition that contains sample tests or test banks, which are frequently very helpful. However, these test banks are sometimes prepared by graduate students hired by the textbook author to produce the test items, and some of these graduate students have had only minimal experience in producing test items. Therefore, many of the test items found in the teacher's edition are potentially problematic. You should go through the test bank to look for possible items. At times the items can be used as written. However, at other times you may encounter a potentially good item that is somewhat problematic as it is currently written. In that case, you can simply start with that problematic test item and edit it to improve it. Since editing items found in teacher's editions often takes less time than writing items from scratch, I encourage you to try that approach.

Ordering the Items

There are no hard and fast rules for the order of items on a test. Research suggests that for most tests, item order has little effect on how students perform on the test. It does not appear to matter if the test begins with a few easy items or a few hard items. Therefore, the order of items should primarily be determined by other practical considerations. For example, it is frequently easier to score a test when items of one format are grouped together. In addition, if you routinely review tests, then it is also helpful to keep items grouped by topic. It is also common to have the more objective items at the beginning of the test and the essay items (if any) at the end. However, in spite of these recommendations, if you find that another way to order the items works best for you and your students, then I encourage you to try it.

Formatting the Test

The two biggest issues in formatting a test are to make the test easy for the students to read and complete, and to make it easy for you to score. Since most of you will be preparing tests on a computer, using a word processing program, formatting will be much easier than it used to be.

There are several things to keep in mind to make the test readable and better for your students. First, do not try to cram too much material onto a single page. Cramming too many items onto a single page can make the material difficult for the students to read. In general, it is best to leave plenty of "white" space. The items need to be clearly prepared so that one item does not blend into another; so, double space between items. In addition, the students should not have to flip pages to complete an item. If an item cannot fit at the bottom of the page, begin it on a new page. Students should not have to flip pages to answer a question based on a diagram, table, map, or chart. The required material should all be on the same page as the questions about it. For younger students, where questions are often brief, some teachers have found that printing the page in a two column format makes the items more readable.

The second issue is to make the test easier for you to score. If you do not use a separate scoring sheet,[1] it can be helpful to format the items in a manner that will ease scoring. Often, the best way to do that is to have the students answer the question in either the left or the right margin next to the item. You can put blanks in the margin to clearly indicate to the students where the answers should be placed. You can then hold your key next to the students' answers and score the items quickly.

Preparing Instructions

Except for the youngest students, all instructions should be provided in writing at the beginning of the test, and when appropriate at the beginning of each new section. The instructions need to be clear, yet concise. The instructions need to describe the number of items and the number of pages on the test. They should include directions on what the students need to do to complete the items and any special instructions (for example, whether they can use a calculator or scratch paper). Instructions should also include the time limits. In the directions before each section, you should also list the point value of each question.

Of course, you should read the instructions to younger students. Do you think that it is necessary to read instructions to older students if the instructions have been written on the test? Many teachers have found that, although they tell their students to read the instructions before starting to take the test, many never do so. Frequently, they are so anxious to get started that they simply skip the instructions. Therefore, I strongly recommend that you read the instructions aloud to the students. It never hurts and, often, it can help.

Proofreading

The last step before printing the test is to proofread it carefully. Take the test yourself as the students would take the test. Doing so sometimes reveals errors that you would easily miss if you were simply reading through the test. Making announcements about typos while the students are taking the test wastes time and distracts some students. Doing so also interferes with the students' concentration.

ADMINISTERING THE TEST

Setting Up an Appropriate Testing Environment

You may recall from Chapter 4 that measurement error can come from three different sources, one of which is environmental effects. A test can only be reliable and valid if it is administered in an appropriate environment. Students need a comfortable, quiet place, free from distractions, to take a test. The room should be well-ventilated and be at a comfortable temperature. There should be few distracting noises or activities going on in the classroom. The room should not be crowded. Students need to feel that they have enough room to work without being on top of one another.

Minimizing Frustration

Teachers also need to minimize student frustration. Frustration often leads to anxiety which tends to have a negative effect on student performance. Testing needs to follow a reasonable schedule. Students need to be given plenty of advanced warning about an upcoming test so that they have sufficient time to prepare. Many teachers provide review sessions the day before the test, which can allow students to judge their level of preparation and gives the students the chance to devote additional time to study, if needed. Although teachers need to stress the importance of tests, it is probably best not to over-emphasize a test's importance. That only serves to heighten student anxiety.

Minimizing Interruptions

It is also important to minimize interruptions during the test. If the test is well prepared and the teacher gives instructions before the students begin the test, there should be no reason for the teacher to have to give additional instructions during the test. What about student questions? In a similar fashion, we do not want students asking questions aloud during the test as that can also interfere with the other students' ability to concentrate. Some teachers, therefore, allow no student questions during a test. I, however, recognize that students sometimes have difficulty interpreting questions even if they are well prepared. Because language is so complex, some students will sometimes interpret a word or phrase to mean something other than what was intended. If the students have a question, they could come to the front of the room to ask for clarification. You can answer the students' questions, in a quiet voice, unless your response would directly provide them with the answer to the question. Some teachers are unhappy with that procedure because they believe that, as students come to the front of the room, they will look at other students' tests. They ask the students instead to raise their hands and then go to them. There are a variety of ways of dealing with student questions that can minimize interruptions.

SUMMARY

A well-developed test requires careful planning. A teacher must decide on the purpose of the test, the type and number of items to be used, and the difficulty level of the items. The teacher must also be sure that the test has sufficient accuracy for the decisions that will be made based on its results. The teacher must prepare the items using objectives or a Table of Specifications, decide on the order of the items, format the test, and prepare instructions. It is also important for the teacher to carefully proofread the test before having it printed. When administering the test, the teacher must set up an appropriate testing environment that allows students to perform at their best. The teacher should also try to minimize both student frustration and interruptions during testing.

EXERCISES

1. Label each of the following as a descriptor for a *power test* (P) or a *speeded test* (S):

    a. _____ Contains a large number of items
    b. _____ Contains fairly simple items
    c. _____ Contains difficult items
    d. _____ Time is not a factor
    e. _____ Appropriate for measuring manual/clerical skills
    f. _____ Contains a specific time limit
    g. _____ More than 80% of students will complete it

2. Put the following steps in the proper order for producing and administering a classroom test:

    a. _____ Prepare the items
    b. _____ Define the purpose of the test
    c. _____ Choose the level of difficulty of the items
    d. _____ Proofread
    e. _____ Prepare instructions
    f. _____ Order the items
    g. _____ Set up an appropriate testing environment
    h. _____ Assure sufficient accuracy
    i. _____ Choose the types of item to use
    j. _____ Choose the number of items to use
    k. _____ Format the test

3. Based on your reading, label the following statements as either true (T) or false (F):

    a. _____ Printing the instructions at the beginning of a test is appropriate for very young students.
    b. _____ Double spacing should be used between items on a test.
    c. _____ Teachers should not allow students to ask questions during a test.
    d. _____ The easiest way to increase reliability is to have a small number of items on a test.
    e. _____ Items with a moderate level of difficulty are ideal in achieving a large standard deviation.

4. Choose a chapter from a textbook in your area and describe a test that you would develop for a specific grade level. Consider all of the factors described in this chapter as you develop your test.

5. Follow-up question 4 above by actually preparing a test from either a list of objectives or from a Table of Specifications.

SPOTLIGHT ON THE CLASSROOM

Mrs. Anthony has been a 4th-grade teacher at Schaffer Elementary School in Leeland, Virginia, for the past 33 years. She understands the importance of developing quality tests for her students. The school purchased new science books for all of the grade levels for the upcoming school year. During the summer months, Mrs. Anthony has decided to read and prepare the new material. She wants to create all of the science tests that she will administer throughout the year.

The book is divided into chapters and units. Mrs. Anthony is developing a test that will be given at the end of each unit, or every three chapters. The tests will be summative evaluations that cover many objectives.

Mrs. Anthony feels that a variety of test items should be used on the tests. She plans to use matching questions for vocabulary, multiple-choice questions to test knowledge and comprehension, and one or two brief essays for slightly higher-level cognitive objectives. Since Mrs. Anthony teaches science to her homeroom class, time is not a factor. However, the children are only 10-years-old, so the test cannot be too lengthy, but still must measure a large number of objectives. She decides to put 10 matching questions, 15 multiple-choice questions, and two very brief essays on the tests. She believes that the tests should take the students about 30 minutes to complete. All of the items Mrs. Anthony plans to create are moderately difficult.

When it comes time to write the questions, Mrs. Anthony begins by referring to the tests in the teacher's edition sample questions. She is able to use only a few of the questions from the book because too many of them are too easy. She spaces the questions far apart, yet keeps the pages neat and even. At the beginning of each section, Mrs. Anthony places bold, clear directions. Finally, Mrs. Anthony proofreads the tests she created and decides that they are ready to use for the new school year!

1. Discuss the test planning and development skills used by Mrs. Anthony.
2. Is there anything wrong or anything you would correct or add to her process?

NOTE

1. Separate scoring sheets are not recommended for younger students. They are simply too confusing.

11

ANALYZING TESTS

INTRODUCTION

After you have given a test to your students and graded it, you are not necessarily finished with the test. You may choose to use the test or items from the test again sometime in the future. Therefore, it is useful to know how well the individual test items measure the students' knowledge of the material. Did the items work as you expected them to do? By analyzing the test, you can gain information on how well you taught the concepts to your students. Test items can tell you many things about student performance. Have you ever asked yourself any of these questions? Are there issues, ideas, and concepts that the students did not master? Are there issues about which the students appear to be confused? Is there material that will require further work? These questions can often be answered by performing a test analysis.

In recent years there has been more emphasis on using teaching techniques that are supported by research, that are data driven. When you complete a test analysis and use that information to alter your teaching and testing, you are using data-driven techniques.

TEST ANALYSIS

You can analyze your classroom tests at several levels. The first level of analysis involves examining the test as a whole. In an ideal world, when you give your students a summative assessment (a chapter or unit examination), you could find that every student obtains a perfect score on the exam. Assuming that your examination is highly valid and appropriately difficult, such a result would tell you that you have been very successful in teaching the material—that every student has successfully mastered the material. In reality, however, you rarely experience such an idealistic situation.

What does it actually mean when your students score very well on an examination? Let's say that the mean on the test was 95% correct with a very small standard deviation. Essentially, all students scored from about 90% to 100% correct. First, you should assume that you have a class that is, at least, somewhat heterogeneous—the students differ from one another in ability. So, how should you interpret such a performance?

There are, at least, two possible interpretations. The first interpretation is that the students may have all done a superb job in mastering the material. You could conclude that they all really knew what they were doing, and were able to demonstrate their skills on the test. However, there remains another possibility. That second possibility is that the test was much easier than you had anticipated. Are the scores much higher than the scores you typically obtain when testing similar students on the same material? Even students who had not fully mastered the material were able to perform well on the test simply because the items were very easy. In many instances, you should be able to rule out this second possibility by examining the individual test items to see how well they match your objectives. However, if you want further confirmation that the students truly mastered the material, you might wait a couple of weeks and then give the students another opportunity to demonstrate that they can actually use their learning in another type of assessment. If they again perform well, you can be more confident about your original interpretation of the data.[1]

Now, let's take a look at the other end of the continuum. What does it mean when students perform poorly on an assessment? One possibility is that you simply did not do a very good job of teaching the material, or that some of the material was more confusing to the students than you had anticipated. If you have not done enough formative assessment (discussed in Chapter 1), you may get a surprise when you give a summative assessment to find that the students perform poorly on some topics. There are some skills that the students simply have not mastered. Although you may be tempted to move on to the next chapter or unit (in order to stay on schedule), in most instances the responsible thing to do is to revisit the topics that confused the students. This is especially important if those topics with which the students are struggling include skills that they will need to use in the future.

When students perform poorly on a summative assessment, you also need to consider the possibility that the test was simply more difficult than you had anticipated. Again, you need to check to see that the test items match the objectives from that chapter or unit. Sometimes teachers give tests that are too difficult, or do not match what they taught. For example, some teachers provide instruction primarily at the knowledge and comprehension levels, but test primarily at the application and analysis levels. In this case, there is simply not a good match between the teaching and the testing. Their tests lack evidence of content-related validity because of this poor match between what was taught and what was tested.

ITEM ANALYSIS

The second level for evaluating a test is to perform an item analysis. Although you can perform an item analysis on any type of item, it is easiest to demonstrate with multiple-choice items. With any type of item you can examine item difficulty and item discrimination. However, with multiple-choice and alternative-choice items, you can look at three characteristics of each item. You can examine item difficulty, item discrimination, and you can perform a distractor analysis. Let us look at each of these separately.

Item Difficulty

Item difficulty is a rather straightforward concept—it is simply reported as the proportion of students who had the item correct. For example, if 73% of the students answered the item correctly, then the item difficulty is listed as .73. The only potentially confusing aspect of item "difficulty" is that its name is, in fact, the opposite—the higher the item difficulty, the easier the item. So, an item with a difficulty level of .88 is an easier item than one with a difficulty level of .55. More students could correctly answer the first item than the second.

> **Definition**
>
> **Item difficulty** is the proportion of students who answered the item correctly.

Why is item difficulty important? There are a variety of reasons why item difficulty could be important, but we are most frequently concerned with how item difficulty is related to item discrimination: A test item should differentiate between students who are well prepared for the exam and those students who are less prepared. The better-prepared students should be able to answer the item correctly more often than the less-prepared students. It turns out that, frequently, items that are moderately difficult better differentiate between well-prepared and less-prepared students than items that are either very difficult or items that are very easy. When items are very easy, most students are able to answer them correctly, including both the well-prepared and the less-prepared students. The same is true with very difficult items, except that most students get the items wrong; both the well-prepared and the less-prepared students are likely to answer them incorrectly. We often (but not always) find the greatest differences in performance between the better-prepared and less-prepared students when the items are moderately difficult. Therefore, you should strive to develop test items that are moderately difficult.

You might ask, what is a moderately difficult item? As I just mentioned, we frequently obtain the best item discrimination and the highest reliability on a test when the items are moderately difficult. But how difficult is moderately difficult? Frederic Lord (1952) demonstrated that, for completion items, we can obtain the best reliability and the greatest ability to differentiate when items have a difficulty level of about .50. However, for true–false and multiple-choice items, guessing can play a role and the items need to be somewhat easier in order to obtain the highest possible reliability. For example, with true–false items, since guessing can play a significant role, we tend to get the best discrimination and reliability when item difficulty is about .85. However, with five-option multiple-choice items, where the effect of guessing is less severe, we tend to get the best discrimination and the highest reliability when item difficulty is about .69.

Item Discrimination

As I just mentioned, a good item tends to discriminate (differentiate) between well-prepared and less-prepared students. You want more of the better-prepared students to get the item correct than the less-prepared students.

Figure 11.1 is an example of an item analysis for Item 17 from a 40-item four-option multiple-choice test that I gave to students in one of my psychology classes. For this

Item 17

Students	A	B*	C	D
Upper 25%	0.00	0.80	0.20	0.00
Lower 25%	0.50	0.20	0.30	0.00
All students	0.36	0.38	0.26	0.00

Figure 11.1 Item analysis for Item 17.

item, option B was the correct choice (indicated by the asterisk). The first row of the item analysis shows the proportion of students from the upper quartile (the 25% of the students who had the highest total scores on the test) who selected each of the four options. None of the best-prepared students chose either options A or D, whereas, 80% of those students chose option B (the correct choice) and 20% chose option C. The next row of the item analysis shows the proportion of students from the lowest quartile (the 25% of the students who had the lowest total scores on the test) who selected each of the four options. None of the least-prepared students chose option D. Of this group, 50% chose option A, 20% chose option B (the correct choice), and 30% chose option C. The last row of the item analysis shows the proportion of all students from the class who chose each of the four options.

How do we determine the item difficulty level? You will remember that the item difficulty is the proportion of students who had the item correct. The last row of Figure 11.1 shows that, among all of the students who took the test, 38% chose option B, the correct answer. Therefore, the item difficulty is listed as .38.

How do we determine item discrimination? The *item discrimination index* is the difference in the proportion of the better-prepared students who had the item correct as compared to the proportion of less-prepared students who had the item correct. In this case 80% (or .80) of the best-prepared students had the item correct, whereas only 20% (or .20) of the least-prepared students had the item correct. The item discrimination index is computed by subtracting the second proportion from the first (Equation 11.1).

$$\text{Item Discrimination Index} = .80 - .20 = .60 \qquad (11.1)$$

Essentially this means that 60% more of the better-prepared students got this item correct than the less-prepared students.

> **Definition**
>
> The **item discrimination index** is the proportion of the better-prepared students who had the item correct minus the proportion of less-prepared students who had the item correct.

You should strive to build tests with high reliability. When selecting test items, you should attempt to use items with higher item discrimination indices because item discrimination contributes to a test's reliability. A test that has many items with a high item discrimination index will have a higher reliability than a test which has many items with a lower item discrimination index.

How high should an item discrimination index be? It could conceivably range from −1.00 to 1.00. An item discrimination index of .40 or higher indicates that it is an exceptionally good item in terms of its ability to discriminate between well-prepared and less-prepared students. Item discrimination indices in the range of .20 to .39 are very desirable and help the reliability of the test. When item discrimination indices are near zero (.00), the item is neither helping nor harming the reliability of the test. However, negative item discrimination indices (yes, they do happen) actually lower the reliability of the test.

Perhaps the most common reason to perform an item analysis is to examine a test that you might want to use again in the future. The item analysis allows you to determine which items are working well and should be retained, which should perhaps be discarded, and which could benefit from some revision. An ideal item is one that is moderately difficult and has a high discrimination index. The emphasis should be on the discrimination index. If this is low or even negative, the item needs to be revised or even discarded. You need to determine, or at least make a good guess at, why the item is performing poorly. Is there an error in the answer key? Does the item include material that was not covered because of time constraints or other circumstances? Is the item poorly worded and potentially confusing? When you use multiple-choice items you can take one additional step in the item analysis: You can also perform a distractor analysis.

Distractor Analysis

With multiple-choice items, the well-prepared students are expected to be able to determine that any distractor (a wrong alternative) is clearly the wrong answer. However, students who are less prepared should view each distractor as potentially correct. So, how should a distractor behave? Essentially, you would like to see a higher proportion of the less-prepared students choose a distractor than the well-prepared students.

In truth, we do not typically complete a distractor analysis unless an item is performing poorly. Let's once again look at Figure 11.1. Option A appears to be working very well as a distractor since none of the best-prepared students chose it and 50% of the less-prepared students chose it. Option C is also working, although not quite as well since 20% of the best-prepared students chose it and 30% of the less-prepared students did. Option D is not working at all since none of the students chose it. Since option D is not working, you might be tempted to change it. However, since this item has an item discrimination index of .60 and is working extremely well, it would be best to simply not touch Option D. Sometimes you simply need to leave well-enough alone!

Before you receive additional practice with item analysis, let's discuss the typical steps you should go through to perform an analysis. Remember, you are primarily trying to find items which discriminate well. Step 1: Does this item display an acceptable item discrimination index? If the answer is "yes," you could stop with the item analysis right there. If the answer is "no," then you should move to Step 2 and look at the item difficulty level. Is the item discrimination index too low simply because the item is either too easy or too difficult? If so, then you might want to revise the item simply to make it easier or more difficult. However, if the item discriminates poorly, yet is moderately difficult, then you should move on to Step 3 and perform a distractor analysis. Are the distractors working as they should?

How can distractors work poorly? One way in which distractors fail to perform is that few, if any, students choose them. These distractors are often implausible. Even the least-prepared students are able to recognize them as clearly wrong. Another potential problem with distractors is where they are partially correct. These can be confusing because even the well-prepared students can sometimes be attracted to them. If any of these problems occur, rewriting the distractor can sometimes improve the question.

Some other distractors, such as "all of the above" or "none of the above," are potentially troublesome. For example, some students who have chosen the correct alternative but are not 100% certain that they are correct may be inclined to go with "none of the above" simply because of their uncertainty. If the "none of the above" alternative were not present, the students would have had the answer correct as they should have. Also, if students identify one alternative as clearly correct and one or more other alternatives as partially correct, they may be inclined to go for "all of the above" as the correct answer. In many situations, this type of alternative simply makes items more confusing than they should be and tends to lower the overall reliability of a test.

Item Analysis Practice

Now that we have gone through the process of performing an item analysis, let us look at a few item analyses to get some practice.

Figure 11.2 represents the item analyses of five additional items from the psychology

Item 19

Students	A*	B	C	D
Upper 25%	0.70	0.00	0.30	0.00
Lower 25%	0.30	0.10	0.50	0.10
All students	0.54	0.10	0.33	0.03

Item 26

Students	A	B	C*	D
Upper 25%	0.20	0.20	0.60	0.00
Lower 25%	0.40	0.30	0.30	0.00
All students	0.23	0.18	0.56	0.03

Item 32

Students	A	B	C	D*
Upper 25%	0.00	0.00	0.00	1.00
Lower 25%	0.10	0.00	0.20	0.70
All students	0.05	0.00	0.13	0.82

Item 35

Students	A*	B	C	D
Upper 25%	0.80	0.10	0.00	0.10
Lower 25%	0.70	0.00	0.10	0.20
All students	0.77	0.03	0.13	0.08

Item 44

Students	A	B*	C	D
Upper 25%	0.15	0.25	0.50	0.15
Lower 25%	0.10	0.40	0.20	0.30
All students	0.12	0.30	0.40	0.18

Figure 11.2 Additional item analyses.

test mentioned earlier. Let's start with **Item 19**. Start by looking at the item's discrimination index. The correct alternative is A. Of the best-prepared students, .70 chose that option, whereas only .30 of the least-prepared students chose A. The difference between .70 and .30 is .40, which is the item discrimination index. Since this is an excellent item discrimination level, you could stop the item analysis right here. However, since you are practicing, we will continue with the other steps.

The second step is to check the item difficulty. Since 54% of all of the students chose option A, the correct answer, the item difficulty is listed as .54. The high item discrimination index is likely to be attributable, in part, to the fact that this is a moderately difficult item.

The third step is the distractor analysis. Option B is not working well as a distractor since only 10% of all the students chose it and none of either the better-prepared or the less-prepared students chose it. Option C is working well since more of the less-prepared students chose it than the better-prepared students. However, 30% of the best-prepared students chose it, which is a cause for concern. Perhaps it appeared to be more correct than it should have done. Option D is not working well either since only one student out of the class chose it. For this item, even though none of the distractors are working as well as they could, the item, as a whole, is still working well. (Sometimes you just get lucky!) In that case, I would probably leave the item as is, but check it again the next time I use it.

For **Item 26**, the correct option is C. Here, .60 of the best-prepared students chose option C, but only .30 of the least-prepared students chose that option, making the item discrimination index .60 minus .30, or .30. Therefore, this item has an acceptable item discrimination index. The difficulty index is also acceptable since 56% of all of the students in the class chose the correct answer.

The distractor analysis indicates that both options A and B are working well as distractors since more of the less-prepared students chose each. However, since none of either the better-prepared or the less-prepared students chose option D, that distractor is simply not doing well. Perhaps you could improve this item by making option D more plausible.

The next item analysis is for **Item 32**. All of the better-prepared students chose option D (the correct option) and 70% of the less-prepared students chose it. Therefore, the item discrimination index is 1.00 minus .70, or .30. This item also has an acceptable item discrimination index.

This item was relatively easy since, of all the students in the class, 82% chose the correct answer. Since this was a relatively easy item, you might be surprised that it still had an acceptable item discrimination index. You may recall that we tend to see better item discrimination with items that are moderately difficult. However, once again, as Frederic Lord (1952) pointed out, with multiple-choice items guessing can play a role. Therefore, he argued, with four-option multiple choice items, you typically obtain the best item discrimination and the best reliability for items with a difficulty index of about .74. Although Item 32 is not very difficult, its difficulty index does not fall far from the ideal difficulty level which allows good item discrimination.

Let's look at the distractor analysis. For this item, option A is somewhat helpful because more of the less-prepared students chose it, but it is not contributing significantly to the item's effectiveness. Option B is not working at all since no student chose it. Finally, option C is helping since none of the best-prepared students chose it and 20%

of the less-prepared students did. If you wanted to improve this item, you should work on making options A and B more plausible.

Item 35 is an interesting item since, at first, it appears to have characteristics similar to the previous item. However, it has a very low item discrimination index because, even though 80% of the best-prepared students had the item correct, 70% of the least-prepared students also had it correct. The item discrimination index is, therefore, only .10. Why is it performing so poorly? This item, with an item difficulty of .77, is slightly more difficult than the last item we examined and, therefore, could still potentially work well. However, since it is not working well we need to look at the distractors.

Both options C and D are each helping the item somewhat since more of the less-prepared students chose them. However, option B is actually hurting the item because it was more attractive to the well-prepared students than it was to the less-prepared students.

To improve this item, you should probably start by trying to make it a little more difficult. Then, closely examine each of the distractors to attempt to make each of them more plausible.

Finally, let's look at **Item 44**. The correct option B was answered by 40% of the less-prepared students, but by only 25% of the best-prepared students. Therefore, this item actually has a negative item discrimination index of −.15. Clearly, there is something wrong with this item. The item was quite difficult since only 30% of all of the students chose the correct option. Why is this item so difficult?

The distractor analysis immediately points to the possible problem with this item. A total of 40% of the students chose option C and 50% of the better-prepared students chose this option. Why is this option so attractive, especially to the better-prepared students? When an item performs like this, you should first check to see if it was keyed incorrectly. Perhaps option C is actually the correct answer. If it turns out that option C was the correct answer, then the mystery is solved.

If the item was keyed correctly and option B was the correct answer, then you must look at the actual item. What was it about option C that made it appear to be a better choice even to the better-prepared students? You may be able to see the problem and change that option. However, at other times you may have to resort to asking the class why they thought that option C was correct. Frequently, they are able to explain how they interpreted the question which made option C appear to be correct. Generally, it has to do with the confusing way the question was phrased. In those instances, rewriting the question stem to make it crystal clear can help. However, if you cannot determine why the question was performing so poorly, it is often better simply to throw out the question and replace it with another question the next time you use that exam.

The Stability of Item Analyses

At this point I should add a word of caution about test analyses and item analyses. Both types of analysis will depend on the students who took the test. For example, I frequently teach two or more sections of a particular course each term. If I give the same test to each section and perform separate analyses on each test, I can get different results. I may find that Item 26 worked well in one section of the class, but rather poorly in the other section. Differences from section to section are more likely if the class sizes are small. If I had 18 students in one section and 22 students in the other section, then I should expect differences in the analyses. However, if the class sizes were much larger (for example, 75 students in each section), then I would expect more similarities between the separate analyses. Therefore, I recommend that you exercise caution in interpreting test and item analyses with very small classes.

SUMMARY

After students complete a test you may choose to perform a test analysis. This allows you to examine how the test performed as an assessment device and sometimes gives you information about how well you taught the unit. Since your goal is to use tests and other assessment devices that are reliable, the students who are the most knowledgeable and the best prepared should earn high scores, whereas those students who are less prepared should earn lower scores.

If you would like to use the test again in the future, you might want to perform an item analysis to determine which items can be used again, which items require revision, and which should be replaced. For almost any type of test item, you can examine the item difficulty and the item discrimination index. In addition, for multiple-choice items you can also perform a distractor analysis.

EXERCISES

The following charts show the results from a 6th-grade world geography exam. (Note: The correct answer for each item is noted with an asterisk.)

Analyze each item using the following steps:

a. Find the item discrimination index.
b. Find the item difficulty.
c. Perform a distractor analysis, when appropriate to do so.
d. Explain what you would change about the item, if anything, and why.

Item 1:

Students	A	B	C*	D
Upper 25%	0.25	0.35	0.40	0.00
Lower 25%	0.40	0.10	0.50	0.00
All	0.30	0.20	0.45	0.05

Item 2:

Students	A*	B	C	D
Upper 25%	0.75	0.05	0.15	0.05
Lower 25%	0.73	0.00	0.20	0.07
All	0.74	0.02	0.18	0.06

Item 3:

Students	A*	B	C	D
Upper 25%	0.52	0.00	0.00	0.48
Lower 25%	0.16	0.00	0.20	0.64
All	0.45	0.03	0.05	0.47

Item 4:

Students	A	B	C	D*
Upper 25%	0.02	0.00	0.05	0.93
Lower 25%	0.10	0.29	0.45	0.16
All	0.05	0.15	0.30	0.50

SPOTLIGHT ON THE CLASSROOM

Mr. Eswein teaches 6th-grade social studies at Fairmont Middle School near Birmingham, Alabama. He has taught the same class for over 10 years, and has altered his tests, as well as his teaching methods, many times. In the past he relied on items from the teacher's edition of the textbook to build his exams. However, this year he has decided that he could build better exam items on his own. His tests typically consist of multiple-choice, true–false, and short essay questions.

This year, his students appear to be having more trouble with his tests and are performing poorly, even though they appear to be equally as talented as his students have been for the past several years. They eagerly participate in class discussions and give every appearance of understanding the material. When he uses various informal assessments in the classroom, his students appear able to understand the material, but still perform poorly on his chapter and unit examinations.

He is now beginning to wonder if his exam items are the source of the problem.

Can you suggest some steps that he could take to evaluate his tests and his exam items?

NOTE

1. When you give a test immediately after instruction, students will tend to perform well simply because the material is fresh in their memory. However, if your assessment is delayed by several weeks, you can expect a decline in the students' performance as a result of forgetting the material. Many educators argue that a delayed test is actually a better indicator of real learning. After all, most of the time we need to use skills learned some time ago.

Section III

ALTERNATIVE ASSESSMENT TECHNIQUES

In the last section we discussed classroom testing—which included the four most common testing formats—how to go about building a test, and, finally, how to analyze a test. This section of the text contains three chapters on alternative assessment techniques. Chapter 12 discusses the details of informal assessment, which includes informal observations and questions. In many classrooms informal assessment is much more common than formal assessment. Chapter 13 discusses performance assessment. This involves any situation in which we ask students to demonstrate their competency by performing some task. Finally, Chapter 14 discusses portfolios. Although portfolios are actually a type of performance assessment, they are sufficiently different to deserve special attention.

12

INFORMAL ASSESSMENT

INTRODUCTION

So far we have discussed formal assessment techniques, such as tests and quizzes. This chapter is the first of three that will help you look at alternative assessment techniques. Let's start by looking at informal assessment and questioning.

What is Informal Assessment?

Informal assessment involves classroom interactions during which teachers observe their students' behaviors. When a teacher walks around the room looking over students' shoulders while they are doing seat work, observes a student reading a paragraph aloud, or observes three students working cooperatively on a class project, that teacher is conducting an informal assessment. Informal assessment can also involve the teacher asking a student a question and paying close attention to the student's response.

Perhaps as much as 90% or more of all the assessment carried on within a classroom is in the nature of informal assessment. While presenting lessons, teachers are almost constantly monitoring their students. We are often doing so for the purpose of formative assessment. We rely on our students' responses to help us determine if the lesson is proceeding as planned. The students are providing us feedback about whether they understand and are able to follow our lesson. They may be telling us, through their body language, that they are confused. If the feedback that you are receiving from your students is ambiguous, then you may choose to ask direct questions to assess their understanding, or you may ask them to use the skills that you are attempting to teach them to see if they have acquired those skills.

Just as it takes time and effort to become skillful at formal assessment, it also takes time and practice to become proficient with informal assessment. For example, as I prepared to write this chapter, I was reminded of the years that I spent as a clinical psychologist in a mental health setting. When a new client first came in for service we performed an intake interview, much of which consisted of what is referred to in the field as a "clinical diagnostic interview." That interview involved a number of prescribed questions that I was to ask the client. However, I also learned to ask follow-up questions to specific comments that the client made. Within about a year, I had become quite expert with the clinical interview and very often had a rather thorough picture of the problem that the client was bringing to me by the time the interview was completed. Often, within about the first 15 minutes, I had the picture that I needed, and simply used the rest of the interview to fill in some of the important details—those that would help me design the most effective treatment plan.

Clearly, the clinical diagnostic interview is more formal than most informal assessments since there is typically a prescribed set of questions to ask. However, even with a more informal approach you can become quite skillful at trying to answer the various questions that you might have about your students. You must recognize that informal questions are not haphazard. Typically you, the teacher, have concerns about how the lesson is proceeding and are trying to ask the appropriate questions that will allow you to assess that progress. You must also recognize, however, that informal assessment is not always accurate. On occasion, you may arrive at a tentative hypothesis about what is going on with one or more of your students and later have to reject or revise that hypothesis based on new information.

TYPES OF INFORMAL ASSESSMENT

Informal assessment comes in two basic variations: informal observations, and questions. I will briefly describe each. Let us take a close look first at informal observations.

Informal Observations

As a teacher, one of your most common activities will be the informal observations of your students. You will be observing students even while you are lecturing or explaining directions for various activities. You will be observing to see if they appear to be paying attention to you and if they appear to understand what you are saying. At other times you will ask the students to do something at their seats, such as work on a problem. You can observe them from the front of the room to see if they are working, or you can roam around the room or up and down the aisles to peer over their shoulders to see if they are completing the task appropriately and correctly. There are many ways in which you can observe your students completing academic tasks.

There are also many student activities that you can observe even beyond the academic realm. For example, you may observe how Micah, a student who recently transferred into your class, is doing in her social interactions with other students. Does she appear to be making friends? You can observe your students for evidence that they appear to be motivated by the lesson. Are they enthusiastically involved with the activities or do they show signs of boredom? You can observe individual students who appear to be having concentration problems to see if you can discover what might be interfering with their ability to concentrate. Certainly, there are many characteristics of the students that you can observe.

Questions

Questioning students is another very common classroom practice. Teachers ask students questions for a large variety of reasons. At times, teachers use questions as a simple tool to keep students involved in the lesson. At other times, teacher questions are designed to elicit the students' current understanding of a concept in order to provide a good starting point for an explanation or lesson. Teachers also use questions to keep the lesson focused on the appropriate level. For example, if the goal of the lesson is to increase the students' abilities to analyze a particular situation, then questions requiring analysis will keep the students focused on that goal. At other times, teachers use questions simply to help the students obtain additional practice at a skill. Clearly, questions can be used for a variety of other purposes.

CHARACTERISTICS OF INFORMAL ASSESSMENT

Although informal assessment may appear, on the surface, to be less structured than more formal assessment procedures, in reality, it has many complexities of its own. Let's consider the following 10 characteristics of informal assessment.

1. *Informal observations and questions are largely designed to alter your teaching to make it more effective.* Most informal observations and questions are designed as formative assessment techniques (see Chapter 1). Essentially, that means that they are designed to give teachers feedback about how their lessons are progressing so that they can make alterations to achieve their instructional goals. You might ask yourself whether the students appear to have understood Step 1 in the procedure that you are teaching. If you are convinced, through informal observations and questions, that they have the ability to do Step 1, then you are ready to move on to Step 2. However, if your informal assessment leads you to believe that they still need work with Step 1, then you can provide additional help and practice in that area.

Formative assessment can be directed at an entire class or it can be directed at particular students. You may determine that, although most of the students are prepared to move on to Step 2, several students still appear to be confused and require additional instruction.

2. *Observations and questions frequently lead to additional observations and questions.* It is unlikely that you will be able to answer the questions that you have about your students with a single observation or question. Often, you will find yourself having to ask a series of questions or make a number of observations until you feel satisfied that you have discovered what you need to know. Perhaps the first question that you ask will allow you to eliminate one or two hypotheses that you have about why a student appears to be confused. Frequently, the student's response to that first question will direct you to additional questions until you have narrowed down the competing hypotheses that you have considered. At other times, you will quiz a student to see if he or she can use a skill that you just taught. Then, you will often quiz other students with similar questions to make sure that they can also use that skill.

3. *Most observations and questions are quickly forgotten.* Since we tend to make so many observations and ask so many questions during a typical day, it would be impossible for us to remember many of the students' responses. We are simply dealing with information overload. Therefore, you should plan to ask questions and make observations that you will be able to use within the very near future, within the next few minutes. As you are presenting a lesson, the most effective observations and questions are those that will allow you to alter the direction that you are currently taking to improve your lesson. Asking questions and making observations today that are designed to change your lesson for next week is much less effective. Unless you immediately make

some notes about how you want to change next week's lesson, it is very likely that when you go to teach that lesson next week, you will not remember much of what you observed today. You may have a sense that there was something that you wanted to alter in the lesson, but not be able to put your finger on exactly what it was.

4. *Most things that occur in the classroom are simply not observed.* You are neither Superman nor Superwoman. You cannot pay attention to everything that is going on within the classroom at any one time. Although teaching is frequently an exercise in multitasking, even teachers are not able to pay attention to everything that is happening within the classroom. Therefore, you must recognize that through your questions and observations you are only registering a small sample of the many behaviors that you could potentially observe. You hope that the behaviors you are observing are representative of those behaviors that you did not have the opportunity to observe, but you cannot be certain of that. Therefore, sometimes your observations and questions will lack reliability and validity and the conclusions that you draw from those observations and questions can be erroneous. You simply must recognize that informal assessment can, at times, lead you to the wrong conclusions or, at least, to conclusions that are incomplete. If you design your questions and observations to be as objective as possible, you should be able to minimize drawing erroneous conclusions.

5. *The more focused that you are on one behavior, the more likely it is that you will miss other potentially useful information.* Under almost any circumstance, you will miss many of the behaviors that you could potentially observe in your classroom. However, when you focus on one student or one particular type of observation, you are concentrating on that student or on that behavior. As a result of that concentration, you are likely to miss even more of what else is going on in the classroom. Therefore, in situations where you need to be closely monitoring the entire classroom, you will be less able to make focused observations. Such focused observations will have to wait until such times when the students are engaged in productive activities and you feel that it is safe to concentrate on a specific student or a specific behavior.

6. *Even while focusing on an observation, you must still maintain critical behaviors.* You are rarely free in your classrooms to ignore some essential activities. You must frequently multitask, quickly shifting your attention from one activity to another. For example, when you are driving on an unfamiliar interstate highway near a big city at rush hour, you find yourself paying attention to many activities, all at the same time. If you notice a driver several cars in front of you driving erratically, you may focus more attention on that erratic driver. However, you will still need to attend to the other drivers, the lane you should be in, your speed, and so on in order to arrive at your destination safely. Such multitasking is essential in the classroom. For example, as a teacher you will need to follow your lesson plan, monitor your pace, and attend to your students all at the same time. These and other tasks are essential and must be monitored even when you are making other observations.

7. *Experience with observations and questions makes you more effective in their use.* The more you use observations and questions, the more effectively you will be able to make use of informal assessment. Many natives of Washington, D.C. and Los Angeles drive on the expressways at rush hour every day. Yet, they experience much less anxiety than do the tourists, simply because the natives have developed effective strategies to deal with the traffic. Their experience helps them assess the situation more quickly and easily.

The same is true for experienced teachers. With experience you become better at making observations and asking appropriate questions simply because you have done it so often. Experienced teachers quickly know what they should observe or what questions they should ask with much less effort than that required from new teachers. You simply get better at it and it requires less effort on your part.

8. *Experience with the behaviors being observed makes you better observers.* Clearly, when you are experienced with the behavior being observed, you are a far better observer than you were when you were a novice. I like the analogy of being an observer or a judge at a diving contest. A dive takes only a matter of two to three seconds from the time the diver leaves the diving board until he or she enters the water. During those two to three seconds, the judge is expected to observe about six different aspects of the dive (the diver's position when entering the water, for example). Clearly, if you have never been a competitive diver yourself, or a diving coach, it would take a lot of experience to be able to pay close attention to so many behaviors in so little time. However, those who are very experienced with diving do it quite well.

The same holds true in the classroom. If you have to observe a behavior with which you are not familiar, you will only be able to pay close attention to one or two aspects of the behavior. However, with greater familiarity, you will be better able to pay close attention to multiple aspects of the behavior and will do so with relatively high reliability.

9. *Preliminary observations and questions may lead you to make tentative hypotheses which can lead to subsequent observations and questions.* As I mentioned earlier, it is rare that a single observation or question will answer a query that you may have about a particular student or the class as a whole. Let's say that you are teaching a new math algorithm in your 6th-grade class and, for reasons that are unclear to you, many of the students appear confused about the procedure and are doing it wrong. Although this is your fourth year as a 6th-grade teacher, you have never seen this sort of confusion before. However, the 6th-grade math curriculum was changed this year as was the sequence when some concepts were to be taught. Your first assumption may be that the students are confusing some step in this algorithm with one of the other math algorithms that you recently taught.

This assumption becomes your first hypothesis. You could question students to see if you are able to support this hypothesis. As you go through the procedure of asking questions and observing their responses, you keep revising your hypothesis until you feel relatively certain that you understand the nature of their confusion. You can then go about eliminating the source of the confusion. With any luck, this leads to a successful conclusion.

This is known as an *iterative* process. You simply keep repeating the process of forming hypotheses, asking questions or making observations that either support or do not support the hypotheses, until you arrive at a satisfactory conclusion.

10. *Even well-supported hypotheses may eventually be determined to be erroneous.* Unfortunately, even after you have completed the iterative process described above and have come to a satisfactory conclusion, there are times when you will eventually find that your conclusions were either wrong or, at least, incomplete. This is a perplexing, and, sometimes, even an amusing situation. You were so sure that you understood what was happening, and only later recognized that you had it wrong. Fortunately, this does not happen too often. However, you must be prepared for it and must be open to the reality

that your observation and questioning skills, along with your logic, are fallible. You will, at times, make mistakes!

PLANNING FOR OBSERVATIONS AND QUESTIONS

Informal assessment, like formal assessment, works better when you plan it. Informal assessment is an integral part of your teaching, and should, therefore, be well integrated into your lesson plans. Your informal observations and questions need to be largely driven by your instructional goals and objectives. You have to be able to choose which behaviors you will observe while attempting to maintain reliability (consistency) and validity (observing the appropriate behaviors).

Choosing Behaviors to Observe

How do you choose which behaviors to observe? At times, the answer to this question appears to be obvious, or what is sometimes referred to as a "no-brainer." However, it is important to understand why you decide to observe some behaviors rather than others.

To begin, you need to differentiate between learning (sometimes known as "capabilities") and performance. You cannot directly observe students' learning or capabilities. What students have learned—what they have the capability to do—lies somewhere within them. They are not accessible to you. Instead, you must ask the students to perform some behavior which you hope will demonstrate their learning or capability. You must choose a behavior (or behaviors) that you believe will demonstrate the students' learning.

In addition, much of the time you would like to choose behaviors that you can measure, or at least evaluate. Some behaviors are easier to measure or evaluate than are others. For example, after students have *learned* a new math algorithm, you can ask them to complete several problems. A student's competency at solving math problems is fairly easy to measure. However, after you teach a unit on creativity, you could ask each student to demonstrate his or her new *capability* with creativity by writing a creative paragraph. Evaluating a student's written paragraph for creativity is considerably more difficult to evaluate than is scoring a math problem.

You also need to develop skills in observing nonverbal behaviors. At times, your students will specifically tell you that they are confused and will ask for further explanation. At other times, however, students will allow you to go on with your lesson even though they do not understand. Therefore, you need to learn to read nonverbal cues from your students, some of which can be quite subtle. You need to learn to recognize signs of confusion, frustration, and inattention. If you are having difficulty reading those nonverbal cues, you can specifically ask students if they are confused. Once you open that door, students will often tell you about the difficulties that they are experiencing.

The Validity Question

This problem of choosing an appropriate behavior to observe can be referred to as the *validity question*. Are you able to demonstrate that the behaviors that you are observing are actually reflecting the appropriate learning or capability? Although this can, at times, be difficult to demonstrate, the simplest way to assure validity is to have a well-developed set of objectives and make certain that you have a close match between the objectives and the questions you are asking or the behaviors that you are observing. For example, let's say that you have the following objective for your 5th-grade social studies class: The students will be able to identify that, on his first trip to the Americas, Christopher Columbus used three ships named the Niña, the Pinta, and the Santa Maria. A valid question would require the students to either recognize or identify the names of all three ships. However, a question concerning the length of the trip would not be a valid question concerning this particular objective.

The Reliability Question

Informal observations and questions also need to display *reliability* or consistency. Although you do not typically expect that your informal assessment techniques will need to display the same high levels of reliability that you frequently expect on a classroom test, you would still like some assurance of reliability. The simplest way to improve the reliability of an informal assessment is to increase the number of observations that you make or questions that you ask each student. Rather than ask a student one question, your results will be more reliable if you ask that same student two or more questions on the same topic. How many questions should you ask or how many observations should you make? If the outcome of the informal assessment is not very important, then you could make fewer observations or ask fewer questions. However, if you are going to make substantial changes in your teaching or important decisions about your students, then you want greater assurance of reliability and should ask more questions and/or make more observations.

You can also increase the reliability of your informal assessments by observing and questioning many different students in your classes. If you only observe a few students, then any conclusions that you make based on those observations may not generalize well. Your conclusions may only describe the few students you observed and not the other students in your class. The more students you observe, the better the chance that the conclusions you reach will generalize to the whole class. In addition, do not always question or observe the same students time after time; choosing students at random will generally result in more reliable conclusions.

TECHNIQUES FOR EFFECTIVE INFORMAL ASSESSMENT

Now that you have learned about informal assessment, you may be asking yourself, "How can I use informal assessment effectively?" Informal assessment works best when you plan it well, when you use it frequently, when you maintain positive interactions with your students, and when you use the results to improve your instruction.

Planning Informal Assessment

Informal assessment should be built into your lesson plans. When developing lessons, plan to include informal assessment techniques any time feedback from students would appear to help. Tie the informal assessment techniques to your goals and objectives and use a variety of assessment techniques. However, you should also have a contingency plan. You should also feel free to use informal assessment techniques any time you are puzzled by what you are observing. If, at some point in a lesson, students appear to be confused, it would be helpful to use an informal assessment technique to gain insight into the problem before continuing with the lesson.

Use Informal Assessment Frequently

Although it is possible to imagine that some teachers might overuse informal assessment, it is much more common to underuse it. Teachers in the primary grades use informal assessment almost constantly. However, as students get older, there is a tendency to use it much less often. Although high school teachers probably do not need to use informal assessment as often as would a 1st-grade teacher, most teachers would benefit by simply using informal assessment more often. When you are teaching, use informal assessment frequently, no matter with what age group you are working and no matter what subject you are teaching.

Maintain Positive Interactions with your Students

Informal observation techniques work best when your students perceive you as a helping person. Your students should believe that your observations of their behaviors and your questions are designed to help them better learn the material and become better at the skills that they are learning. You do not want your students to become fearful or apprehensive every time you ask them a question or observe them. They need to believe that it is all right for them to be confused or to make a mistake—that the reason that you are asking questions or observing them is to help them overcome confusion.

This also means that you have to be careful how you respond to them. They should *never* feel that you are putting them on the spot, embarrassing them, or criticizing them. You are simply there to help them! If you have some students who are especially sensitive to potential criticism, try to do most of your observations and questioning privately. Once they see you as a helping person, they will be more comfortable responding in front of their classmates. In addition, it is good classroom policy that students should never criticize one another.

While we are discussing maintaining positive interactions with students, let us consider wait-time. In the past, teachers, after asking a question, only allowed about one second of wait-time before providing the student with a hint or moving on to another student. However, the most recent generation of teachers have been encouraged to wait between 5 and 15 seconds before expecting a response (Riley, 1986). When teachers show more patience, students often provide better, more thoughtful answers and frequently remember the material better.

Use the Results of Informal Assessments to Alter Instruction

Students also need to believe that the answers that they provide to your questions and the behaviors that you observe are important to you. They need to feel that you are listening carefully and watching closely. One way to convince them that what they do is important is to alter your instruction based on what you hear or observe. When they see you as being concerned about the source of their confusion, and actually doing something about it to help them, they view the whole process as helpful, and will be more willing to participate in the interactions. As a result, instruction will improve.

SUMMARY

This chapter discussed informal assessment, which includes both informal observations and classroom questions. This type of assessment occurs frequently in the classroom, often many times each day. Ten characteristics of informal assessment were discussed, including that it is a type of formative assessment. It is designed to give you, the teacher, information about how your lessons are proceeding. We also discussed how it differs from formal assessment, and how to make your informal assessment techniques both valid and reliable by building them into your daily lessons. Finally, we considered techniques that you can use to make your use of informal assessment more effective.

EXERCISES

1. Identify each of the following as an example of either *informal assessment* (I) or *formal assessment* (F).

   a. _____ Give the students a 20-point pop quiz to see how well they remember the state capitals.
   b. _____ While reading a story out loud to the class, ask the students questions to check for understanding.
   c. _____ While the students are working in small groups, walk around and examine the students' ability to communicate with one another.
   d. _____ Have the students complete a worksheet after the class reads a chapter about the water cycle.
   e. _____ Before beginning a unit on the human body, ask the students a variety of questions to see how much they already know.

2. Identify each of the following statements as either true (T) or false (F).

   a. _____ Your observations in the classroom should NEVER be wrong.
   b. _____ Observations and questions should be used to make your teaching more effective.
   c. _____ You are most likely to see a large portion of what goes on in the classroom.
   d. _____ Most observations and questions are forgotten.
   e. _____ Teachers must frequently multitask when they are observing and questioning their students.

3. Fill in the blank with one of the following words: *reliability* or *validity*.

   a. The easiest way to improve _____ is to increase the number of observations you make and questions you ask.
   b. When checking for _____, you need to make sure that you have a close match between your list of objectives and the questions you are asking or observations you are making.
   c. Your observation has high _____ if you are able to show that the behavior that you observed reflects the appropriate learning or capability.
   d. Your results will have higher _____ if you ask the same student two or more questions on the same topic rather than ask that student one question.

4. You are designing a lesson for a 3rd-grade classroom on the reading skill, fact versus opinion. List the types of formal and informal assessment you could incorporate into the lessons to be sure that the students have developed the skill.

SPOTLIGHT ON THE CLASSROOM

Breann Roberts is a senior elementary education major at the University of Minnesota. This semester she is student teaching in a 3rd-grade classroom in Big Lake, MN. Ms. Roberts knows that more than paper-and-pencil testing should be utilized in the classroom. Each night, Ms. Roberts creates elaborate lesson plans with material introductions, hands-on activities, lesson reviews, and assessments.

Ms. Roberts is beginning a unit on multiplication, and has decided that this is the perfect opportunity to try out her ideas on informal assessment. It is a new topic for the students and is also a topic where the achievement of mastery is critical.

To introduce the lesson on the first day, Ms. Roberts breaks the class into small groups. She writes a few word problems on the board and tells the students to work together to see what they can accomplish. As the students are working, Ms. Roberts walks around the room listening to and observing the groups. She has a checklist in hand to keep track of the steps that each group is taking to solve the problems.

The next day, Ms. Roberts begins math class by asking students questions to see what they remember from the day before. She has some of the students come to the board to explain mathematics homework problems involving multiplication. Ms. Roberts uses the students' responses over the past two days and her observations to determine which concepts she needs to review that day.

As you can see, Ms. Roberts has a good idea about how to use informal assessment in the classroom. In what other ways could she use informal assessment with her lessons?

13

PERFORMANCE ASSESSMENTS

INTRODUCTION

This chapter, which is the second of three chapters on alternative assessment techniques, will discuss performance assessments. Performance assessments, sometimes known as performance appraisals, are used when teachers watch a student perform some task and then rate the student's performance. When is performance assessment more appropriate than a traditional paper-and-pencil test? We will also discuss the advantages and the limitations of performance assessment. Finally, we will discuss how to go about developing and using effective performance assessments.

You may note that performance assessment and informal observations (discussed in the previous chapter) appear to be somewhat similar. Informal observations typically involve teachers observing only one part of a complex behavior, whereas performance assessments typically involve the observations of entire complex behaviors. In addition, informal observations are typically performed as formative assessment, whereas performance appraisals are more typically used as summative assessments. However, there are times when the two do overlap.

WHAT ARE PERFORMANCE ASSESSMENTS?

Ms. Johannson is a high school chemistry teacher who wants to evaluate her students' chemistry lab skills. She could use a traditional paper-and-pencil test of laboratory procedures. However, she realizes that such a test actually measures the students' *knowledge* of lab procedures, not necessarily their *ability to use* the lab skills effectively. Therefore, she decides that she will ask each student to perform a laboratory procedure, observe them, and rate each student's performance in carrying out each step safely, appropriately, and effectively. Ms. Johannson has decided to use a performance assessment.

Performance assessments are alternatives to traditional paper-and-pencil tests. During a performance assessment, the students are asked to carry out some activity while they are being observed by a teacher. At times, the teacher is focused primarily on the process that the students perform to complete the task. At other times, the teacher is focused on the outcome—the finished product that resulted from the students' activities. In most circumstances, performance assessments are used in situations where traditional paper-and-pencil tests are simply not appropriate. However, there are, on occasion, activities that can be evaluated with either form of assessment device.

TYPES OF PERFORMANCE ASSESSMENT

Oosterhof (2001) points out that performance assessment can typically be characterized on three dimensions. The first dimension involves assessing *process versus product*. The second dimension involves using *simulated versus real settings*. Finally, the third dimension involves using *natural versus structured settings*.

Process vs. Product

As I mentioned in the last section, teachers can either focus on the process that the students follow as they go through each step in the procedure, or they can focus on the product that results from the procedure. Ms. Johannson, the high school chemistry teacher, was primarily interested in the process that her students went through to complete the laboratory procedure. However, Mr. Czyszczon (pronounced Season), the mechanical drawing teacher, might be more interested in the finished drawings that his students completed. In most situations, teachers focus either on one or the other, on process or on product. However, there are times when teachers might focus on both.

Simulated vs. Real Settings

Whenever it is possible, you would like to observe your students perform a task, which they learned, in a real setting. For example, a driver's education teacher must eventually take his or her students out on the road and observe them drive on real roads with real traffic. This is sometimes referred to as *authentic* assessment. You are observing your students using the skills that they have learned in a real-life situation, as you expect they will do in the future. However, there are many times when it is not possible, feasible, or practical to observe each student in a real setting. For example, when training pilots to fly a jumbo jet, we want them to be able to experience an emergency, respond appropriately, and land the jet safely. We would like pilots to be able to experience a wind shear (a strong vertical wind) upon landing and still get the plane safely onto the runway. However, we cannot create wind shears at will, nor would we really want a pilot to have to deal with a wind shear unnecessarily. Obviously, we don't want to risk anyone's life or a $100 million jet. Therefore, the airline industry has developed very lifelike flight simulators that allow pilots to learn to deal with such emergencies without any of these risks or problems.

There are many examples of classroom use of performance assessment using simulated settings. When teaching CPR, students typically use a special dummy rather than practice their skills on people who are in life-threatening situations. In my college educational psychology class, I have my students teach mini-lessons to some of the other members of their class, even though the lessons are typically more appropriate for elementary-aged or high school-aged students. Can you think of situations where you completed a performance assessment in a simulated setting?

Natural vs. Structured Settings

Some performance assessments are completed in a natural setting, whereas others are more effective when teachers use a structured setting. At times you might prefer to observe a student perform a behavior without giving the student many instructions. For example, a driver's education teacher might simply instruct his student to drive around anywhere the student wants for the next 15 minutes. In this case, the student is being assessed in a natural setting. However, at other times you may want to observe certain behaviors. Now, our driver's education teacher wants to observe his student making a left turn into a parking lot from a busy street. In this situation, the teacher would tell the student where he wants him to drive. In this second case, the student is being assessed in a structured setting.

Teachers frequently use a natural setting to observe a student's typical behavior. However, if there are certain behaviors that you would particularly like to observe, with a natural setting the behaviors may or may not occur. In such a case, a structured setting is more appropriate, because you can be certain that you will be able to observe the behaviors that you wish to evaluate.

WHEN ARE PERFORMANCE ASSESSMENTS APPROPRIATE TO USE?

There are many different situations where we can use performance assessment. At times, a performance assessment can simply substitute for a paper-and-pencil test. For example, Toby missed the spelling test which was given in class yesterday because he was absent. Today, instead of giving him the paper-and-pencil test that you used yesterday, you could give him an oral test. Strictly speaking, any oral test is actually a performance assessment, although it may simply be an oral version of a traditional written assessment.

However, an oral version of a written test is not always equivalent to the written version of a test. Our abilities to write about something and our abilities to talk about the same thing are not always equivalent. Some students perform better when writing, whereas others perform better when speaking. Therefore, oral tests are more appropriate in some situations than in others. They may be especially appropriate for students with certain disabilities. Perhaps a student does not perform well on written tests, in part, as a result of a disability. In this case, her written test scores do not adequately reflect her learning. However, if she can perform better on an oral version of the same test, then that oral test is a more appropriate way to measure her learning.

Although the oral test is simply a version of performance assessment, performance assessments are more appropriate when they are measuring higher-level skills and other skills that cannot easily be measured with written tests. Some of the skills that can probably best be measured with performance assessment are listed below.

- acting skills
- balancing
- counting
- drawing and art skills
- experimenting
- graphing skills

- interviewing
- measuring
- monitoring
- musical skills
- physical education skills
- programming skills
- ranking
- sorting
- speaking skills (English or a foreign language)
- writing skills

This is only a short list of skills that can often best be measured through performance assessment. Can you generate a more complete list?

Many of the techniques described in this chapter could also be applied to other miscellaneous assessment techniques. For example, many homework assignments and papers can be handled in the same way in which performance assessments are handled. In a broad way, many of them can also be considered performance assessments.

ADVANTAGES AND LIMITATIONS OF PERFORMANCE ASSESSMENT

Advantages

Perhaps the most important advantage of performance assessment is that it allows you to directly measure skills which could only be measured in an indirect fashion with a paper-and-pencil test. This would include many higher-level cognitive skills and most psychomotor skills. Imagine trying to evaluate tennis skills with a paper-and-pencil test. With many performance assessments, students are expected to be able to demonstrate that they are actually able to use the skills that they have been learning.

A second advantage of performance assessment is that it can sometimes affect how students learn material. For example, if students know that after studying a unit they are going to be tested primarily at the knowledge level, they will often simply try to memorize the material for the test. Unfortunately, often much of the material is forgotten soon after the test. If, instead, the students know that they will be expected to demonstrate their ability to use the material, much of what they learn goes into procedural memory, and is better remembered. Therefore, if students are expected to use the skills, they sometimes learn material differently and remember it better.

A third advantage of performance assessment is that it allows you to measure process as well as product. Paper-and-pencil tests are best at measuring the outcomes or products of learning. It is much more difficult to measure process (the steps the students went through to arrive at the outcome) with paper-and-pencil tests. However, performance assessment frequently does an excellent job of measuring process since you can actually observe the student going through the process.

Limitations

Perhaps the most serious limitation of performance assessments is that they are very time-consuming to conduct. With a paper-and-pencil test, you can have your students all take the test at the same time. Perhaps it takes 20 minutes for all 25 students in your class to take the paper-and-pencil test. If, instead, you were to use a performance assessment with each student it would take much longer. If you try to measure the same skills with a five-minute performance assessment for each student, it would take 125 minutes to complete the assessment process on all 25 students. Many performance assessments can take even longer.

A second limitation of performance assessment is that often they cannot be scored objectively. In various ways, scoring many performance assessments is similar to grading global essays. In order to determine a score, you must often rely on non-objective judgment, which often leads to lower reliability.

A third limitation also has to do with the scoring. When doing a process assessment, you must observe the student while he or she is completing the task. Typically, no record of what has occurred is available for later review. Therefore, you are relying on your observation skills and your memory. This can also reduce the reliability of performance assessment.

A fourth limitation of performance assessment is related to the Domain Sampling Model that we discussed earlier in the text (see Part I, Chapters 5 and 7). When you ask a student to demonstrate her ability to perform a task, in most cases you can only sample the student's performance. For example, a driver's education teacher does not have the time to observe each student drive in a number of diverse situations with various levels of traffic, various road conditions, various weather conditions, and so on. You can only observe some behaviors. You never know if how the student drove in one situation generalizes to how she would drive in other situations. This limitation also tends to reduce the reliability of performance assessments.

In addition, many students approach performance assessments with more anxiety than they approach a classroom test. Performance assessments are almost always one-on-one and many students feel that they are on the spot. They often experience something similar to "stage fright." Those same students may experience less anxiety with a classroom test where they can feel some sense of anonymity. As mentioned earlier in the text, student anxiety tends to reduce the reliability of a test.

PLANNING AND DEVELOPING PERFORMANCE ASSESSMENTS

There are a number of issues to keep in mind when you go about developing performance assessments.

Tie Assessment to Objectives

First, as you would with any other assessment technique, the best way to plan for a performance assessment is to tie it to your objectives. If your performance assessment is based on your objectives for the lesson, you will have better reliability and content-related evidence of validity. You want to make certain that your assessment is measuring the skills that you taught.

Measure Important Skills

You will also want to make certain that the skills that you are assessing are important skills. They should be authentic skills, ones that the students will actually be expected to use in real life. Even if you are unable to measure these skills in an authentic (real-life) manner, you still need to choose authentic skills to measure. Performance assessments frequently require you to make a considerable amount of effort, and you really do not want to be putting in that much effort measuring trivial skills. In addition, if the students perceive that you are measuring important skills, they will also be more willing to exert effort to learn those skills.

Establish Precise Skills to Measure

Although performance assessment is sometimes used to measure broad, general skills, as is true with most other assessment techniques, it can be most effective when you precisely define those skills that you wish to measure. For example, if the broader skill that your students are expected to perform consists of a number of steps or sub-skills, you must be certain to spell them out clearly. That will help you focus your observations and will also make scoring the performance assessment more reliable. Earlier in the chapter, we discussed Ms. Johannson evaluating her students' chemistry lab skills. She could choose one broad skill to observe that requires five separate steps that must be completed in order. She would then have five precise steps to evaluate for each student and could also evaluate whether each student performed the steps in the correct order.

Focus on Process or Product Only

Another issue concerns whether you will be evaluating process or product. Although teachers sometimes evaluate both, that is frequently a very ambitious goal. Your assessment will be more effective if you focus on only one. A focus on process is often the most effective when it is used for a diagnostic or formative assessment. You want to make certain that the students are performing the tasks correctly, identify which tasks are giving them difficulty, and provide additional assistance with those troublesome tasks. With summative assessment (when giving a grade), you can focus on either process or on product, largely based on the nature of the skill.

Define the Tasks for the Students

Another important issue is to communicate your expectations clearly to your students. Although it is always helpful to communicate your expectations to your students, when they are preparing for a performance assessment, it is especially helpful if they know precisely what it is you expect them to be able to do. They are better able to learn, prepare, and practice those skills, when they know what you expect from them. They will also frequently be able to continue to use those skills in the future.

SCORING PERFORMANCE ASSESSMENTS

Performance assessments can be a challenge to score because they are frequently more complex than most paper-and-pencil tests. However, there are several approaches that can make scoring performance assessments more objective and, therefore, more reliable. Let's take a look at checklists, rating scales, and rubrics.

Checklists

For some performance assessments you can create a list of the behaviors, skills, or features that you expect to see in either the student's performance or in the finished product. With a checklist you simply list the behaviors (skills, features) and check them off as you observe each one. Once you have completed the checklist, you will have

Student:	Sarah James	Yes	No
1.	Park the car on a level surface.	✔	
2.	Put the car in gear and set the parking brake.	✔	
3.	Chock two appropriate tires.	✔	
4.	Get the new tire and assemble the jack.	✔	
5.	Place the jack in the appropriate spot and raise car partly.	✔	
6.	Remove the wheel cover and loosen the lug nuts.	✔	
7.	Raise the car until the tire is off the ground.	✔	
8.	Remove the lug nuts, storing them in a safe place.	✔	
9.	Remove the old tire and replace it with the new tire.	✔	
10.	Replace the lug nuts and tighten.	✔	
11.	Lower the jack part of the way.		✔
12.	Finish tightening the lug nuts and replace the wheel cover.	✔	
13.	Finish lowering the jack.	✔	
14.	Remove the chocks.		✔
15.	Store the jack, chocks, and the old tire.		✔

Figure 13.1 Mr. Worrell's checklist for changing a tire.

a list of behaviors that the student displayed during the assessment as well as a list of behaviors that the student did not display.

In Chapter 3 we discussed a driver's education teacher, Mr. Worrell, who developed a list of the steps for changing a tire on a car. After teaching the students how to change the tire, he decided to ask his students to change a tire while he rated their performance. He also developed a checklist to use to rate each student's performance. In Figure 13.1 you can see a completed checklist for one of his students, Sarah James. From this checklist you should easily be able to see that Sarah only forgot three steps in the process. She did not partially lower the car before tightening the lug nuts and she forgot to remove the tire chocks and store them.

Checklists are most appropriate when the assessment involves observing behaviors and finished products that include a variety of steps or characteristics. Checklists require a dichotomous response ("yes" or "no," "present or not present") and do not allow the teacher to make any judgment about how well each skill was completed. It was either completed or not completed. Sometimes you can compute a total score based on the number or percentage of skills that were appropriately completed, although that does not work well in all situations. At other times you can simply give the checklist to the student as a report on how well he or she performed each skill.

Rating Scales

A second way to score performance assessments is with the use of rating scales. These are very much like checklists, which were discussed in the last section, but with one additional characteristic. As with checklists, you start out with a list of skills. However, after each skill, you are expected to rate each student on how well the task was performed. The scales have three or more points on them. For example, how would you rate this chapter for readability using the following scale?

1. Extremely difficult to read.
2. More difficult to read than other chapters.
3. About the same difficulty as other chapters.
4. Easier to read than many chapters.
5. Very easy to read.

These types of rating scale are very popular and are frequently referred to as Likert-types scales. They are named after Renis Likert (1932) who invented and popularized this rating scale technology. I have seen some Likert-types scales with as few as 3 points and others with as many as 11 points. However, scales with 5 to 7 points are most common since they may have the best psychometric characteristics.

Rating scales have two advantages over checklists. First, they allow the teacher to make a finer judgment and are not simply limited to dichotomous responses. Perhaps the student completed the skill, but not as well as he or she should have done. In this case, you can give a 3 or 4 on a 5-point scale rather than the full 5 points. A second advantage is that rating scales are frequently more reliable than checklists simply because the scores can cover a larger range. For example, if a student is rated on 10 skills with a checklist, scores could range from 0 (displayed none of the skills) to 10 (displayed all skills). However, if those 10 skills are each rated on a 7-point scale (with possible scores between 1 and 7 for each skill) then total points could range from a low of 10 (all 1s) to 70 (all 7s). This typically results in a larger standard deviation among scores which often results in higher reliabilities.

Figure 13.2 is an example of a rating scale that Ms. Smith uses to evaluate informative speeches in her speech class. Each category also contains those characteristics that she expects to see in a good informative speech.

For teachers, both checklists and rating scales work best when you use consistent polarity. For example, on a checklist, a "yes" rating should always indicate good performance and a "no" rating should indicate poor performance. If some of the items have a reversed polarity, you could become more easily confused when completing the form. The same goes for rating scales. High scores should indicate good performance and low scores poor performance for each item. Reversing the polarity on some items increases teacher confusion when completing the forms and introduces measurement error into the scoring.

Rubrics

With some performance assessments, neither checklists nor rating scales are appropriate. In those instances you may wish to resort to the use of a rubric. Although the term, rubric, is used in many different ways, it typically refers to a holistic scoring plan (Andrade, 2000). Let's say, for example, that you assigned your students to complete a project. Although the students do have some choices that they can make about the project, you have outlined for them some essential characteristics that you expect to see in their finished work. In this case, you could build a rubric that is based on your expectations. What specific characteristics would you need to see in a project in order to give it an A grade? What would you need to see in a project in order to give it a B grade, and so on? The more details that you include in the rubric, the easier it will be to use. If the rubric is too general, you will find yourself very dependent on your personal

5 – Excellent
4 – Good
3 – Average
2 – Fair
1 – Poor

1. Introduction   5 4 3 2 1
   The best introductions include a unique opening; arouse the listener's attention; provide direction; convey a central purpose; and are relevant to the audience.
2. Organization   5 4 3 2 1
   The best speeches have a clear format; have good transitions; are easy to follow; contain only relevant information; have visual aids that support the organization; and contain an introduction, a body, and a conclusion.
3. Delivery   5 4 3 2 1
   The best speakers use a natural stance; display natural eye contact; use natural gestures; display a positive attitude; are self-confident; demonstrate interest and enthusiasm; use an appropriate voice tone; and do not overly rely on notes.
4. Research   5 4 3 2 1
   The best speakers cite their sources during the speech; use high quality, credible, and unbiased sources; and effectively select details to be presented.
5. Conclusion   5 4 3 2 1
   The best conclusions connect with the introduction; summarize the main points; offer questions as appropriate; and do not fade out or apologize.
6. Visual Aids   5 4 3 2 1
   The best visual aids are appropriate to the topic; essential to understanding the speech; work smoothly into the speech; are large enough, neatly done; and are clean, uncluttered, and clearly labeled.

TOTAL POINTS: _____

Figure 13.2 Ms. Smith's rating scale for evaluating an informative speech.

judgment, and the reliability will be lower. See Figure 13.3 for an example of a rubric for a high school American history term paper.

Rubrics, however, can sometimes be confusing. For example, in Figure 13.3 you see a rubric for an American history term paper. In order to earn an A, the paper must display six characteristics. What do you do if the paper displays five of the characteristics, but falls short on the sixth? In that case you must build a plan that allows for such inconsistency. One possible plan would be to assign points for each characteristic. For example, if the student met five of the characteristics at the A level, but only met the sixth characteristic at the C level, appropriate points could be assigned to each. If an A is worth 4 points and a C is worth 2 points, the student would have earned 22 points (five As and one C) out of a total of 24 points required for an A. This would then probably translate to a grade of A minus. This is just one of many ways to deal with such inconsistencies.

Rubrics are useful in many situations. For example, they can also be used for scoring global essay exams. However, it does take some experience to learn to develop and use rubrics effectively. Many teachers are disappointed the first time that they develop a rubric, typically because it was either too general or too specific. However, with practice, they can become better at it.

Whether you use a checklist, a rating scale, or a rubric, you should keep some points

Paper Grade	Necessary Characteristics
A	Introduction is complete and engaging. Topic is sufficiently narrow and relevant. Each sub topic is thoroughly discussed. Ideas flow logically from one paragraph to another. The conclusion is integrative. At least 8 relevant sources are used appropriately.
B	Introduction is relatively complete, but not very engaging. Topic is too broad or not very relevant. Some sub topics are not discussed well. Ideas flow relatively well from one paragraph to another. There is a conclusion, although not very integrative. At least 6 relevant sources are used appropriately.
C	There is some attempt at an introduction. Topic is either very broad or not relevant. Most sub topics are not discussed well. Many paragraphs appear unrelated to others. There is some attempt at a conclusion. At least 4 relevant sources are used appropriately.
D	There is no introduction. Topic is much too broad and not relevant. Sub topics are largely lacking. There is little logical flow throughout the paper. There is no conclusion. At least 2 relevant sources are used, although not necessarily appropriately.

Figure 13.3 Mr. Samuels's rubric for American history term papers.

in mind. Any scoring plan designed for a performance assessment needs to be well organized and easy to use. When you are observing a student performing a skill, there is not much time to look away from the student to record your responses. Every time you look away from the student you could be missing some important observations. However, if your scoring plan is well organized and if you know it well, you should be able to very quickly make a note on the scoring plan, and then return to your observation. If the skill occurs very quickly, you will often have to focus your full attention on the student. Once the student has completed the performance, you can then immediately fill out the scoring plan. Although this requires you to rely on your memory, with practice you can do this reliably.

SUMMARY

Performance assessments are a way to rate students' performance and are used by teachers when they observe students performing a behavior or skill. Performance assessments are most often used to evaluate students when more traditional paper-and-pencil tests are simply not appropriate. Performance assessments can be used to evaluate either process or product. They can be used in either simulated or real settings, and they can allow teachers to observe behavior as it occurs naturally or the teacher can structure the setting. The primary advantage of performance assessments is that they allow the teacher to evaluate skills that cannot be evaluated well with paper-and-pencil tests. The primary limitation is that they take considerable time to complete. Teachers prepare performance assessments by listing the skills or characteristics that they expect to see in the students' performance. Finally, teachers are frequently assisted in scoring performance assessments with the use of checklists, rating scales, and rubrics.

EXERCISES

1. State whether a paper-and-pencil assessment or a performance assessment would be more appropriate in the following situations:

   a. A home economics teacher wants to make sure her students are correctly using the measuring utensils while baking.
   b. A physical education teacher wants to make sure his students know the rules of baseball.
   c. An English teacher wants her students to be able to correctly pronounce each word that is on this week's spelling test.
   d. A music teacher wants to see if his students can play the notes of the treble clef and the bass clef.
   e. A geography teacher wants to see if his students can draw a sketch of the state in which they live.

2. Come up with an example of how a teacher can use a performance assessment in the following activities and objective:

   a. a 4th-grade social studies activity where students need to locate different cities on a world map;
   b. a 5th-grade volcano science experiment designed to demonstrate the basic structure of a volcano;
   c. a 9th-grade physical education class where students are learning how to play volleyball;
   d. a 3rd-grade math class reviewing multiplication tables;
   e. a preschool class sorting three dimensional wooden shapes.

3. Create a brief checklist or rating scale that you would use if you were to assess children on their ability to make a peanut butter and jelly sandwich.

SPOTLIGHT ON THE CLASSROOM

Ms. Smith is a professor at the University of Arizona and primarily teaches public speaking to first- and second-year college students. Her course consists of lectures, discussions, presentations, and tests, and is broken into units.

For a unit on persuasive speeches, she begins with lecture and discussion about persuasive speaking and describes the various characteristics of an effective persuasive speech. Students are then expected each to present a persuasive speech to the rest of the class. Each speech is graded by the use of a rubric that is specific for persuasive speeches, but is general enough to allow students to use creativity. At the end of the unit, she gives the students an objective test on the characteristics of public speaking and, as in this unit, the particular characteristics of a persuasive speech.

Currently, she is using formal assessment in terms of her classroom tests and performance assessment in terms of the students' speeches. Can you think of other ways that she might build performance assessments into her class?

14

PORTFOLIOS

INTRODUCTION

Students in fields like art, advertising, architecture, fashion design, and photography have always been encouraged to develop professional portfolios. These students are expected to include in their portfolios examples of some of their very best work and enough examples to show their versatility. They use their portfolios on job interviews and as a way to sell their services to potential clients. Over the past 20 years, educators in many fields have attempted to adapt the portfolio model as an alternative to traditional paper-and-pencil assessments (Sweet, 1993). Portfolios have some distinctive advantages as an assessment device, but also have a number of limitations.

In this chapter, the last of three on alternative assessment techniques, we will discuss portfolios as an assessment technique. You will learn more about the essential characteristics of portfolios, their advantages, and their limitations. We will also consider where portfolios may be used in an appropriate manner and how to assist your students in developing their portfolios.

WHAT MAKES PORTFOLIOS DISTINCTIVE?

Why have many teachers become fascinated with portfolios? What makes them unique? Almost all of the assessment techniques that we have discussed take a snapshot of a student. They give you a picture of what a student is like at one given point in time. They do not typically give you the ability to see how a student's skills have grown throughout the year. Portfolios, on the other hand, have the potential to demonstrate that growth. If students are encouraged to include samples of work (e.g. writing samples) produced throughout the year, you, the teacher, have the ability to evaluate that growth. Frequently, even more importantly, it gives both you and your students a way to demonstrate that growth to important third parties, such as school administrators and parents. Many teachers find this characteristic of portfolios attractive.

Some teachers are also suspicious about the apparent artificiality of many paper-and-pencil assessment devices. They frequently feel that most classroom tests lack authenticity and do not accurately reflect their students' abilities.[1] Those teachers sometimes see portfolios as being more authentic and better able to measure their students' abilities to use the skills that they have learned in the classroom.

These are some of the reasons why individual teachers and, sometimes, entire schools have adopted the use of portfolios. Other potential advantages of portfolios are described in the next section.

ADVANTAGES AND LIMITATIONS

As is true with the other assessment techniques, portfolios have both potential advantages as well as limitations.

Advantages

Most assessment techniques have the tendency to focus on students' weaknesses. Rather than focusing on the test items that a student answered correctly, teachers tend to focus more on the items that were answered incorrectly or on skills that students have not yet mastered. Therefore, there is a focus on a student's weaknesses. On the other hand, with portfolios, students are encouraged to include samples of their best work. Therefore, there is more of a focus on a student's strengths.

A second advantage of portfolios is that they are tailored to each student's individual needs. Most classroom assessment techniques are designed to be given to all of the students in the classroom at the same time and are measuring shared educational goals and objectives. However, if you organize your classroom so that individualized goals are set for each student, then typical classroom tests may not work well. However, portfolios are specifically designed for each student based on the goals and objectives that have been set up for that student. Portfolios, therefore, might be a good assessment alternative in a classroom that is more focused on individualized educational goals.

Another advantage of portfolios is that they frequently help students learn how to evaluate their own work. Most students are relatively naïve about how to evaluate their work. They are often uncertain about exactly what teachers are looking for in work samples and are surprised at the grades that they receive. However, in developing portfolios, students work—with assistance from their teachers—to develop criteria to use to evaluate work samples. They are expected to be able eventually to look at various samples of their own work, evaluate each sample, and include their best samples. Without the use of portfolios, some students might never develop this skill.

There is still one other potential advantage of portfolios: They provide teachers with an alternative form of assessment. Good teaching typically requires flexibility! You will encounter students who, for one reason or another, simply do not perform as well as they should with more traditional assessment techniques. In those cases, you will want to have possible alternative assessment techniques available. In fact, some states now allow portfolio assessment to substitute for more traditional required standardized assessment devices for certain students. That type of flexibility is important in education.

Limitations

Portfolios also suffer from potential limitations. Portfolios are actually a specific type of performance assessment, which we talked about in the previous chapter. Although teachers often view portfolios as a way to measure and demonstrate student progress, portfolios work best at measuring student outcomes—products. With portfolios you can include samples of early work as well as samples of more recent work. The differences in the work samples are expected to demonstrate progress—growth. However, this approach gives you very little information about the processes that took place that allowed the student to make that growth. Even when students include a first draft of a paper along with the finished product, we are left without any information about what occurred that allowed that progress. Therefore, portfolios typically show us the finished product of growth, not how the growth occurred.

Another limitation is that portfolios are very time-intensive. They involve a lot of one-on-one time between the teacher and the student. First, the teacher and the student must sit down and plan out the portfolio. Effective portfolios require a collaborative effort. Second, at least once in the process of developing the portfolio, the student and teacher must meet to check on its progress. Such a progress meeting could easily last 30 minutes. Finally, the teacher needs to evaluate each portfolio. A careful review of a portfolio can also take a considerable amount of time.

A third limitation of portfolios is that they are difficult to score reliably. If the portfolio is expected to stand on its own to demonstrate student progress, then a teacher evaluation may not be necessary since the progress might be self-evident. However, in most cases, a portfolio is used as an assessment device and is used to help develop a grade for a student. In that case, you will have to evaluate and grade it. Even with the use of a well-developed grading plan or rubric, it is difficult to grade portfolios reliably. Although there are not many published reports on portfolio reliability, when such studies have been completed, inter-rater agreement typically produces reliabilities of below .50, which are unacceptably low.

COMPONENTS OF PORTFOLIOS

There are many different ways to organize portfolios, depending on the subject matter, and the desired goals. However, I am going to provide you with a general model that can be used in many settings. The best portfolios typically have three components: a list of goals, the work samples, and annotations.

The List of Goals

When planning out a portfolio, the first thing that you must do is to decide on the purpose of the portfolio. What specific educational goals do you want to demonstrate? For example, let's say that you are a high school English teacher working with juniors and seniors. Your personal goal for your students might be to teach them how to write a variety of types of essay: descriptive, narrative, persuasive, and comparison and contrast. Therefore, you might encourage your students to develop portfolios that show their skills with each of the four types of essay that you taught. The students would then essentially have four goals—to demonstrate competence with each type of essay.

In the above example, each student in your class could conceivably have the same goals. In reality, teachers tend to use portfolios in a more flexible manner; each student could set her or his own goals. It is typically recommended that the setting of goals should be a collaborative effort between teacher and student. Frequently, you need to solicit ideas about goals from your students. However, since students often have little experience with portfolios, you will have to help them set reasonable goals that they will be able to demonstrate through the portfolio. When the process is completed both you and your student will have a firm understanding of what the student will need to do.

Once the goals are set, they can often serve as a table of contents for the portfolio.

Work Samples

The most substantial part of the portfolio will be the work samples, which should be arranged by the goals. For the example that I provided earlier, the student would want samples of each of the four types of essay.

When there are many work samples to choose from, selecting those to include can be difficult for your students and you will need to work with them to teach them how to make that choice. Portfolios typically include a student's best examples. Therefore, you will need to teach the students how to evaluate their work samples. For example, if they want to include examples of descriptive essays, you will need to teach them about the characteristics of good descriptive essays and how to go about determining if their essays adequately display those characteristics. As students learn to decide which work samples to include, they are learning important evaluation skills: How do I evaluate my own work?

Deciding which work samples to include should be a collaborative effort between you and the student. Frequently, the work samples will already have been evaluated by you, the teacher. However, since one of your goals is to help your students learn to evaluate their own work, you may have to meet with each student several times to make certain that the student is appropriately evaluating the samples that he or she may wish to include.

Annotations

The last section of the portfolio will include annotations, which are similar to footnotes. For each work sample your student should include an annotation. The annotation could contain anything about the work sample which the student would like to communicate to anyone reading the portfolio. For example, it can include the date when each piece was prepared, which would be important for evaluating growth. It can also include a rationale as to why that particular work sample was chosen. For some types of portfolio the annotations might be very brief, perhaps only a few sentences. However, for other types more explanations are required and annotations will be longer. The annotations are typically placed in the back of the portfolio.

WHEN IS PORTFOLIO ASSESSMENT THE MOST EFFECTIVE?

There are educators who argue that portfolio assessment can work effectively with students of all ages and in almost all academic disciplines. However, an educator who is a little more conservative or skeptical is likely to argue that portfolios will probably work better in some situations than in others. For example, portfolios have traditionally been used in fields heavily dependent on creativity, probably because they have been an effective tool for helping students display their creativity. In school they can continue to be effective when creativity is one of the primary educational goals. However, they need not be limited to the arts. They can work well with writing and creative problem solving in many different disciplines.

In addition, portfolio assessment will probably work better with older students than with very young students. Most portfolios require students to analyze their work samples and then evaluate them. Most often, both analysis and evaluation require abstract thinking skills which are simply not present in most children under the age of about 12. Unless analysis and evaluation are kept at the concrete level, younger children simply do not yet have the ability to deal with them. Therefore, when portfolios are used with younger students they need to be simpler and more concrete. Since younger students typically lack the ability to evaluate their own work, the use of portfolios is probably less effective with that group. However, if students are introduced to the use of portfolios in the early grades, they will probably be able to use them more effectively when they are older.

HELPING STUDENTS DEVELOP THEIR PORTFOLIOS

Unless students have already had considerable experience with portfolios they will typically need a great deal of help from you, the teacher, and often they will not even know how to get started. Therefore, you will have to guide them along the way.

One of the first areas where they will need help will be in setting appropriate goals. Often, you will set some general parameters for them and perhaps even suggest the types of goal that they should set for themselves. However, most students, and especially younger students, have often had little experience in setting meaningful goals. Left on their own, students will typically set goals that are much too broad. You will have to help them narrow their goals and develop goals that are appropriate for a portfolio assessment. It is also important to help your students set goals that are personally meaningful in order to keep them motivated to complete the task.

Another area where your students will need help is with the selection of work samples to include. They will need guidance in evaluating work samples to see which ones actually display the capabilities that they are trying to demonstrate. As I mentioned earlier, students are frequently unaware of what to look for in a work sample to judge its quality. Sometimes you will be able to work on this with your entire class. Having students work together in groups with a peer evaluator can be helpful. However, at other times, you will have to work with students on this on a one-on-one basis. This aspect of portfolio development is one you want to emphasize since learning to judge the quality of their work is one of the most important skills that your students will learn from this activity.

Your students will also need assistance with annotations until they get the hang of it, and will need assistance with putting their portfolios together. It can be helpful to have several different sample portfolios available in the classroom for students to look at as models. In general, you will need to provide more assistance when students start each new part of the portfolio. However, once they learn how to do it on their own, they will require less help from you.

SCORING PORTFOLIOS

Perhaps one of the most difficult parts of the process for you, the teacher, will involve scoring the portfolios. At times, the portfolios may not need to be scored. For example, if the aim of the portfolio is to demonstrate to parents their child's growth with certain skills over the year, the portfolio can speak for itself and may not need a formal evaluation by you. In this case, however, you will want to be involved with your students throughout the process to make certain that they are developing their portfolios appropriately.

In many instances, however, you will be expected to score and evaluate the portfolios that you assign to your students. You should approach scoring portfolios as you would other performance assessments by the use of checklists, rating scales, or rubrics. They will allow you to be more consistent in evaluating different students' portfolios.

Even with the use of checklists, rating scales, and rubrics, unless you are highly organized, the scoring and evaluating of the portfolios will probably take much longer than you would like. There are, however, a few ways in which you can make the process more efficient. For example, if you provided students with a list of criteria for evaluating work samples, have the students include the lists of the criteria with each work sample that you plan to evaluate. Another way to make portfolios more efficient to score is to have the students complete them electronically (Montgomery & Wiley, 2008). There are now a number of software programs that work well with portfolios. Electronic portfolios can also contain video clips which would make them especially useful when students wish to highlight performance skills (e.g. theater). Electronic portfolios allow you, the teacher, to work on scoring the portfolios outside of the classroom, without having to physically drag them with you. Finally, it will also help if you clearly communicate to the students the criteria that you will use for your evaluations. When they know exactly what you are looking for, they are more likely to set up the portfolio in a manner that will make those important characteristics stand out.

THE FUTURE OF PORTFOLIO ASSESSMENT

I must admit that I am uncertain about the future of portfolio assessment. Although portfolios have some special strengths—they are a way to teach students to evaluate their own work and a way to communicate progress—they certainly will not replace most traditional assessment techniques. In addition, they are not appropriate in all settings. It may turn out simply to be an educational fad which excites some educators for a few years, but is eventually abandoned by most because it is unwieldy or unworkable. However, with experience, portfolio assessment also may evolve into a very useful tool, especially within some disciplines. Only time will tell!

SUMMARY

Portfolios have been used in the creative fields for many years. However, since the late 1980s, educators in many fields have started to use portfolio assessment. Portfolios typically involve students developing a collection of work samples to use to demonstrate specific educational goals. Portfolios have become popular because they provide a way to demonstrate student growth and because they can be an effective way to communicate that growth to others, such as parents. Portfolios also have some limitations. They can be very time-consuming for both students and teachers. They are also difficult to evaluate reliably. Although portfolios can come in many different forms, one popular form includes educational goals, work samples, and annotations. Portfolios are typically scored by using checklists, rating scales, or rubrics.

EXERCISES

1. Which of the following is an advantage of portfolio assessment?

    A. Portfolios typically focus on the student's strengths and weaknesses.
    B. Students never have to evaluate the portfolio themselves.
    C. Portfolios are designed for individualized goals and needs of the students.
    D. Portfolios are quick and easy to make and evaluate.

2. Which of the following statements is true about portfolios?

    A. Portfolios are quick and easy to make and evaluate.
    B. Portfolios usually show the finished product of growth.
    C. It is easy to evaluate portfolios reliably.
    D. None of the above.

3. Which of the following is typically used to score portfolios?

    A. checklists
    B. rubrics
    C. rating scales
    D. all of the above

4. Complete the following statement: Portfolios are becoming more popular in the classroom because they are a way to demonstrate and communicate student _____.

    A. growth
    B. health
    C. behavior

5. Imagine that you are a 9th-grade science teacher. You are planning a unit on air and water pollution. Create an assignment for each of the following assessment types that you could use in this unit.

    A. performance assessment
    B. informal observations
    C. portfolios

6. Generate a list of items or material that could be included in a 4th-grade writing portfolio.

SPOTLIGHT ON THE CLASSROOM

Judi North, a social studies teacher at Leeward High School, started using portfolios in her 10th-grade American history classes this year. Over the past few years her students have complained that most of the American history that they have studied had little to do with their lives. They also complained about memorizing names and dates, only to forget them the day after the test.

In response to their complaints, Ms. North designed a portfolio assignment. For each of the eight historical periods that they study in her class, each class member must pick an issue and demonstrate how it relates to some issue that we are dealing with currently or very recently here in the U.S. Once the students got used to working on these projects, they became much more interested in U.S. history. However, since the projects take so much time, Ms. North has stopped giving the chapter tests that she used in the past. She decided that the students' grades will be based solely on their portfolios.

During her free period she often chats with her colleague, Miguel Hernandez, another social studies teacher. She described this portfolio project with excitement and told him how pleased she was with her students' new enthusiasm. Mr. Hernandez pointed out to her that he was also interested in using portfolios, had read a lot about them, and discovered that they, unfortunately, had a reputation for having very low reliabilities when graded. On the other hand, traditional classroom tests tend to be much more reliable.

Now Ms. North faces a dilemma. She recognizes that in order for grades to be valid, they must be based on reliable measures. How can she maintain her students' new enthusiasm and still grade them reliably?

NOTE

1. Psychometricians often argue that teachers' suspicions about the artificiality of classroom tests are generally exaggerated. The majority of classroom tests do display acceptable levels of both reliability and validity and are typically correlated with the students' abilities to use these skills in real life.

Section IV

ADDITIONAL MEASUREMENT ISSUES

This last section of Part I includes several other measurement issues that are each sufficiently unique not to fit well into any of the other sections. Chapter 15 discusses how to teach your students better test-taking skills. Many students lack these skills, which can have a negative effect on the reliability and validity of your tests. When you teach these skills to your students, it can positively impact on the educational environment in many ways. Chapter 16 discusses the many standardized tests that you are likely to encounter in your teaching career. The characteristics of these tests, and how they can be used effectively, are considered. Finally, Chapter 17 discusses the numerous alternative ways in which you are likely to see test scores reported. I discuss the advantages and disadvantages of each approach as well as how you should interpret these alternative approaches.

15

TEACHING STUDENTS TEST-TAKING SKILLS

INTRODUCTION

Many teachers believe that all students instinctively know how to take tests. This is just not so. This point was made clear to me when I was in graduate school. One of the first classes that I took was an advanced educational psychology class taken by both beginning graduate students and some upper-level undergraduates. Since there were about 60 students in the class, most of the test items were multiple-choice, which worked well for me. I had attended a large undergraduate institution where I had taken many multiple-choice exams. However, one of my classmates was from England and had almost no experience with multiple-choice exam questions. She earned a low score on the first exam simply because she had no idea how to approach this type of test. She left many questions blank simply because she was not absolutely sure of the correct alternative. The idea of taking an educated guess was completely foreign to her. In her experience, if you were uncertain of the answer, you simply did not guess. Luckily, after that first disastrous experience, her new American friends taught her the art of taking multiple-choice tests and making educated guesses. Her scores on the remaining exams improved dramatically.

Many students need to learn how to take tests. Some students learn those skills from friends, family members, or teachers. Others learn how to do it themselves, simply because they are very good at adapting to challenges in their environment. Unfortunately, many students simply do not learn effective test-taking skills and strategies, or not enough of them. Other students actually use ineffective test-taking strategies that result in test scores much lower than those that they should have obtained based on their knowledge and level of preparation.

As a teacher, you want your students' performance on your tests to reflect their skills in the content area and in their level of preparation. You do not want them to be penalized because of their poor test-taking skills. This represents error variance and decreases the reliability of your tests. As much as possible, you want your tests to tap into your students' true scores.

In this chapter, you will learn some of the test-taking skills and strategies that you can teach your students. You will also learn how you can better prepare your students to take your tests and how you can help them improve their test performance.

GENERAL TEST-TAKING STRATEGIES

There are a number of general test-taking strategies that your students can learn, such as how to budget their time, how to read directions carefully, and how to read questions carefully.

Budgeting Time

You may recall that earlier in the text I mentioned that most classroom tests should be power tests (tests which most students will be able to finish) and students should be given plenty of time to finish. In reality, however, some classroom tests are rather long for the allotted time and a number of students do not finish. Therefore, your students need to learn how to budget and monitor their time when taking tests. This can be especially important when students get stuck on a particularly difficult question or problem and spend much too much time on it. Some students spend so much time on one very difficult item that they never get to complete other much easier items, and end up with an uncharacteristically low score on the test.

You can teach your students some ways to avoid that and similar problems. First, they can learn how to estimate how much time they should spend on each item. For example, if the test consists of 25 items and the students have 30 minutes to complete it, then they should figure that they need to be completing about one item per minute. If the students start the test at 1:15 p.m. and move consecutively through the items, then they should check to see how much time is left after they complete item 13, the half-way point on the exam. If it is not yet 1:30 p.m., then they are moving at an appropriate pace. If, however, it is past 1:30 p.m., then they need to speed up.

Dianna Van Blerkom (2009) recommends that, when time is a factor and when there are different types of item on a test, students should employ other time-budgeting strategies. For example, if one item is a high point-gainer (let's say that it is worth 50% of the total test score), then students should answer that question first. Go for the high point-gainers first. In other situations, the questions may each be worth the same number of points, but some questions are easier than others. In that case, students should answer the easiest questions first to be assured of obtaining those points. As students answer the easier items, they should mark the other items for later review. Then, as time allows, they can work on the more difficult and time-consuming questions.

Reading Directions

Very often, students assume that they know what they are doing and begin a project or task without first reading the directions. It is only when they run into problems that they go back and read the directions, recognize that they have been doing it incorrectly, and have to go back and start at the beginning. In most cases, the time loss does not affect the student's grade. However, on a test with time limits, failure to read the directions could have serious consequences. You need to help your students get into the habit of reading the directions on a test. I typically read the directions aloud to my students, but not all teachers do that. Therefore, you need to use some teaching techniques to get your students used to reading test directions. One method that can be effective is to vary the directions. Or, you could require students to underline key words in the directions.

Reading Items Carefully

Your students also need to learn how to read questions carefully. Earlier in the text, I advised you to write your questions in as clear and as concise a manner as possible. In spite of that advice, there are many test questions that can be a challenge to read. Some questions are grammatically complex, contain modifying words that can affect the meaning of the question, or simply contain unnecessary information. In any of those situations, careless reading of the question may lead to incorrect responses.

There are skills that you can teach your students concerning reading questions carefully. For example, in a complex item, teach your students to identify and underline that part (or those parts) of the item in which the question is actually being asked.

Example 1

Although fought in January, 1815, after the treaty had been signed, <u>the Battle of New Orleans was a part of which war?</u>
(Answer: The War of 1812)

You can also teach your students to underline important words that could alter the meaning of the question. Words such as "least," "except," "always," "not," or "never" can be especially important. Many students tend to read test items too quickly and don't actually answer the question that was asked. Underlining key parts of the question helps some students to slow down and read more carefully.

Example 2

Which of the following was <u>not</u> one of the major causes of World War I?

A. numerous alliances between countries

B. the rapid industrialization of Europe

C. competition for colonies and influence in Africa and Asia

D. strong militarism with the military often stronger than the civil governments

E. powerful nationalism

(Answer: B)

Still another aspect of reading items carefully is to try to determine the intent of the writer. At the beginning of the year, students don't know their teachers very well, which makes it more difficult for them to determine the teacher's intent on a question. After some time students learn what to expect from their teachers and become better at determining their intent. However, a student does not need to become a mind reader to figure out what the teacher expected as a correct answer. Frequently, students simply need to remind themselves, "What did the teacher emphasize while teaching this material?" Teachers tend to emphasize the most important material and tend also to test that same material.

Another strategy that you can teach your students will help them deal with potentially ambiguous items. Encourage them to ask the teacher for clarification. For example, a student might recognize that an item can be interpreted in two different ways. If the student asks the teacher about which of the two ways the question should be answered, he or she is more likely to choose the correct alternative. Some teachers might not allow such questions during a test, but many will.

In addition, when students point out ambiguous items to their teachers, it encourages teachers to write better items. Certainly, if that teacher wants to use that item again in the future, he or she will attempt to prepare a better item, free from ambiguity.

Checking Tests before Turning Them In

Another test-taking strategy that you can teach your students is to check their tests before turning them in. Of course, at times there is simply not enough time for students to go back over their tests, but when enough time is available they should be encouraged to check their tests. Sometimes students find that they have made clerical errors or simply forgotten to complete a question. At other times, especially with tests involving problem solving in math and science, it helps to check for computational errors. When students feel rushed or nervous, it is easy to make careless mistakes. These kinds of error have an impact upon the reliability of the test.

When checking a test, students sometimes decide to change the answer that they originally supplied for an item. Is it better to change an answer or leave it as it is? The research suggests that about 50% of the time when students change their answers, they go from a wrong answer to a right answer. Of course, that also means that about 50% of the time students change a right answer to a wrong answer. Perhaps the most cautious advice is to encourage students to avoid changing answers unless they find that they made an error in originally reading the item or if they find that they made a computational or similar error.

TEST-TAKING STRATEGIES FOR SPECIFIC TEST FORMATS

Now that we have considered some general test-taking strategies, let's discuss strategies specific to various testing formats. This section of the chapter will cover the short-answer, essay, multiple-choice, and true–false formats.

Strategies for Short-Answer Tests

As you probably recall, short-answer tests come in several forms and include completion items and fill-in-the-blank. In the completion and fill-in-the-blank formats, the answers typically consist of a single word or phrase. In the short-answer format, the answer could be as long as a sentence. Teaching your students the following strategies could help their performance on short-answer tests.

When attempting to answer fill-in-the-blank questions, students should start by reading the question and saying the word "blank" at the appropriate point. Then the students should try to think of words or phrases that would best complete the statement, keeping in mind the material that was taught. Many times the grammatical structure of the sentence will help the students determine which type of word (e.g. a noun) is required. Finally, the students should reread the question with the words that they inserted into the blanks to make sure that the answer makes sense.

Math and science problems also often fit into the short-answer format. Estimation skills can frequently help with these types of question. For example, in Chapter 2 I mention that the standard deviation of a set of scores is typically between one third and one sixth of the range. Because it takes only a few seconds to compute the range, doing so will tell you if the answer that you computed for the standard deviation is likely to be correct. There are many estimation skills that you can teach your students in both science and mathematics. Putting one or two practice questions on the first few tests and having the students do them as a class can help them better understand how to use these strategies.

Strategies for Essay Tests

Essay questions require students to have good organizational and writing skills. Students need to learn to write in a clear, logical, and succinct fashion. However, even students who are still in the process of developing those skills can learn to write better essay answers.

To answer an essay question, students need to make certain that they understand what is being asked. What is the issue that they must address? The next step is to take a few moments and plan out the answer, perhaps using a brief outline written in the margin. Then, as they write out their answers, they need to do so by describing their main points and providing supporting details for each. A good plan to follow is main point 1, then supporting details, followed by main point 2, and supporting details, and so on. Concluding with a brief summary of the main points brings the essay to a logical end. Teachers tend to give well-organized essay answers higher grades than those that are less so.

Students sometimes have time-management problems with essay items. How much time should I allow myself to answer an essay question? Perhaps the simplest guide is to use the point value of the essay. For example, if an essay is worth 30 points on a test of 100 points, then students should allow themselves about 30% of the available time to answer the essay. At times, that may mean keeping the essay answer brief because the item is not worth many points. However, if a student can make the relevant arguments in just a few sentences, that student is likely to score well.

As time allows, students should get into the habit of proofreading their essay answers. Even a quick proofreading can reveal errors in the essay that could result in lower scores. Proofreading takes only a few minutes and is frequently worth the extra effort. Having students rewrite their essay answers after they have been graded (with appropriate suggestions for improvement from the teacher) can be very beneficial. Once students learn how to structure an essay answer and have a better idea of how much detail you expect them to provide, they should be able to communicate more accurately their mastery of the material.

Strategies for Multiple-Choice Tests

There are a number of strategies that students can learn to improve their performance on multiple-choice items. Many multiple choice items can be treated like a short-answer item; that is, the students can read the stem (the question) and attempt to provide the correct answer without looking at the alternative answers. If they are able to successfully do that, then finding the correct alternative is often relatively easy. Students also need to read all of the alternative answers before choosing the correct one. At times, they may think that one alternative appears, at first glance, to be correct until they have read the other alternatives and recognize that another alternative is a much better answer. With more difficult items, students can also learn to cross out the clearly incorrect alternatives, allowing them to focus only on those alternative answers that may be correct. This process of elimination often leads to the correct answer.

Although, earlier in the text I discouraged the use of "all of the above" and "none of the above" as alternatives in multiple-choice items, they do show up with some frequency. Sometimes students have difficulty with items that contain those alternatives simply because they have never learned to apply simple strategies. For example, if when reading the alternative answers the students find any alternative that is correct, then they can immediately exclude "none of the above" as correct. In a similar fashion, if in another item they find that any alternative is wrong, they can immediately exclude "all of the above" as correct. Although these strategies appear very logical and self-evident to us as teachers, they are not always obvious to our students. Therefore, teaching them these strategies frequently helps their test performance.

Matching items are essentially a variation of the multiple-choice format, but are unique enough to require their own strategies. First, it is very important to read the directions. Some teachers set up matching items so that each alternative can be used only once. At other times the alternatives can be used many times. To avoid confusion, students should work from one column only. For example, let's say that the question has to do with explorers. The column on the left lists places that were explored and the column on the right lists the names of the explorers. If the first item in the left-hand column was, "fought the Incas in Peru," the student should know immediately that the answer is Juan Pizarro (or one of his brothers), and look for his name in the right-hand column. If the alternatives are used only once, then the student should cross off his name. The student should continue with that process, moving down the list on the left, and completing the ones that he or she knows. Then, on returning to the more difficult items, the student will have fewer explorers to choose from, which should help. Of course, if the final two items on the test do not match, the student should go back and look for errors. Although matching tests appear to be easy, an error early in the matching process typically leads to other errors.

Strategies for True–false Tests

True–false test items also frequently present a challenge to students, but you can teach your students how to approach them more effectively. For example, students need to understand that if any part of the statement is false, then the entire statement is false. In addition, statements that contain absolute words such as "all," "always," "completely," "forever," "never," "no one," "only," and "totally," are typically false. (This particular strategy sometimes applies also to multiple-choice items.) Very few things are absolute. On the other hand, statements that contain adjectives that imply an indefinite degree ("frequently," "generally," "many," "may," "often," "usually," and "sometimes") are typically true. Teaching students to identify and underline the word or phrase that makes the statement incorrect can help them better identify statements that are false. If they are unable to identify such a word or phrase, the statement is probably true.

Another strategy that can sometimes work on true–false items is to try to rephrase the statement to make it false by adding a word like "not." The student should then read the statement each way. Which way appears more reasonable? If one alternative is much more reasonable than the other, the more reasonable one is probably correct. Asking students to correct false statements on tests or explain why a statement is true helps them learn to answer true–false items more effectively.

FAMILIARITY WITH TESTING APPROACHES

At the beginning of this chapter, I shared a story of a British graduate student facing her first multiple-choice test at a large American university. She performed very poorly simply because she had never before taken a test in that format. However, with some help from her friends, and with some experience, she was soon able to handle multiple-choice items as well as the other types of item with which she was familiar.

The point is that students need to develop familiarity with testing formats and testing mediums before they can be successful. When computer-based testing was introduced in the 1980s, researchers found that students typically performed less well on computer-ized versions of a test than they did on the paper-and-pencil versions of the same test. However, today's students have had much more experience with computers and com-puter testing than did their counterparts of 20 years ago. As a consequence, researchers no longer find any difference in performance between taking a computer version of a test or a paper-and-pencil version (Mead & Drasgow, 1993; Wang, Jiao, Young, Brooks, & Olsen, 2007).

In a similar manner, when faced with a new or unfamiliar testing format or testing medium, you must expect that students will need time to learn how to deal effectively with them. However, you can make the process go more smoothly by giving them opportunities to practice with the unfamiliar new tests.

APPROACHES TO TEACHING TEST-TAKING SKILLS

How do you actually go about teaching the various test-taking skills that we have discussed? By using a combination of practice and discussion, you can turn your students into good test-takers.

One way to start is to give your students a practice test. However, don't tell them in advance that it is a practice test because you want them to prepare for it as if it were a real test. After the test (either the same day or the next day) you can then review it. At that point, you explain to them that it was a practice test and it was designed to help them learn how to take that type of test. As you review each item, ask for volunteers who know the correct answer. If the students supply the correct answer, ask them follow-up questions concerning how they determined that it was the correct answer. You could ask other students how they figured out the correct answer. Perhaps there were words in the item that helped them determine the answer. If none of the students mention a particu-lar strategy that you think might help, you could supply it yourself and encourage them to try that strategy with later items. Some students might argue that another alternative or answer was correct. In this case, you might engage in a class discussion as to why these other alternatives are incorrect.

Another approach is to have students take a practice test in small groups of three to four students. Make sure that the groups are heterogeneous for test-taking skills. Encourage the groups not only to determine the correct answer for each item, but also to share their decision-making process and the strategies that they used. After the groups have finished, you can then review the test as a full class, sharing strategies.

No matter which approach you use, it must involve more than you, the teacher, simply talking to the class. Students are more likely to use these skills and strategies if they have discussed them with their peers and if they have had a sufficient amount of practice.

SUMMARY

This chapter discussed test-taking strategies. Many students do not earn the grades that they should have received on tests simply because they do not know how to take tests effectively. Some students learn good test-taking skills and strategies from family, friends, or teachers. However, because many students have limited knowledge about how to effectively approach a test, you need to teach them these strategies. Students need to learn general test-taking strategies related to budgeting their time, reading directions, and reading questions carefully. There are also specific strategies that you can teach your students about various testing formats. Students need to learn how to effectively approach short-answer items, essay items, multiple-choice items (including matching), and true–false items. Students tend to perform better with various item formats and various testing modalities as they gain more experience with similar tests. Finally, students can often learn good test-taking skills by taking practice tests and engaging in discussions with their peers.

EXERCISES

State whether or not each of the following is an effective test-taking strategy to teach students. If it is not, explain what you would do differently.

1. Mr. Yang tells his students that if they get stuck on a particular question, they should stick with it until they come up with the correct answer, no matter how long it takes.
2. Before beginning each test, Ms. Bolini has one student read the directions out loud to the entire class.
3. During a test, Mrs. Ackers tells her students when there is 10 minutes left before the end of class. At this point, she also advises the class to go back through the test and check their answers.
4. Mr. Gregorich does not allow his 10th-grade earth science students to write or make any marks on their test booklet.
5. Mrs. Popowicz advises her students not to waste time reading all of the alternatives on a multiple-choice exam. She says that as soon as they see an answer they like, they should mark it and move on to the next question.

SPOTLIGHT ON THE CLASSROOM

Mrs. Quader is a new 8th-grade social studies teacher at Sharpsville Middle School in Sharon, Kansas. After giving her students their first exam, she noticed that many performed poorly. She examined several characteristics of the test items and changed some questions to make the test more reliable and valid. However, she feels that the students may simply need to learn a few test-taking skills to raise their scores.

The first exam was worth 50 points. It consisted of 20 multiple-choice questions worth 1 point each, 2 short-essay questions worth 5 points each, 10 matching questions, and 10 true–false questions, all worth 1 point each. Although the students were given 50 minutes to complete the exam, about 25% of them left items blank, indicating that they may not have had time to finish.

What tips and techniques could Mrs. Quader teach her students about test taking to improve their scores on the next exam? What could Mrs. Quader do during the exam or change about the exam to improve the scores on the next test?

16

STANDARDIZED TESTS

INTRODUCTION

Standardized tests are widely used in American education. During a routine year, local school districts often require students to take one standardized achievement test that the school will use for planning and another standardized achievement test dictated by the state to meet the requirements of the federal No Child Left Behind (NCLB) legislation. In addition, some students may be required to take a standardized aptitude test or other tests. In this chapter, you will learn more about the general characteristics of standardized tests as well as the various types of standardized test. A discussion of what teachers and schools should look at when selecting which standardized test to use and how to use them efficiently is also included. Finally, you will learn more about the roles that standardized tests have taken in the age of NCLB and other federal mandates.

GENERAL CHARACTERISTICS OF STANDARDIZED TESTS

In many respects standardized tests are similar to the regular tests that you will use in your classroom. On occasion, you will even find items on standardized tests that are very similar to items that you have written yourself. However, while you are often on your own to prepare a classroom test and only have an hour or two to do so, most standardized tests require a team of experts and may take a year or longer to develop. As a result, standardized tests are both technologically and methodologically very sophisticated. In addition, they are often able to obtain much higher reliability and validity than you could expect to obtain with your classroom tests.

A number of standardized tests are developed by large testing companies such as Educational Testing Service in Princeton, New Jersey or the American College Testing Service, in Iowa City, Iowa. Other tests are developed by smaller companies that are almost as sophisticated as these very large firms. There are literally hundreds of standardized tests available today. Some are very general and widely used; others are more specific and used less frequently. In order to help you understand the process involved in developing a standardized test, let me tell you about an experience that I had developing some standardized tests.

A Case Study in Developing a Standardized Test

In the mid 1980s, the American Institute of Architects (AIA) wanted to develop and promote continuing education for practicing architects. Today, in most professions, in order to maintain one's professional licensure, one must take a certain number of hours of approved continuing professional education every few years. Since the AIA is the primary professional organization that licenses architects, it recognized that it needed to develop a mechanism to help practicing architects identify areas of professional practice where they might need help. Its first step was to put together a panel of well-known professional architects who were recognized both for their expertise and their work in training future architects. Many on the panel were themselves the authors of text-books used to train architects; all had spent considerable time actually working in architectural firms.

The first step was for the panel to meet for a workshop over several days. The goal of that workshop was to identify those areas in which many architects could use add-itional training. When attending school to study for a degree in architecture, students learn skills primarily related to designing buildings. However, when they get out into the real world, many architects find that they actually spend most of their time attend-ing to the business of being an architect and relatively little time designing buildings. For example, they need to learn how to develop and deal with a budget for a project proposal. They also need to learn how to manage a project, which includes managing contractors and subcontractors. When this panel had finished, they had identified about 22 areas where they thought that architects could benefit from continuing education.

Once the planning panel finished its job, the AIA selected one of those 22 areas. It then selected a new panel of architects, each of whom was chosen because he or she was a noted expert in that particular area. That new panel was convened for a two-day workshop in order to develop a list of objectives for that particular skill area. Once that panel was satisfied that they had a relatively complete set of objectives, the AIA set about developing a test that could be distributed to architects to help them determine whether they might benefit from additional training in that area.

In order to develop that test, the AIA contracted with a firm that specialized in developing and administering tests in business settings. I was subcontracted through that firm to actually develop the test items. However, since I had essentially no train-ing in architecture, I needed help. Therefore, the panel designated several members as consultants and provided me with a list of books that were considered the best in that area.

After obtaining the books and reading the relevant sections, I attacked each objective, one at a time. I was expected to develop two five-option multiple-choice items for each of the 30 objectives that had been identified so that there would be two forms of the test. If I had trouble developing items or was confused about an objective, I called one of the consultants to ask for help or clarification. Usually, I was able to prepare about three items for every eight-hour work day. Once the items were prepared, I sent them to my supervisor at the testing service so that he could review them and suggest alterations. Then we sent the entire set of 60 items to each member of the panel so that they could be reviewed. That was followed by a lengthy conference call during which we made additional alterations to the items.

At that point we had a preliminary set of 60 items, two for each objective. This preliminary test was then administered to two groups: 100 practicing architects and 100 first- or second-year architecture students. In such a situation we would expect that the practicing architects would perform much better on the test items than the novice architecture students. We also performed an item analysis on the pre-tested items. We then used the results of that pre-testing to make further revisions to the items. The revised item set was again distributed to our panel of experts so that they could suggest any final necessary revisions. Once that was completed, we had our finished test. We did this for a number of different areas prescribed by the original panel. For each test, it typically took nearly an entire year until the test was ready for use.

Steps in Building a Standardized Test

The case study just described is merely an illustration of some of what goes into building a standardized test. The tests that I helped to develop were only for the purpose of helping practicing architects identify areas where they could probably benefit from continuing education. However, most standardized tests are designed to help make much more important educational decisions and, therefore, need to be developed with even more pre-testing and pilot testing.

Most standardized tests are designed by teams. Some members of the teams are testing experts, whereas other members are content experts. The teams must develop a set of objectives and develop items to measure those objectives. The items need to be pre-tested on the types of student who will eventually be taking the tests to assess if they work as expected. Once the test items have been pre-tested and revised, the entire test needs to be given to a large norm group in order to set age or grade norms. Once those steps are completed, the test is ready for use.

Setting Interpretation Standards

Historically, most standardized tests were designed to be norm referenced. For example, if a 5th-grade student took this particular test, he or she would be compared to a large group of other 5th-grade students throughout the country. If a student scored at the 70th percentile, it means that the student did as well or better than 70% of the 5th-grade students in the norm group.

Other tests are designed to be criterion-referenced where a test is expected to measure students' proficiency with a predetermined domain. For example, to develop a 5th-grade math test that is criterion-referenced, the test developers must start by identifying the topics and objectives that are typically taught in 5th-grade classes throughout the country. The difficulty with this approach is that the 5th-grade math curriculum varies from state to state and frequently from school to school within a state. The test developers, therefore, end up with a list of topics and objectives that is typically too long. Although a particular topic may be taught in 40% of 5th-grade classrooms throughout the country, it is not taught in all 5th-grade classes. As a result, most 5th-grade teachers could not possibly cover all of the topics and objectives on the list. Perhaps they can only reasonably be expected to cover from 70% to 80% of the objectives (sometimes even fewer). However, as long as their schools recognize that not all of the objectives that were tested were taught, they can still make appropriate interpretations from the tests.

More and more standardized tests today are being designed to be interpreted from either or both perspectives. They can be interpreted as either norm-referenced or as criterion-referenced. Test publishers like that dual approach since they can sell their tests both to schools looking for norm-referenced tests and to schools looking for criterion-referenced tests.

Standardized Test Administration

Standardized tests are designed to be administered in a routine manner. There is a specific set of directions that teachers (or others administering the tests) are expected to follow. The directions are so specific that a student taking the test in a rural school in southern Ohio should have exactly the same testing experience as a student taking the test in urban San Diego, California. Many of the tests are relatively easy to administer and teachers can do so with only minimal training. Other tests (e.g. individual intelligence tests) require a considerable amount of training and can only be administered by those professionals certified as having such training (e.g. a psychologist, a reading specialist, a speech-language pathologist).

ACHIEVEMENT TESTS

The type of standardized test that you, a teacher, will encounter most frequently will be standardized achievement tests. Of the various types of standardized test that are discussed in this chapter, these are the closest to the regular classroom tests that you will give your students. Standardized achievement tests are designed to measure what students have learned over a relatively short period of time (typically a year) in a specific subject matter. They can be either norm-referenced or criterion-referenced. They come in two general types: single-subject area and survey batteries.

Definition

Standardized achievement tests are designed to measure what students have learned over a relatively short period of time (typically a year) in a specific subject matter.

Single-Subject-Area Achievement Tests

Teachers at both the elementary and secondary levels will sometimes give single-subject-area achievement tests. For example, an organization such as the National Association of Biology Teachers may develop a comprehensive biology exam based on the typical biology curriculum taught in high schools throughout the country. Such an exam could be used by biology teachers as a comprehensive final. It would also allow teachers and schools to see how their biology curriculum stacks up against biology courses taught throughout the country. Such single-subject tests are made up of many items on one subject and, as a result, they tend to have relatively good reliability.

> **Definition**
> A **single-subject-area achievement test** is a standardized achievement test that is limited to a single content area.

Sometimes schools use several single-subject-area achievement tests. They may use one for reading, another for math, another for science, and still another for social studies. These tests tend to have high reliability and validity. However, there is one drawback to this approach. The school cannot effectively compare students across subject-matter areas because each test is based on a different norm group. For example, let's say that for one school the mean reading achievement test score for 4th-grade students is at the 50th percentile and the mean math achievement test for the same group of students is at the 65th percentile. The school might want to interpret that to mean that their 4th graders are doing better in math than they are doing in reading. However, since each test interpretation was based on a separate norm group, such a conclusion may not be warranted.

Survey Batteries

The standardized achievement tests that are most frequently used in elementary schools (and only somewhat less frequently at the secondary level) are known as survey batteries. The tests, which can take two or more hours to administer, typically measure several reading skills, several language arts skills, and several mathematics skills. Sometimes they measure students' skills in health, science, and social studies as well. Most of the test batteries are available for various grade levels. A typical package might include a test for 1st grade, a test for 2nd and 3rd grades, a test for grades 4 through 6, a junior high school version (grades 7 through 9), and a senior high school version (grades 10 through 12). Many of the tests are also available in equivalent forms. That typically means that two or more parallel items are prepared for each objective with one or more item for each objective on each form of the test. As a result, a student could take the test twice without actually having the same items both times.

> **Definition**
> **Survey batteries** are standardized achievement tests that measure a variety of skill areas in one single test.

These survey batteries have been very popular and are widely used because they have a number of advantages. Since the norms for these tests are based on the same set of students, teachers can see how their students are doing in the various subject areas. For example, let's say that the school system looks at the average scores for all the 3rd-grade students within their system. They may discover that, in comparison with national norms, their 3rd-grade students are doing well in reading and language arts. However, in comparison to their progress in reading and language arts, the 3rd-grade students are doing less well in math. This might be an indicator that the school should look at its 3rd-grade math curriculum and how math is being taught in the classrooms.

These survey batteries can potentially be one of the most useful tools in the school's assessment package. It allows teachers to monitor individual students to identify their strengths and weaknesses. It can allow schools to monitor teachers' grading practices. For example, it would be desirable to see that for a particular class there is a relatively high correlation between the grades students received in math and their mathematics achievement test scores. The survey batteries also have the potential to help teachers. For example, if students are randomly assigned to classes, and for the last three years Mrs. Green's 6th-grade students have had the lowest average math achievement scores, the administration might decide that Mrs. Green might need some help in developing her math curriculum or that she might require some additional training to make her more effective at teaching math.

The survey batteries also have limitations. For example, since they typically measure from five to nine different skills, they cannot contain as many questions for each skill as would a single-subject-area test. Therefore, the individual subtest scores are less reliable. That means that you need to exercise caution when making educational decisions about individual students based on their subtest scores. Another limitation is that the survey batteries do a better job of monitoring some skills than others. They appear to monitor reading, language arts, and math skills better than they monitor other skills like social studies and science. Still another limitation is that the survey batteries need to match the school's curriculum. If a school chooses a survey battery simply because other neighboring schools use it, but the school's curriculum is not a good match for the curriculum on which the test is based, then the test scores have very little meaning.

Some of the most common survey batteries used throughout the United States include the following (Linn & Miller, 2005):

- *California Achievement Tests*;
- *Iowa Tests of Basic Skills*;
- *Metropolitan Achievement Tests*;
- *Stanford Achievement Tests*;
- *TerraNova* [Comprehensive Tests of Basic Skills];
- *The 3-Rs Test*.

DIAGNOSTIC TESTS

Diagnostic tests are a specific type of achievement test that are so specialized that they form their own category. These tests are designed to be administered to students who are struggling in one of the skill areas and are intended to identify specific sub-skills with which the student might be having difficulty. For example, Sonya, a 2nd-grade student, is struggling with reading. Although Sonya's teacher has observed Sonya read, she is still uncertain which specific reading skills are giving Sonya her greatest trouble. Therefore, the teacher decides to give Sonya a reading diagnostic test to identify the areas in which Sonya needs extra help.

> **Definition**
>
> **Diagnostic tests** are achievement tests designed to be administered to students who are struggling in one of the skill areas and are intended to identify specific sub-skills with which the student might be having difficulty.

Although survey batteries also measure a few reading skills, the diagnostic reading tests measure many more sub-skills, and do so with many more items. This makes them more reliable and better at diagnosing specific reading problems.

Diagnostic tests are also widely used in schools. There have been attempts, over the years, to develop diagnostic tests in almost every subject-matter area. However, those that have had the widest use are in the areas of elementary reading, language arts, and math. Although some of the diagnostic tests can be administered to an entire class at one time, most are designed for individual administration—one teacher and one student working alone together. Some of the tests require relatively little training and can be administered by many teachers. However, other diagnostic tests require a considerable amount of training and are usually administered by an educational specialist.

Reading Readiness Tests

One type of diagnostic test that has been somewhat controversial is the reading readiness test, sometimes referred to as readiness tests. These tests were originally designed to be used late in kindergarten to determine whether students had acquired enough pre-reading skills to begin reading instruction.

> **Definition**
>
> **Reading readiness tests** are diagnostic tests designed to be used in kindergarten to determine whether students are ready for reading instruction.

Until the late 1960s, reading instruction in the United States did not typically begin until 1st grade. In most states kindergarten attendance was not mandatory, and in many regions of the country relatively few children attended kindergarten. However, as kindergarten attendance soared in the later part of the 20th century, many schools throughout the country began reading instruction during kindergarten. The reading readiness tests were then used to choose those students who were ready for early reading instruction and those who needed additional work with pre-reading skills.

Many schools went one step further. They administered the reading readiness test near the end of kindergarten to determine whether students were ready for 1st grade. If the students scored high enough, they were permitted to move up to 1st grade the following fall. However, when students did not achieve high scores, other options were considered. Some students were expected to repeat kindergarten, attend a transitional 1st grade, or even sit out of school for one year while they matured. The problem with these approaches is that they each appear relatively ineffective. Research suggests that students develop reading skills most quickly if, after a year of kindergarten, they are promoted to 1st grade regardless of how they score on reading readiness tests. The reading readiness tests do not have sufficient predictive validity to be used for future grade placement. They work best as diagnostic instruments. The results of the tests should be used only to offer suggestions for further instruction in pre-reading skills.

APTITUDE TESTS

The other major category of standardized test is aptitude tests, also frequently known as ability tests. Whereas achievement tests are subject-specific and tend to measure what students learned formally (most often in class) over a relatively short period of time, aptitude tests are broader and measure what students often learned more informally (both in and out of school) over a longer period of time. In addition, although achievement tests are designed to tell us what students have already learned, aptitude tests are designed to help predict what students will be able to learn in the future. Finally, whereas students' scores on achievement tests are typically very dependent on the quality of experiences that they have had (e.g. good instruction), their scores on aptitude tests are often less dependent on the quality of their experiences.

> *Definition*
>
> **Aptitude tests** are broad measures of what students have learned (often informally) over a long period of time and are designed to predict what students will be able to learn in the future.

Theoretically, it appears that achievement tests and aptitude tests are quite different from one another. However, the reality is that they are frequently quite similar to one another and both are dependent on the quality of a student's educational experiences. Lee Cronbach (1984) suggested that there is a continuum of achievement–aptitude tests. At one extreme are the pure achievement tests that measure knowledge in subject matters such as social studies, English, math, and science. At the other extreme are the pure aptitude tests that deal with skills such as abstract reasoning. However, there are tests in the middle of the continuum that appear to measure both achievement and aptitude. These tests measure skills like verbal and quantitative problem solving. Because of this, there is often overlap between achievement tests and aptitude tests.

There is a common myth concerning aptitude tests: Many people believe that aptitude tests have the capacity to tap into and measure innate God-given abilities. Aptitude tests are neither magical, nor do they have omniscient powers. A student's score on an aptitude test is still very dependent on the quality of his or her experiences. Let's say that two students are born with identical brain structures and identical potential. However, one student is raised in a family where family members rarely talk or read to him, where he has very limited opportunities to explore his environment, never gets to watch television or visit a zoo or a museum, and so on. He has never attended pre-school nor has he had many opportunities to interact with peers. Finally, he has rarely been given toys that encourage him to use his imagination. The other child has family members who talk to him and read to him all of the time and have done so since he was an infant. He is given many opportunities to explore his environment and watches many educational television shows and videos with the family. He has been to a number of zoos and museums. He has been on a number of family outings to interesting places and has attended pre-school. Finally, he has many toys that encourage the use of his imagination. If, at age 6, both boys are given an aptitude test, the second boy will probably score much higher than his counterpart.

Aptitude tests come in two general varieties. The first is the individual aptitude test that is administered one-on-one. These tests typically involve an educational specialist, such as a school psychologist, working alone with one child. The second type of aptitude test is the group test. With these tests, an entire classroom full of students can be tested at the same time.

Individual Aptitude Tests

Individual aptitude tests are often best known as intelligence tests. These tests are typically administered in a quiet room by a psychologist to one child. The psychologist has an entire kit of material and typically presents 10 or more subtests to the child. The tasks change often, helping to keep the child's attention. The psychologist recites the directions to the child who then responds either verbally, by drawing, or by manipulating the materials. Typical items can include vocabulary (What is a poem?), general knowledge (Who is the president of the United States?), similarities (What do a dog and a goldfish have in common?), arithmetic (Jack had 12 baseball cards, but gave 3 to his brother Tom. How many did he have left?), block design, and finding missing items in a picture. The most common versions of these tests take about an hour to complete.

Definition

Individual aptitude tests (often known as intelligence tests) are designed to be administered by a specialist to one child at a time.

The two individual intelligence tests that are both the most widely used and respected are the *Stanford-Binet Intelligence Scale* (5th edition) and the Wechsler scales, especially the *Wechsler Intelligence Scale for Children* (4th edition) known as the WISC-IV.

The Stanford-Binet, which was originally published by Lewis Terman in 1916, is the grandfather of all modern intelligence tests. This test was Terman's upgraded version of the intelligence test developed by the French psychologist, Alfred Binet, a few years earlier. The Stanford-Binet is still considered to be one of the best intelligence tests ever devised. For many years, the Stanford-Binet only provided a single I.Q. score with a mean of 100 and a standard deviation of 16. Today, however, it provides scores for 10 subscales, five factors for both the verbal and nonverbal domain. Those five factors are Fluid Reasoning, Knowledge, Quantitative Reasoning, Visual-Spatial Processing, and Working Memory.

The Wechsler Intelligence Scale for Children was originally developed by David Wechsler in 1949. The 4th edition contains 10 standard subscales and 5 additional subscales that can be used as needed. The WISC-IV is designed for children between the ages of 6 and 16. There are also two other versions of the Wechsler scales: the *Wechsler Preschool and Primary Scale of Intelligence—Revised* (WPPSI–R) for children between ages 2 and 6, and the *Wechsler Adult Intelligence Scale* (3rd edition) (WAIS-III) for older adolescents and adults.

The Stanford-Binet, the Wechsler Scales, and a number of other individual intelligence tests require the administrator to have considerable training. Therefore, most classroom teachers will not be giving these tests. In addition, these tests can take up to 90 minutes to administer and additional time to score. As a result, individual intelligence tests are rarely administered to all students within a school. In many schools, only students who are being evaluated as possibly displaying a disability and students being considered for gifted education are tested with these instruments.

Group Aptitude Tests

Other aptitude tests are known as group aptitude tests because they can be administered to an entire class of students at one time. These tests were, in the past, also sometimes referred to as intelligence tests. However, critics pointed out that, for many reasons, it was best not to refer to these tests as intelligence tests. Today, these group tests are referred to as learning ability tests, school ability tests, cognitive ability tests, or scholastic aptitude tests.

Definition

Group aptitude tests are aptitude tests that can be administered to an entire class of students at one time.

For the youngest children, the teacher reads the question to the students and they respond on an answer form. Typically, beginning in 3rd grade, students read the questions themselves. Since the older students must read the questions in order to respond, these tests are sometimes criticized as being overly dependent on reading skills. If the student is a strong reader, his or her score probably reflects the student's learning ability. However, if the student is a poor reader, his or her test score is probably deflated by the reading problems and is not an accurate representation of the student's ability to learn.

In spite of this limitation, group aptitude tests are very popular in schools for several reasons. First, for many students, they predict their learning ability almost as well as the individual aptitude tests. Second, they are much less expensive to administer. Finally, they can be administered to an entire class and scored quickly.

Some of the most common group aptitude tests that you will encounter are the following (Linn & Miller, 2005):

- *Cognitive Abilities Test*;
- *Henmon-Nelson Test of Mental Ability*;
- *Otis-Lennon School Ability Test*;
- *School and College Ability Test*;
- *Tests of Cognitive Skills*.

Some of the group aptitude tests are designed to be very broad ranged. They not only focus on academic skills, but also on many non-academic skills that people use in various occupations. Historically, schools have given students these broad range aptitude tests in about 8th grade. They are designed to help students begin to make choices about potential careers. Based on their skills, students are better able to determine the type of curriculum they should take in high school. Historically, schools have offered about four choices: academic (college preparation), general, commercial, and industrial arts.

OTHER TYPES OF STANDARDIZED TEST

Although you, as a teacher, will most frequently encounter achievement and aptitude tests in the schools where you teach, you may also, on occasion, encounter some other standardized tests. For example, you may occasionally see attitude scales and career interest inventories.

While *attitude scales* are quite popular in many fields, they are not used that frequently in schools. However, specific attitude scales could be used in conjunction with drug and alcohol awareness programs, sex education programs, and drivers' education training. In each case, a part of these programs is to help students develop more responsible attitudes. Therefore, schools sometimes administer attitude scales before the students start the program and then again at the conclusion of the program to see if the program has been able to change the students' attitudes. Schools may also use attitude scales for students who are not performing well in school. At times, these scales allow school personnel to determine what types of motivational issue are affecting students and recommend programs that may help these students.

Many high schools use *career interest inventories.* These inventories are designed to help students assess their interests and skills and match them to others who have been successful in a number of careers. These career interest inventories may reinforce a student's previous ideas about a career or introduce students to career options that they may have never even considered.

USING STANDARDIZED TESTS EFFECTIVELY IN THE SCHOOLS

There are a number of issues that school personnel must consider in order to use standardized tests effectively. Critics sometimes argue that too many standardized tests are administered to students. However, all of the standardized tests that have been discussed in this chapter can benefit both schools and individual students if they are administered, interpreted, and used appropriately. This means that school personnel need to know how to select the tests that will best meet their purposes. They need to know how to administer and interpret test scores appropriately. Finally, they need to know the sort of decisions that can appropriately be made based on the outcome of each test.

Selecting Standardized Tests

Perhaps one of the most difficult parts of using standardized tests is selecting the appropriate tests. Before choosing a standardized test, school personnel need to decide on the purpose of the test. Are they giving the tests simply to monitor the progress of their students in order to assess their curriculum? Are they using the tests to monitor individual students and identify which students need extra help? Are they using the tests to help decide on the best class placements for students for the next year? These are only a few of the reasons that tests are given. However, a test that monitors student progress well will not always be the best test for placement decisions for next year.

With many achievement tests, school personnel will obtain the most satisfactory results when they attempt to match the test to their curriculum. If there is a poor match between the material that is covered on the test and the school's curriculum then the test result will be nearly impossible to interpret. Test publishers, however, provide hand-books that include a great deal of information, including a list of topics that are covered at each grade level. This makes the selection of the appropriate tests somewhat easier.

When school personnel are looking for norm-referenced tests, they should also care-fully look at the description of the norm group that was used. If the students in the school roughly match the description of the characteristics of the norm group, an appropriate interpretation of the test scores will be possible. However, if the students in the school are somewhat atypical in terms of socioeconomic status, ethnic diversity, English language learners, and so on, it may be difficult to interpret scores appropriately. Some tests provide a variety of norms, including norms for different regions of the United States.

Another source of information about published tests is the *Mental Measurement Yearbook* series and *Tests in Print*. These are each published regularly by the Buros Institute and contain a great deal of information about each test. They also typically include at least one or two reviews of each test. They are available in many libraries and online.

Making Predictions Based on Test Scores

One of the more common reasons for the use of standardized tests is to help make placement decisions. In general, aptitude tests are the best at predicting future school performance. When Alfred Binet designed the first intelligence test in the first decade of the 20th century, it was for exactly that purpose. It was designed to predict how students would perform in school. Today's aptitude tests continue to do a very good job of predicting future performance.

At times, however, some achievement tests can actually do a better job of predicting future performance for some tasks. Aptitude tests are typically best at predicting general academic performance in the distant future. For example, you give a group of 2nd-grade students an aptitude test early in 2nd grade. You then track their performance for the next several years. You will probably find moderately high correlations between their aptitude test scores and their grade-point-averages in 3rd, 4th, and 5th grades. However, if you want to predict how one of your 2nd-grade students will perform in 3rd-grade arithmetic, a better predictor will often be his or her score from the arithmetic achieve-ment test taken late in 2nd grade. Achievement tests frequently do a better job of predicting performance in the same subject-matter area in the near future than will aptitude tests. On the other hand, a student's achievement test score in arithmetic will not predict how that student will perform in reading the next year.

Using Standardized Tests Appropriately

As I mentioned earlier, most of the standardized tests that have been discussed can benefit both schools and their students if used appropriately. However, school personnel tend to create problems when they try to use tests inappropriately or make decisions that are unwarranted by the test scores. For example, readiness tests can be used appropriately to identify which students need additional help with reading readiness skills. However, these tests are not very appropriate for making decisions about whether students are ready for enrolment in kindergarten or 1st grade. In much the same way, many achievement tests are appropriate for monitoring student progress within a school or an entire school system but, in most instances, are not appropriate for comparing schools with one another. Before school personnel decide to use a test to make important decisions, they should probably consult the test manuals and reviews of the tests. In some cases, they may need to consult a measurement expert about whether the tests that they plan to use were actually designed with such decision making in mind.

THE EFFECTS OF *NO CHILD LEFT BEHIND* AND OTHER FEDERAL MANDATES

During the past few years, public schools have felt increased pressure to use standardized testing. In January, 2002, President George W. Bush signed the No Child Left Behind (often simply referred to as NCLB) legislation. Although this law was simply a reauthorization of the Elementary and Secondary Education Act (which was originally put into effect in 1965), it added provisions that brought standardized testing to the forefront. NCLB required schools to test children annually in the areas of reading and math in grades 3 through 8 and at least once in high school. Also, beginning in the 2007–2008 school year, schools were required also to test students in science at least three times between grades 3 through 11.

According to the NCLB Act, students are expected to show adequate yearly progress. In addition, if schools do not meet a standard for adequate yearly progress, a number of steps can be taken, some of which are viewed rather negatively by teachers and school administrators.

As a result of NCLB most states have added new testing programs. Although most schools throughout the country were using standardized achievement tests prior to 2002, many of those tests were not adequately designed to measure the skills that NCLB required schools to measure. Therefore, most states have adopted new tests for the sole purpose of meeting the requirements of NCLB. In addition, there has been so much pressure on schools meeting the adequate yearly progress standards that school boards, school administrators, and teachers tend to see these new tests as extremely important. Critics have argued that in many schools teachers are now "teaching to the tests." Only material that will be covered on the tests will be taught. As a result, many elementary teachers are now spending much more time teaching reading and math. Critics also point out that this new emphasis on reading and math has left little time for instruction in social studies and science. Some schools have also reduced or eliminated instruction in music, art, health, and physical education.

Although NCLB is still a relatively new piece of legislation, it does represent a change in the culture of schools. As a country, it can take us a number of years for our institutions to react to and adapt to cultural changes. Either schools will learn how to operate with NCLB or, if not, the law will be amended into one that will better meet the needs of both our students and our schools.

NCLB is just one example of a federal mandate that has had an effect on the use of standardized testing in schools. However, it is not the only example. Legislators at both the state and federal level have often viewed standardized testing as an approach to school improvement. Sometimes these mandated testing programs have led to real school improvement, whereas at other times they have not worked as well. However, you must realize that these and other mandates will probably continue well into the future and, as a teacher, you will be the most effective if you learn to "go with the flow."

SUMMARY

In this chapter, you learned about the characteristics of standardized tests. Many of them are sophisticated cousins of the regular classroom tests developed by teachers. Standardized tests are typically developed by teams consisting of experts in both testing and in the subject-matter being tested. Most standardized tests are either norm-referenced or criterion-referenced, or sometimes both.

There are several different types of standardized test. Achievement tests and aptitude tests are the most common types used in the schools. Achievement tests are designed to measure what students have learned over a relatively short period of time in a specific subject-matter area. Aptitude tests, on the other hand, are designed to measure what students have learned informally over a longer period of time. Each of these tests has several subtypes. Achievement tests come in the form of single-subject-matter tests and survey batteries. Aptitude tests can be administered either individually or to an entire group. Other standardized tests also include reading readiness tests, diagnostic tests, attitude scales, and career interest inventories.

School personnel need to consider several issues if they want to use standardized tests effectively. First, they need to be careful in selecting standardized tests that will meet their needs. They also need to recognize that some tests are better to use when making certain decisions and other tests will work better at helping them make other decisions.

The No Child Left Behind Act of 2002 and other federal and state mandates have resulted in mandatory standardized testing in most U.S. schools. In addition, the pressures to achieve standards at various grade levels have often resulted in curricular changes and suggestions that some teachers now "teach to the test."

EXERCISES

Match the items in the two columns:

Part A

1. _____ Diagnostic test   a. Predicts what students will be able to learn
2. _____ Achievement test   b. Identifies a specific area where students struggle
3. _____ Aptitude test   c. Measures what students learned over a short period of time in a specific subject area

Part B

1. _____ Diagnostic test   a. survey batteries
2. _____ Achievement test   b. individual or group tests
3. _____ Aptitude test   c. reading readiness

Part C

1. What are the two types of interpretation standard for standardized tests? Define each of these.

2. What is the first thing a school should decide before choosing a standardized test?
3. What recent law, signed by President George W. Bush, has caused many schools to add new testing programs? What are some things that this law requires? What are the objectives of these tests? How is your state measuring these objectives?

Part D
Given the following situations, state what kind of test would be most appropriate. Explain your answer.

1. The guidance counselors at Steelville Elementary are preparing to schedule classes for next year's 8th-grade students. The students need to be assessed to find out which type of math class they will need.
2. To gain information about all of the 6th-grade teachers at Franklin Middle School, the principal wants to find out how well the 6th-grade students are doing in reading, math, and science. She wants to test the students to see if the overall class is stronger in one subject than another.
3. Mrs. Cappioli notices that one of her students is having trouble in math. In order to help her, Mrs. Cappioli needs to find out the specific areas where the student is having the problem.

SPOTLIGHT ON THE CLASSROOM

Murrysville, North Carolina is a growing, southern city. The population has grown from 10,000 people to 90,000 people in just the past 10 years. New school districts have been rapidly established across the area to accommodate for the rapid growth in population. The Bayside Area School District was recently established in 2005.

The school board at Bayside has finally settled in and is comfortable with the curriculum the school has implemented. They have been participating in the No Child Left Behind standardized testing procedures to meet state requirements. A group of school board members and administrators have got together and feel it is time to put their curriculum and teaching to the test. They feel the most effective way to do so is to administer standardized tests in various subject areas in various grade levels. They want to compare their students' achievement to that of other students around the country. The school would like to monitor the progress of their students in order to assess their new curriculum.

School administrators and officials have decided that the most suitable solution would be to use a survey battery. Is this a good choice for this situation? What are the advantages and disadvantages? What else would you recommend?

17

ALTERNATIVE WAYS TO REPORT TEST SCORES

INTRODUCTION

Raw scores are not always the most effective way to report a test score. If you are a parent and your child reported to you that she received a score of 25 on her last social studies test, you would probably need to ask her a few questions about the test so that you could put her score in perspective. How did she do compared with the other students in her class? Was her score about average, above average, or below average? What does her test score mean? Over the years, statisticians and psychometricians have developed a number of alternative ways to report test scores that are all designed to make the scores easier to interpret.

In this chapter you will read about many of these alternative ways to report and interpret test scores. The chapter will cover percentile ranks, z-scores, T-scores, SAT scores, Normal-Curve-Equivalent scores, Stanines, and grade-equivalent scores. You will also learn about the advantages and disadvantages of each of these alternative ways to report scores. This chapter will also describe the Standard Error of Measurement, the sampling distribution of observed scores, and how to use them to build confidence intervals—still another way to report and interpret test scores.

In today's educational environment, where there is so much emphasis on test scores, it is critical to have alternative methods for reporting and interpreting test scores. These test scores must be interpreted by teachers, students, parents, school administrators, government officials, and the public.

PERCENTILE RANKS

A popular way to report test scores is as percentile ranks, primarily because both students and parents find them easy to interpret. Many students learn to interpret percentile ranks in their middle-school years, soon after they learn how to compute percentages. Students quickly learn to interpret percentile ranks: If he or she scored at the 55th percentile, the student did as well or better than 55% of the students who took the test.

> **Definition**
>
> A **percentile rank** indicates the percentage of students who had that score or lower.

If you read Chapter 20, which describes frequency distributions, you learned to calculate percentile ranks. In essence, to calculate percentile ranks, you need to develop an expanded frequency distribution which includes columns for % and C%. Remember that C% (cumulative percent) is also known as percentile rank. Let's review an example from Chapter 20.

Take a look at Figure 17.1, which includes an expanded frequency distribution of the scores that Mrs. Wan's 20 chemistry students earned on their last chemistry quiz. Columns for cumulative frequency (CF), cumulative proportion (CP), and cumulative percent (C%), also known as percentile rank, have been included. The C% column represents the percent of students who had that score or lower. You may also remember that C% refers to the upper limit on the raw score column. For example, what raw score corresponds to the 50th percentile? You might be inclined to say that a score of 11 is the 50th percentile. However, because there are 10 scores above 11 and only 7 scores below 11, it cannot be the 50th percentile. The actual 50th percentile is 11.5 (the upper limit of the interval that extends from 10.50000 to 11.49999). There are 10 scores above it and 10 scores below it.

Percentile ranks, like most of the standardized scores discussed in this chapter, are relative placement scores. They show where a student fits in with a larger norm group. However, unlike the other standardized score scales discussed in this chapter, percentile ranks are not very useful for comparing students with each other because they typically involve unequal intervals.

Let's try an example that demonstrates the unequal interval dilemma. You have administered a test to a large group of students and the frequency distribution

X		F	P	%	CF	CP	C%
15	I	1	.05	5	20	1.00	100
14	II	2	.10	10	19	.95	95
13	III	3	.15	15	17	.85	85
12	IIII	4	.20	20	14	.70	70
11	III	3	.15	15	10	.50	50
10	II	2	.10	10	7	.35	35
9	II	2	.10	10	5	.25	25
8	II	2	.10	10	3	.15	15
7		0	0	0	1	.05	5
6	I	1	.05	5	1	.05	5
5		0	0	0	0	0	0
4		0	0	0	0	0	0
3		0	0	0	0	0	0
2		0	0	0	0	0	0
1		0	0	0	0	0	0

Figure 17.1 Expanded frequency distribution of chemistry quiz scores.

Table 17.1 Test scores for four students

Student	Test Score	Percentile Rank
Lisa	70	50
Juan	75	84
Kim	80	98
Drake	85	99

approximates the normal curve. The mean on this test is 70 and the standard deviation is 5. You are especially interested in four students: Lisa, Juan, Kim, and Drake. Their scores and percentile ranks are listed in Table 17.1.

You will notice that Lisa scored at the mean, Juan scored one standard deviation above the mean, Kim scored two standard deviations above the mean, and Drake scored three standard deviations above the mean. Five points on the raw score scale separate each student from the student either right above or right below him or her. However, if you look at the percentile rank scale, there is a very different story. Juan scored 34 percentile ranks higher than Lisa. However, Kim scored only 14 percentile ranks higher than Juan and Drake scored only 1 percentile rank higher than Kim. Equal distances on the raw score scale do not correspond to equal distances on the percentile rank scale. Since most students tend to obtain scores near the middle of the distribution (near the 50th percentile), even small differences in raw scores at the middle can result in large differences in percentile ranks. However, similar differences in raw scores near the tails of the distribution (the very high and very low scores) result in relatively small differences in percentile ranks. Many fewer students obtain scores in the tails of the frequency distribution. As a result of these unequal intervals, you should not attempt to compare students with one another using their percentile rank scores. Such comparisons can lead to drawing inappropriate conclusions.

STANDARDIZED SCORES

Let's say that the students in your 7th-grade class are administered the Hayes-Lucas Reading Test. One student, Musa Hamdi, receives a score of 235. However, since you are not familiar with this test, you have no way to put Musa's test score into perspective. Since this test is expected to be interpreted from a norm-referenced perspective, you will probably attempt to discover the mean and standard deviation for the norm group of 7th-grade students. However, if you look carefully at the score report, you will probably also see that Musa's test result is reported in several alternative ways. Some of the scores that are reported use scales that psychometricians call standardized scores.

Standardized scores have that name because the raw scores are transformed into new scores that are based on the mean and standard deviation of the raw scores. For example, if Musa's raw score of 235 was transformed into a type of standardized score known as a T-score (to be discussed later), that T-score might be 65. A T-score of 65 means that Musa scored 1½ standard deviations above the mean on the Hayes-Lucas Reading Test. In fact, any time a raw score is converted to the T-score scale, any T-score of 65 would represent a raw score 1½ standard deviations above the mean. Therefore, anyone who is familiar with a particular type of standardized score scale can immediately interpret it.

> **Definition**
> **Standardized scores** are raw scores that are transformed into a new scale that is based on the mean and standard deviation of the raw scores.

z-Scores

The most basic type of standardized score is a z-score (also discussed in the chapter on correlation; see Part II Chapter 22). To convert a raw score into a z-score, you simply subtract the mean of the raw scores from the raw score you wish to convert and then divide the result by the standard deviation of the raw scores. Essentially, you first convert a raw score into a deviation score. You are determining how far the raw score is above (+) or below (−) the mean. Then you divide the deviation score by the standard deviation of the raw scores.

> **Definition**
> A **z-score** is computed by subtracting the mean of the raw scores from the raw score you wish to convert and then dividing the result by the standard deviation of the raw scores. $z = \dfrac{X - M}{SD}$

Here is an example. Let's say that the last time you gave your students a test, the mean on the test turned out to be 75 and the standard deviation was 4. If Lien earned a score of 77, you can convert her raw score of 77 into a z-score by subtracting the mean of the test scores (75) from it and dividing the result by the standard deviation of the test scores. Here is the formula. In this chapter, let's use X to represent the raw score, M to represent the mean, and SD to represent the standard deviation (Equation 17.1).

$$z = \frac{X - M}{SD} = \frac{77 - 75}{4} = \frac{2}{4} = .5 \tag{17.1}$$

Lien's raw score (77) is 2 points above the mean of the raw scores (75). Therefore, her deviation score is +2. You then divide her deviation score by the standard deviation of the raw scores (4). This results in Lien's z-score being .5, which signifies that her raw score put her 1/2 of a standard deviation above the mean.

Z-scores will always have a mean of 0 and a standard deviation of 1. This signifies that you can always interpret a z-score as standard deviation units below or above the mean. A positive z-score denotes a score above the mean, whereas a negative z-score denotes a score below the mean.

Let's use another example. In this case Alec, who is also in your class, earns a score of 70 on the same test. Let's compute Alec's z-score (Equation 17.2).

$$z = \frac{X - M}{SD} = \frac{70 - 77}{4} = \frac{-7}{4} = -1.75 \tag{17.2}$$

Because Alec's raw score of 70 is 7 points below the mean, his deviation score is −7. After this deviation score is divided by the standard deviation (4), it is converted into a z-score of −1.75. This indicates that Alec scored 1¾ standard deviations below the mean on this test.

Z-scores typically range from a low of about −3.00 to a high of about 3.00. Statisticians and psychometricians tend to use z-scores frequently because of their ease of interpretation. However, if you attempted to use z-scores in your classroom, you would probably run into some resistance. With z-scores a score of 0 (zero) is good. It indicates that the student scored at the mean. However, your students have probably been accustomed to interpret a 0 as very bad. In addition, z-scores are both positive and negative, and are typically expressed with two decimal places. These are characteristics that might make z-scores unpopular with students.

Standardized scores (such as z-scores) have another advantage that we have not yet discussed. If you want to compare how the students in your class performed on two different tests, it can sometimes be difficult to do so because the tests typically have different means and standard deviations. For example, one student, Pawel, had 80% correct on each test. That may lead you to believe that Pawel was very consistent from one test to the other. If the mean on the first test was 85 and the standard deviation was 5, it means that Pawel scored one standard deviation below the mean on the first test. His z-score would be −1.00. However, if the mean on the second test was 75 and the standard deviation was once again 5, it means that Pawel scored one standard deviation above the mean on the second test and his z-score would be +1.00. Although his raw scores on each test were the same, his z-scores indicate that compared to his classmates, he performed better on the second test than on the first test.

T-Scores

Because z-scores might be unpopular with both students and their parents, psychometricians have developed a number of alternative standardized scores that should be more palatable to students and parents. One of these alternatives is T-scores. T-scores are designed to have a mean of 50 and a standard deviation of 10. As a result, T-scores typically extend from a low of 20 to a high of 80. When I was in college, T-scores were very popular, and most of our exams were reported as T-scores.

> **Definition**
> **T-scores** are standardized scores with a mean of 50 and a standard deviation of 10.

In order to compute a T-score, the raw scores must first be converted into z-scores. Take a look at the following example. Let's say that you gave a test in your high school French 2 class. Pia earned an 87. The mean on the test was 82 and the standard deviation was 6. In order to convert Pia's test score into a T-score, you must first convert her raw score into a z-score (Equation 17.3).

$$z = \frac{X - M}{SD} = \frac{87 - 82}{6} = \frac{5}{6} = .83 \qquad (17.3)$$

Pia's z-score of .83 can now be converted into a T-score. In order to convert a z-score into another standardized score scale (such as a T-score), you simply take Pia's z-score and multiply it by the standard deviation of the new scale, and then add the mean of the new scale to that product. Here is the general conversion formula (Equation 17.4).

$$NewScore = z(SD_{NewScore}) + M_{NewScore} \quad \text{[general conversion formula]} \qquad (17.4)$$

More specifically, to convert a z-score into a T-score you insert the standard deviation of T-scores (10) and the mean of the T-scores (50) into the general conversion formula. Therefore, the formula for T-scores becomes (Equation 17.5)

$$T = z(10) + 50. \qquad (17.5)$$

To calculate Pia's T-score, you simply substitute her z-score of .83 into the formula (Equation 17.6).

$$T = z(10) + 50 = .83(10) + 50 = 8.3 + 50 = 58.3 \qquad (17.6)$$

Since the typical convention is to report T-scores as whole numbers, you would report Pia's test score as T = 58.

How would you interpret a T-score? Remember the mean of T-scores is 50 and the standard deviation is 10. Therefore, any score above 50 is above the mean and any score below 50 is below the mean. Because the standard deviation is 10 and Pia's T-score was 58, you know that she scored eight-tenths of a standard deviation above the mean. With only a bit of practice, you too will be able to quickly interpret a T-score.

SAT Scores

There is another type of standardized score with which many high school and college students are familiar—the SAT scores. The Scholastics Aptitude Test (SAT, also known as the Scholastic Assessment Tests), which was designed as a college entrance examination for the College Entrance Examination Board, is taken by many college-bound high school students each year. Essentially, the SAT uses a standardized score with the mean of 500 and a standard deviation of 100.[1]

Definition

The **SAT** uses a standardized scale with the mean of 500 and a standard deviation of 100.

If you wished to convert a raw score into a SAT equivalent score, you would first need to convert the raw score into a z-score. The z-score could then be converted into a SAT equivalent score with the following formula (Equation 17.7):

$$SAT = z(100) + 500. \qquad (17.7)$$

How do you interpret a SAT scale score? Jon, a student you know, received a 625 on the Verbal section of the SAT and asks you to interpret that score for him. You point out to him that since the mean of the SATs is 500 and the standard deviation is 100, he scored 1¼ standard deviations above the mean. He has done quite well!

NORMALIZED STANDARD SCORES

In Chapter 19, we discuss the various characteristics of frequency distributions. Here, you will learn a way that you can use frequency distributions to interpret test scores.

If you gather data on some characteristic of a very large group of students (300 or more) and plot the frequency distribution as a frequency polygon or as a histogram, the graph will typically display the characteristics of the Normal distribution. The Normal distribution is a particular type of bell-shaped probability distribution that results when chance factors dominate. Since most human characteristics are determined by a complexity of forces, they often distribute themselves along the Normal curve. However, with smaller groups (less than 300), it is not uncommon to find that the plot will vary somewhat from the Normal distribution. In the last section on standardized scores, there was no discussion about the shape of the distribution of scores. You can interpret z-scores, T-scores, and SAT scores accurately even if the data are not Normally distributed. However, researchers have found that, at times, it is difficult to make fair comparisons for students from year to year or among students from different schools even when using standardized scores, in part, because the frequency distributions do not always have the same form. For example, one large-scale study, known as the National Assessment of Educational Progress, has been tracking the achievement of students in the United States for nearly two decades. As a part of that project, researches frequently want to compare student achievement from year to year or from one region of the country to another. Such comparisons can lead to subtle misinterpretations if the frequency distributions have different forms. It is much like trying to compare the sweetness of apples and oranges. Because each fruit has distinctive characteristics, such comparisons are problematic. With data, it has been argued that such comparisons are most appropriate when the various distributions have the same form.

One approach that has been offered to address this problem is to take a frequency distribution of scores (regardless of its original shape) and transform it into a Normal distribution.[2] To accomplish this task, the raw scores are first transformed into percentile ranks (discussed earlier in this chapter). Then, using a standard Normal curve table, the percentile ranks can be transformed into what are known as normalized z-scores (see Table 17.2 for an abbreviated Normal Curve Table). For example, let's say that a raw score of 78 is computed to have a percentile rank of 42 (42% of the students had a 78 or lower). Based on the abbreviated Normal Curve Table (Table 17.2), you can see that a percentile rank of 42 corresponds to a z-score of −.20. Therefore, the raw score of 78 transforms to a normalized z-score of −.20. Once all of the raw scores have been transformed into normalized z-scores, they can then be transformed into another scale that is easier to interpret. Two scales that are based on Normalized z-scores are Normal Curve Equivalent scores and Stanine scores.

Table 17.2 Abbreviated Normal Curve Conversion Table: z-scores to percentile ranks

z	%tile rank	z	%tile rank
−2.50	1	0.10	54
−2.40	1	0.20	58
−2.30	1	0.30	62
−2.20	1	0.40	66
−2.10	2	0.50	69
−2.00	2	0.60	73
−1.90	3	0.70	76
−1.80	4	0.80	79
−1.70	4	0.90	82
−1.60	5	1.00	84
−1.50	7	1.10	86
−1.40	8	1.20	88
−1.30	10	1.30	90
−1.20	11	1.40	92
−1.10	14	1.50	93
−1.00	16	1.60	95
−0.90	18	1.70	96
−0.80	21	1.80	96
−0.70	24	1.90	97
−0.60	27	2.00	98
−0.50	31	2.10	98
−0.40	34	2.20	99
−0.30	38	2.30	99
−0.20	42	2.40	99
−0.10	46	2.50	99
0.00	50		

Definition

Normalized z-scores are derived from raw scores by first converting the raw scores to percentile ranks. Then, using a Normal Curve Table, the percentile ranks are converted to z-scores. The resulting set of scores will always take the form of the Normal distribution.

Normal Curve Equivalent Scores

Normal curve equivalent (NCE) scores were developed to resemble percentile ranks. Like percentile ranks, NCE scores have a mean of 50 and range from a low of 1 to a high of 99. In fact, percentile ranks and NCE scores are identical for values of 1, 50, and 99. However, although percentile ranks have unequal intervals (discussed earlier in the chapter), NCE scores have equal intervals. Theoretically, the equal interval characteristic of NCE scores allows more reasonable comparison of scores from different populations.

Normal curve equivalent scores are designed to have a mean of 50 and a standard deviation of 21.06 (which allows the scores to extend from 1 to 99. Based on the general conversion formula, the formula for computing NCE scores is as follows (Equation 17.8):

$$NCE = 21.06(z_n) + 50 \text{ (where } z_n \text{ is a normalized z-score)} \qquad (17.8)$$

Definition

Normal Curve Equivalent scores are based on normalized z-scores. They range from 1 to 99 with a mean of 50.

As teachers, you will not typically have to compute NCE scores, which are more likely to be used in research, especially large-scale research studies. However, some standardized tests will report scores as NCEs and, as teachers, you need to be prepared to interpret them.

Stanines

Another scale which is also based on normalized z-scores is widely used in many classrooms throughout parts of the United States. Stanines, which stands for "standard nine" or "standard nine-point scale," is a scale that runs from 1 to 9. It has a mean of 5 and a standard deviation of 2. The formula for computing a Stanine is as follows (Equation 17.9):

$$\text{Stanine} = 2(z_n) + 5 \text{ (where } z_n \text{ is a normalized z-score)} \qquad (17.9)$$

Definition

Stanines are standard scores based on normalized z-scores. They extend from 1 to 9 with a mean of 5 and a standard deviation of 2.

Stanines are fairly popular with school personnel, parents, and students. A number of standardized tests report their scores as Stanines, which are fairly easy to interpret. Essentially, Stanines of 1, 2, and 3 are interpreted as below average; Stanines of 4, 5, and 6 are interpreted as average; and Stanines of 7, 8, and 9 are interpreted as above average. Although Stanine scores lack some of the precision found with most of the other scales that have been discussed in this chapter, it is their simplicity that often makes them popular.

It is interesting to note that the use of Stanines appears to vary throughout the United States. Although they are very popular in many regions of the country, they are used much less frequently in the northeastern states.

GRADE EQUIVALENT SCORES

Another popular way to report standardized test scores is to use Grade Equivalent Scores. These are different from any of the scales that were previously discussed in this chapter. Grade Equivalent Scores were designed for easy interpretation. However, at times, they are also easy to misinterpret.

Perhaps you have heard a story like this. Stu is a 3rd-grade student and on a recent standardized reading test he received a Grade Equivalent Score of 5.5 in reading comprehension. You may have also been told that his score indicates that Stu's reading comprehension is equivalent to that found in the average 5th-grade student in the fifth month of school. In fact, teachers, parents, and students are often told that that is exactly the appropriate way to interpret Stu's score.

However, such an interpretation is often inappropriate. Most standardized tests are normed only for certain grade levels. Perhaps the reading test that is administered for 3rd-grade students has only been normed for 3rd-grade and 4th-grade students. If it has never been normed for 5th-grade students, the 5.5 is only an estimate that has been extrapolated from the data that have been normed. It is likely that Stu is not really reading as well as the typical 5th-grade student. Rather, that Grade Equivalent Score of 5.5 actually indicates that his reading skills are well above average for a 3rd-grade student. In reality, Grade Equivalent Scores indicate whether a student is showing average, below average, or above average performance. The further the Grade Equivalent Score is from the student's actual grade level, the further the student is performing below or above average. However, in most cases, Grade Equivalent Scores should not be interpreted literally.

Grade Equivalent Scores do, however, offer some advantages. They allow you to view individual students and gain a fairly clear picture about how the student is performing in each subject area. If you look at composite scores for an entire class, Grade Equivalent Scores allow you to look at your curriculum to see if there are areas where you need to place greater emphasis. In addition, Grade Equivalent Scores are the only type of score that was discussed in this chapter that you can expect to change from year to year for each student. This allows you to see the growth the students have made from one year to the next.

Up until this point, various types of standardized score and percentile ranks have been discussed. In the next section you will be introduced to an alternative way to report scores that recognizes that tests most often have reliabilities of less than 1.00.

BUILDING CONFIDENCE INTERVALS

Psychometricians have frequently expressed concern that educators and the public sometimes place too much importance on individual test scores. For example, in some states students must obtain a score of 130 on the Wechsler Intelligence Scale for Children (4th edition) (WISC-IV) in order to qualify for gifted programs. Therefore, a student who scores a 131 will qualify, whereas another student who scores a 129 will not. In reality, is there any difference between the two students? Is one student actually gifted and the other one not?

Error Variance

You probably recall from the chapter on reliability (see Chapter 4) that there is a difference between an observed score and a true score. An observed score is the score that the student actually achieves. However, psychometricians point out that the variations found among observed scores actually come from two sources: the variation among true scores, and measurement error (also known as error variance). The true scores are the scores that the students would obtain if the test had perfect reliability. Measurement error is anything that causes the observed score to deviate from the true score. That relationship is expressed with the following formula (Equation 17.10).

$$Variance_{Observed} = Variance_{True} + Variance_{Error} \qquad (17.10)$$

Let's try a hypothetical example to show how this works. In Table 17.3, the test scores for 10 students on a 40-item test are listed. The observed scores vary from a low of 26 to a high of 40. Columns for the students' true scores and their measurement error are also included for demonstration purposes. In reality, you never know a student's true score or measurement error. Theoretically, measurement error will always have a mean of zero (0) since it is randomly distributed. The positive measurement errors and negative measurement errors will always balance out to zero. In addition, both the true scores and the observed scores will have the same mean.

In this example, does the observed-score variance equal the true-score variance plus the error variance? See Equation 17.11.

$$Variance_{Observed} = Variance_{True} + Variance_{Error}$$

$$20.56 = 9.56 + 11.00 \qquad (17.11)$$

It does!

Standard Error of Measurement

The standard deviation of the measurement error is known as the Standard Error of Measurement (SEM). We would like to know the SEM because it is an indicator of reliability. In the previous theoretical example, you were able to compute the SEM directly from the data in the table because you had all the information that you needed.

Table 17.3 Test scores for 10 students

Student	True Score	Measurement Error	Observed Score
Rachel	37	−1	36
Samuel	35	5	40
Lisa	31	3	34
George	38	−4	34
Lynn	33	−2	31
Jose	35	2	37
Julie	29	−3	26
Lee	28	1	29
Sylvia	32	−5	27
Michael	34	4	38
Mean	**33.20**	**0.00**	**33.20**
Stand. Dev.	**3.09**	**3.32**	**4.53**
Variance	**9.56**	**11.00**	**20.56**

Since you had a theoretical column of measurement errors, you simply needed to compute the standard deviation of that column. In reality, however, you never know the students' true scores, nor do you know how much measurement error exists for each student. All you really know are the students' observed scores. However, you can estimate the SEM as long as you have obtained an estimate of the reliability.

Definition

The standard deviation of the measurement error is known as the **Standard Error of Measurement (SEM).**

In Chapter 4, you learned that theoretically reliability is the proportion of observed score variance that comes from the true-score variance. The formula looks like this (Equation 17.12).

$$Reliability = \frac{Variance_{True}}{Variance_{Observed}} \tag{17.12}$$

For the example that you have been using, you can compute the reliability using that formula (Equation 17.13).

$$Reliability = \frac{Variance_{True}}{Variance_{Observed}} = \frac{9.56}{20.56} = .46 \tag{17.13}$$

Let's say that this was an actual test and that you estimated the reliability using one of the techniques described in Chapter 4. Let's also say that the estimated reliability is .46. With that information, you can estimate the SEM using the following formula (Equation 17.14).

$$SEM = SD\sqrt{1 - Reliability} \tag{17.14}$$

With this formula you can estimate the SEM (Standard Error of Measurement) as long as you know the standard deviation of the observed scores and the reliability. In this case you know both. The standard deviation of the observed scores is 4.53 and the reliability is .46. You can put these values into the equation to compute an estimated SEM (Equation 17.15).

$$SEM = SD\sqrt{1 - Reliability} = 4.53\sqrt{1 - .46} = 4.53\sqrt{.54} = 4.53(.735) = 3.33 \tag{17.15}$$

Here the computed SEM is 3.33. You can compare that to the actual SEM from the theoretical model which was 3.32 (essentially identical considering rounding errors).

Using the SEM to Build Confidence Intervals

The next step is to use the SEM to build a confidence interval. The important point to remember is that unless a test has perfect reliability, an observed score is simply an estimate of the true score. If a student with a certain true score were to take the same test an infinite number of times, the student would have a variety of observed scores. If you were to plot the student's observed scores on a frequency polygon, the scores would form the shape of the Normal distribution. This frequency polygon is called the "sampling distribution of observed scores." The mean of the distribution would be the student's true score and the standard deviation of the distribution would be the SEM. Therefore, if you were to give a student any test an infinite number of times you would know his or her true score. It would be the mean of the sampling distribution.

Typically, you only give a student a test once. However, if you know the SEM of the test, you can estimate the student's true score from his or her observed score. On the Normal curve representing the student's observed scores, 68% of the scores will be within one SEM of the true score, 95% of the scores will be within two SEMs of the true score, and 99% of the scores will be within three SEMs of the true score.

You can use this information to build a confidence interval. Let's say that a student, Jim, takes the WISC-IV and obtains a score of 110. You now know that his observed score is 110 and from that you can estimate his true IQ score. On the WISC-IV, the SEM is typically reported to be about 3.0. If you start with Jim's observed score and move one SEM below and above it, you can say that his true score falls within that range with 68% confidence. (Remember that 68% of the observed scores will fall within one SEM of the true score on a sampling distribution of observed scores.) Therefore, you could say that, based on Jim's observed IQ score of 110, you are 68% confident that his true IQ score is between 107 and 113 (110 ± 3).

If you would like to make a statement with greater confidence, you could increase the range of scores to two SEMs on either side of the observed score. Using two SEMs on either side of the observed score allows you to build an interval with 95% confidence. Therefore, you could say that, based on Jim's observed IQ score of 110, you are 95% confident that his true IQ score is between 104 and 116 (110 ± 6).

If you would like to make a statement with even greater confidence, you could increase the range of scores to three SEMs on either side of the observed score. Using three SEMs on either side of the observed score allows you to build an interval with 99% confidence. Therefore, you could say that, based on Jim's observed IQ score of 110, you are 99% confident that his true IQ score is between 101 and 119 (110 ± 9).

Factors Affecting the Width of Confidence Intervals

There are two factors that affect the width of confidence intervals: the level of confidence and the size of the SEM. If you want a fairly narrow confidence interval then you must set a lower confidence level. As the confidence level increases (e.g. 68% to 99%), so does the size of the confidence interval. The other factor that affects the width of a confidence interval is the size of the SEM. Take another look at the formula for computing the SEM (Equation 17.16).

$$SEM = SD\sqrt{1 - Reliability} \qquad (17.16)$$

If the test has perfect reliability, the reliability is 1.0. If you plug 1.0 into the above formula, you will see that the SEM will be zero (0). Therefore, with a perfectly reliable test, the observed score and the true score will be exactly the same. However, as the reliability decreases, the SEM increases in size until it reaches the size of the standard deviation of the observed scores. Therefore, tests with high reliability will have narrower confidence intervals, whereas tests with lower reliability will have wider confidence intervals.

Consider the following example of how confidence intervals have been used in education. At one point, up until the mid 1970s, the American Association for Mental Retardation (AAMR) had set an IQ score of 70 as the cut-off for mental retardation. In most states, a student who obtained an IQ score below 70 could be considered eligible to receive special educational services for students with mental retardation. However, a student who obtained an IQ score of 72 would not be considered eligible for such services. More recently, in recognition of confidence intervals, the AAMR says that any students who obtain IQ scores in the range of 70 to 75 or lower are eligible for services. After all, some of the students who obtain IQ scores in that range would have true IQ scores in the mental retardation range and should be eligible for special services.

Finally, we should return to the question that I asked at the beginning of this section. Should a student with an observed IQ score of 129, or even 126, be considered eligible for services for gifted students if the cut-off score is 130? If we build a 95% confidence interval for a student who obtains a WISC-IV IQ score of 124, the interval extends from a low of 118 to a high of 130 (124 ± 6). Therefore, it is possible that students who obtain IQ scores as low as 124 on the WISC-IV actually have true scores as high as 130. If the goal of your gifted program is to meet the needs of any student who might be gifted, it would be prudent to make gifted programs available to any student who obtains an IQ score in the range of 124 to 130 or higher, especially if there are other indications that the student might be gifted.

SUMMARY

In this chapter you learned about a number of alternative ways to report raw scores. Each of the alternative scoring scales is designed to make it easier for teachers and other professionals to interpret scores.

A number of these scales are known as standardized scores because the raw scores are adjusted by the mean and standard deviation. The basic standardized scores are z-scores, which essentially report scores in standard deviation units and extend from a low of about −3.00 to a high of 3.00. Another standardized score is the T-score, which has a mean of 50 and a standard deviation of 10. T-scores typically range from a low of about 20 to a high of about 80. The last standardized score is the SAT score, which has a mean of 500 and a standard deviation of 100. SAT scores typically range from a low of 200 to a high of 800.

At times, a set of scores is converted into normalized z-scores which results in any distribution, regardless of its original shape, being converted into a Normal distribution. Normalized z-scores can then be converted into either Normal-Curve-Equivalent (NCE) scores or into Stanines. NCE scores range from 1 to 99 and have a mean of 50. They resemble percentile ranks, but have equal intervals. Stanines range from 1 to 9 and have a mean of 5 and a standard deviation of 2. They are popular because they are easy to interpret.

Other popular ways to report tests scores are as percentile ranks and grade-equivalent scores. Percentile ranks indicate where a student is placed within the group who took a test. They are quite popular, but should not be used to compare students with one another because they frequently have unequal intervals. Grade-equivalent scores are an attempt to translate students' scores into grade-level performance.

Confidence intervals are an alternative way to report scores and can be developed from an observed score to estimate a true score. Psychometricians like to use confidence intervals because they more accurately represent the fact that observed scores are only estimates of a student's true score. This chapter also demonstrated how to develop and use confidence intervals.

EXERCISES

Scores on a test are close to being normally distributed, $M = 73.0$ and $SD = 5.0$. The test was administered to 100 students. Use this information to answer the following questions.

1. Approximately how many students scored between 68 and 78?
2. Approximately how many students scored below 63?
3. What is the likely percentile rank of the following raw scores?

Raw Scores	Percentile Rank
58	
63	
68	
73	
78	
83	
88	

4. What are the z-score equivalents to the following raw scores?

Raw Scores	z-Score Equivalent
59	
62	
68	
70	
74	
84	

5. What would be the T-score equivalent for the following raw scores?

Raw Scores	T-score Equivalent
58	
61	
69	
73	
82	
88	

6. What would be the Stanine equivalent for the following raw scores?

Raw Scores	Stanine
63	
68	
73	
78	
80	
83	

7. Alex had a score of 70 on the test. What are some of the various ways you could use to describe his test performance to his parents? Prepare five descriptions of his test performance.

SPOTLIGHT ON THE CLASSROOM

The Portland School District has recently decided to stop using the standardized achievement tests that it has been using for the past decade. Instead, it wants to develop a series of tests that better match its particular curriculum. The chief school administrator gathered a number of well-respected teachers, principals, and school administrators to work on this project over a summer and was able to obtain federal and state financial support to pay for the project.

The testing committee have now nearly finished their work, but still have several important decisions to make. They cannot decide how they should report the test scores. They have considered percentile ranks, z-scores, Stanines, Normal-curve equivalents, and grade-equivalent scales. They call you in for your advice because they understand that you have some background in measurement. They ask you to explain the advantages and limitations of each of the reporting scales that they have considered. What would you tell them?

NOTES

1. Actually, the computation of SAT scores is somewhat more complicated because the test is not re-normed each time it is administered. However, with each administration, if you treat the mean as 500 and the standard deviation as 100, any interpretation of test scores based on those numbers will have relatively high validity.

2. This procedure is somewhat controversial. Some have suggested that since this process involves a non-linear transformation of the raw scores, it results in a distortion of the data and may not result in the hoped for benefits of better comparisons.

Part II
Descriptive Statistics

18

THE LANGUAGE AND LOGIC OF STATISTICS

INTRODUCTION

When approaching any new subject we often have to learn the language of that subject matter. To better understand the logic of statistics, we need to start with some basic vocabulary, including the terms *constant, variable, population, sample, parameter,* and *statistic.* We will also examine a model that will explain how these concepts fit together and, at the same time, explain the difference between descriptive and inferential statistics. Finally, we will examine scales of measurement, or several different ways to think about numbers or data.

The basic goal of statistics is to summarize data. Let's say that you just came home from a tough day at teaching. Your spouse, who is very interested in your career, asks you, "How did your students do on that social studies test you gave today?" You respond by saying, "Alicia received an 85, Bob a 79, Carmen a 95, Dee a 75, Elaine a 90, and so on." It is likely that your tactful spouse will nod, appreciating all of that information. However, it is also likely that your spouse really only wanted a brief summary of the test results. Did the students do well? This would be especially true if you taught five different social studies classes and had a total of 125 students. Statistics gives us the tools that we need to summarize data.

BASIC LANGUAGE AND LOGIC

Constants and Variables

Let's look at some basic language of statistics starting with constants and variables. A *constant* is any value that remains unchanged. For example, the numbers 2, 10, and 31.7856 are all constants. So are the values of π (3.14159) or Avogadro's number (6.02×10^{23}). If there are 28 students enrolled in your class, then that is also a constant. In statistics it is a typical convention to symbolize constants with letters from the beginning of the Roman alphabet (a, b, c, d) or with Greek letters (α [alpha], μ [mu], σ [sigma], and ρ [rho]).

> **Definition**
> A **constant** is any value that remains unchanged.

A *variable* is a quantity that can take on any of a set of values. For example, variables for students in a college class would include heights, weights, ages, GPAs, and scores on the first examination. Each of these would tend to vary among students. It is a typical convention to symbolize variables with letters from the end of the Roman alphabet, with x, y, and z often being used most often.

> **Definition**
> A **variable** is a quantity that can take on any of a set of values.

Populations and Samples

Populations and samples are frequently confused with one another. A *population* is the entire set of people or observations in which you are interested or which are being studied. Examples could include everyone living in the United States (people), the ages of all of the current residents of Brownsville, Texas (observations), or the GPAs for all students enrolled at the University of Connecticut. Although we often think of populations as being quite large, they can also be small. For example, the first examination grades for all the students in your 6th-grade class can also be considered to be a population. The size of the population is the number of people or observations and is typically indicated by the uppercase letter N (for number). For example, the number of students currently enrolled at the college where I teach is 2,951. We express this population size as N = 2,951.

> **Definition**
> A **population** is the entire set of people or observations in which you are interested or which are being studied.

A *sample* is a subset of the population. We generally use a sample when we are interested in studying a population, but when it would be too impractical, time consuming, or expensive to gather information on all of the members of the population. For example, you might be interested in how 3rd graders in Pennsylvania will perform on a new state test. Since it is cheaper and easier to use only a few schools to first try the test, the 3rd graders in those selected schools can serve as a sample for all 3rd-grade students in Pennsylvania.

For another example, we could use the students in a particular classroom as a sample of all of the students attending that school. However, that brings us to an important distinction. You could use the students in a particular class as either a sample or a population, depending on the question that is asked. If you are interested in all of the students in a school, then the students in one particular class serve as a sample of that larger population. However, if you are interested only in that particular class, then the students in that class are the population. We typically represent the size of the sample with the lowercase letter n. For example, if there are 27 students in a class, we can represent this sample size as n = 27.

Definition

A **sample** is a subset of the population.

Although populations (at any given point in time) are stable, samples typically fluctuate. For example, let's say that we would like to determine the average age of students at a particular college. If the student directory from the college computer system contained age information, it could likely give you that average with just a few simple commands. However, if that information were not available by way of the computer, it would be difficult and time consuming to gather the ages of all of the students to calculate the average. In that case you would be likely to find a sample of students, gather their ages, compute an average, and use that as an estimate of the population average. The average age of the population (at a given point in time) would be a fixed number, a constant. Let's say that it is 20.2 years. The sample value, for any given sample, however, is unlikely to be exactly 20.2. It will typically be somewhat higher or lower. This will be especially true if the sample is from a class of first-year students or from an evening class consisting primarily of nontraditional adult students. If you gather many different samples from the same population and compute the mean on each sample, the means will vary from one sample to another.

Obviously, you would have to be cautious in how you gathered the sample. One type of sample is known as a *random sample*. In a random sample every member of the population has an equal likelihood of being selected for that sample. Essentially, you have to use some type of random process—one completely free of any possible bias. One way to develop a random sample is to assign every member of the population a unique number starting at 1 and continuing to N (the number of members in the population). You then use some type of random number generator to select numbers, as in a lottery, until you have filled the sample. Statisticians have found that, in the long run, random samples tend to do the best job of mimicking the population. They are the most likely to be representative of the population and unbiased.

Definition

A **random sample** is one in which every member of the population has an equal likelihood of being selected.

Now, let's return to the idea of *sampling fluctuation*. Remember, earlier we said that the average age of a population would be stable, a constant. We also said that the average age of any one sample is likely to be different from the average of most other samples as well as the average of the population (even for random samples). Therefore, we say that the *sample average* displays sampling fluctuation; it varies among samples.

Definition

Sampling fluctuation refers to the fact that any measure taken on a particular sample from a population is likely to vary among samples from that same population.

It turns out that small samples tend to display more sampling fluctuation than do larger samples. Let's say that you were to choose a sample size of three (n = 3) to estimate the average age of students at a college. You might stand outside a first-year lecture course and question the first three students who leave the classroom. If their ages were 18, 17, and 19, your average would be 18. On the other hand, let's say that you stand outside another classroom where there are more nontraditional students. The first three students to leave that classroom are 25, 20, and 30. In that case the average age would be 25. However, neither of these samples is typical. With small samples, atypical observations (very high or very low) will affect the average more than they would with larger samples. If your sample consisted of two 20-year-old and one 35-year-old student, then the sample mean would be 25. However, with a larger sample there is a greater likelihood that the atypical observation (the 35-year-old student) will be offset by more typical observations (students in their late teens and early 20s). For example, if our 35-year-old student turned up in a sample of 10 students, that student would be less likely to pull up the average. Let's say that the ages for our 10 students are 19, 35, 18, 18, 20, 21, 20, 19, 22, and 20. Then the average age for our sample would be 21.2, only one year above our hypothetical average age of 20.2.

In general, averages computed on larger samples will fluctuate less from the population average than will averages computed from smaller samples. This is an important point. Although you cannot avoid sampling fluctuation, larger samples will show less sampling fluctuation than smaller samples. Since you would like your samples to be representative of the population, you would like less sampling fluctuation. This brings us to our first general principle of statistics: *larger samples are preferred over smaller samples because they are less influenced by sampling fluctuation.*

Parameters and Statistics

Now that you understand the differences between populations and samples, we need to move on to distinguish parameters from statistics. *Parameters* are descriptive indices (e.g. a mean or standard deviation) of a population. The average age of the college population that we have been discussing is such a parameter. Parameters (at any given point in time) are stable, fixed, unvarying. Therefore, they are constants. They are conventionally indicated with either uppercase Roman letters or Greek letters. Parameters that we will be using will include N, P, μ, σ, and ρ.

> *Definition*
> **Parameters** are descriptive indices (e.g. a mean or standard deviation) of a *population*.

Statistics are descriptive indices (e.g. a mean or standard deviation) of samples. Statistics will vary from sample to sample. Therefore, they are variables. Statistics are typically denoted with lowercase Roman letters. Statistics that we will be using will include n, p, s, and r.

> *Definition*
> **Statistics** are descriptive indices (e.g. a mean or standard deviation) of *samples*.

Generally, we are more interested in parameters than statistics because we typically want to know about the characteristics of populations. There are two ways that we can go about determining population parameters. Those two routes are represented in the Figure 18.1 (Games & Klare, 1967).

The first route is the simplest and is represented on the far left side of the diagram. It involves simply and directly describing the characteristics of the population. If the population of interest is reasonably small, you can simply gather the required information from all members of the population, and from the information that you gather on all the members of the population you can calculate the population parameter (e.g. the average age). As a psychologist, I find that this is rarely feasible. Most of the populations in which I am interested, as a psychologist, are large. However, as a teacher, this route is readily available to me since most of the time the population in which I am interested is a single classroom. Therefore, teachers can frequently use Route 1.

Route 2 is somewhat more complicated. This is the route that you must take when it is impractical to make observations on all members of the population. In this case you start with the population and develop a random sample from that population. You then

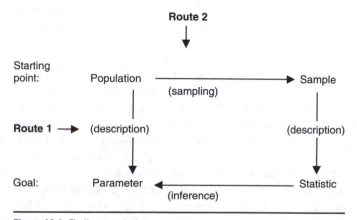

Figure 18.1 Finding population parameters.

make observations on the desired characteristic of all members of that sample and calculate the sample statistic (e.g. the sample mean). Finally, you use inferential statistics to make a probability statement concerning the likelihood that the sample statistic is representative of the corresponding population parameter. You need to ask, "Is the statistic a good estimate of the population parameter?"

This brings us to the differences between descriptive and inferential statistics. *Descriptive statistics* involves directly calculating parameters from populations or statistics from samples. (When you calculate a parameter directly from a population, that process should be referred to as descriptive **parameters**. Nevertheless, the field is known as descriptive **statistics**.) You are simply describing the appropriate population or sample. Look back at Figure 18.1. Route 1 from the diagram is an example of descriptive statistics. *Inferential statistics* involves making estimates of population parameters from sample statistics, and is represented by Route 2 on Figure 18.1. Researchers use both descriptive and inferential statistics frequently. However, for teachers, the populations in which they are interested are most typically single classrooms. Since it is relatively easy to gather information on all members of the population (the students in one's classroom), teachers are typically able to follow Route 1 and use descriptive statistics. Since this text is primarily aimed at classroom teachers, you will be dealing exclusively with descriptive statistics. If you were to take a statistics course in a psychology department or an advanced education course on statistics, you would also learn about inferential statistics since the focus would be more on research, using samples to make estimates about populations.

Definitions

The process of directly describing the characteristics of either populations or samples is referred to as **descriptive statistics**.

The process of using samples to estimate the characteristics of populations is referred as **inferential statistics**.

MEASUREMENT SCALES

Data may show up in a variety of forms. Therefore, over the years we have developed a variety of scales of measurement—terms that we use to describe data.

Categorical Data

One type of data is known as *categorical* data, sometimes also known as *nominal* data. This simply involves sorting observations into logical groups and naming those groups (hence the term "nominal" for naming). An example would include sorting the students in a class into males and females. Therefore, your class may contain 14 males and 12 females. If you decide to play an educational game in the classroom, you might sort the students into two groups, Group 1 and Group 2. Some students are given the label as members of Group 1, whereas other students are labeled as members of Group 2. Other examples of categorical data would include forming the students within your class into groups based on eye color or career aspirations. The groups can be labeled with either names (e.g. male, female) or numbers (e.g. 1, 2). However, when we use numbers to label the characteristics of categorical groups, the numbers are simply being used as substitutes for names and, therefore, do not possess the typical mathematical properties of numbers. It would not make any sense to try to manipulate the numbers mathematically since the results would be nonsensical.

Definition

Categorical or **nominal** data involves sorting a larger group into smaller groups, not based on numbers (e.g. males and females).

Ranked Data

Another form of data is known as *ranked* or *ordinal* data. Let's say that we line up the students from a class in order by height. We could label the tallest student number 1, the next tallest number 2, and soon we have ranked all of the students. In this case the numbers really represent relative placement (first, second, third, etc.). With ranked data we frequently have unequal intervals between the numbers (unequal spaces between the rankings). For example, let's suppose that the tallest student in our 1st-grade class is Paul who is 48 inches tall. The second tallest is Sally who is 47 inches tall. Tom is third at 42 inches high. In this case number 1, Paul, is only one inch taller than number 2, Sally. However, number 2, Sally, is five inches taller than number 3, Tom. That is what we mean by unequal intervals. If we only examine the ranked data we know that Paul is taller than Sally, who is taller than Tom. However, we don't know how far apart they are in actual height.

For another example of ranked data, consider 50 high school students participating in a 10K (10 kilometer) race. As the runners come across the finish line, they are ranked 1st place, 2nd place, 3rd place, and so on. However, the distance between the finishers may vary. The 2nd-place runner may only be a split second behind the winner, whereas the 3rd-place runner might be a minute or more behind the first two finishers.

Definition

Ranked or **ordinal** data involve sorting a group by rank (e.g. setting up a class of students by height or the order in which runners complete a race).

Since ranked or ordinal data do show unequal intervals, we are somewhat reluctant to perform mathematical manipulations on that type of data. For example, an average rank and an average height could mean something different for students in your classroom. Let's try an example to demonstrate this point. Let's say that we have a small college classroom with 11 students, some of whom play basketball. Let's look at their heights which I have arranged in order (see Figure 18.2).

If we look at the average rank in the group, it would be Roberto who is ranked sixth. He is 69 inches (5 ft. 9 in.) tall. However, if we calculate the average height, we find that the average is 70.9 inches. So, in reality, Tanya is actually closer to the average in height for

Name	Height (inches)	Rank
Mark	80	1
Amal	79	2
Kurt	78	3
Paul	77	4
Tanya	71	5
Roberto	69	6
Terri	68	7
Cheryl	67	8
Tony	66	9
Ping	63	10
Trish	62	11

Figure 18.2 The height of 11 students from a college class.

the class than is Roberto. Mathematical manipulations of ordinal or ranked data can lead to erroneous conclusions.

Numerical Data

A third type of data is known as *numerical* or *metric* data. When we use numerical data the numbers are meaningful. If we return to our previous example of our 1st-grade classroom, we could record the students' actual heights. You may recall that Paul was 48 inches tall, Sally was 47 inches tall, and Tom was 42 inches tall. Using each student's actual height, in inches, would be numerical data. All numerical data displays equal intervals, and can therefore be mathematically manipulated. Some statisticians insist on a further breakdown of numerical data into interval and ratio scales. With *ratio scales* there is a meaningful zero point. For example, height would be ratio data. Someone who is 60 inches tall would be twice as tall as someone who is 30 inches tall. However, not all scales have a meaningful zero point. For example, IQ scales have no meaningful zero point. We cannot say that someone with an IQ of 100 is twice as smart as someone with an IQ of 50. IQ scales were simply not set up that way. Scales without a meaningful zero point are known as *interval scales*. Within the context of this text, we are not likely to run into too many instances where the difference between interval and ratio scales will affect what we do or how we interpret data. The one exception will include many standardized tests such as IQ tests.

I should also point out that, on occasion, psychometricians have developed measurement scales that do not fully conform to the definitions that I have provided.

Definitions

Numeric or **metric** data involves data with equal intervals between points on the scale.

Interval data is numeric data without a meaningful zero point.

Ratio data is numeric data with a meaningful zero point.

If you are given a choice about gathering data in either a numeric or in a ranked form, I would recommend that you gather data in the numeric form. When we transform numeric data (e.g. heights) into ranks, we are frequently losing information and may come to an erroneous conclusion as we did in the height example mentioned above. As a general rule, it is better to have more information than less when making decisions.

Discrete Data vs. Continuous Data

There is still one additional distinction that we need to make concerning metric (numeric) data: That is the distinction between discrete and continuous data. *Discrete data* is data that can appear only as whole numbers. Examples would include the number of students in a class and the scores on most examinations. *Continuous data*, on the other hand, can be expressed with fractions or digits after the decimal point. Examples could include height (68.5698 inches) when measured with a very precise instrument, or when my wife instructs me to stop at the grocery store to pick up 1½ pounds of ground sirloin for a recipe we plan to make that evening. Some mathematicians object to treating discrete data as you would continuous data because you can occasionally obtain results that are meaningless. However, a good compromise comes from the idea of rounding. For example, we often treat continuous data as if it were discrete. We typically report someone's height to the nearest inch. Therefore, we could just as easily treat discrete data as if it were rounded off. If a student obtained a score of 76 on an examination (discrete data), we would say that this score of 76 represents any score between 75.50 and 76.49999. We say that we are reporting the score as 76, the midpoint of the interval between 75.50 and 76.4999.

Definitions

Discrete data involves information that can only be represented as whole numbers (e.g. the size of a family).

Continuous data involves information that can be represented as decimals and fractions (e.g. I weigh 162.3 pounds).

Of course, this also means that we need to be careful how we report continuous data. For example, we typically report ages from our last birthday. However, this may lead to errors of as much as six months when computing averages. Therefore, we should report all continuous data, such as ages, to the nearest whole number. For example, if you were 19 years and 7 months old, you should report your age as 20 years. We will use this convention for the remainder of this text. I would further recommend that you use it whenever treating data.

SUMMARY

This chapter provides an introduction to statistical concepts that will be important in understanding measurement principles. A subject matter such as statistics has its own vocabulary. This chapter described a number of important terms. For example, a constant is a value that does not change, whereas a variable is a value that can change from one individual to the next. A population is the entire set of information in which we are interested, whereas a sample is a subset of that population. A parameter describes a population, whereas a statistic describes a sample.

The chapter also described a model that helps us differentiate between descriptive and inferential statistics. When doing research, we frequently rely on inferential statistics, whereas in the classroom we will mostly use descriptive statistics.

In the field of measurement we use several different scales. Data can typically be characterized as categorical, ranked, or numeric. Numeric data can also be further described as either interval data or as ratio data. Finally, statisticians and psychometricians sometimes differentiate between discrete and continuous data.

EXERCISES

1. Which of the following are populations, which are samples, and which could be either? (Mark **P** for a population, an **S** for a sample, and an **E** for either.)

_____ a. The ages of all the students in your high school graduating class on the day you graduated for a report to the newspaper on the characteristics of your graduating class

_____ b. The total number of hours that five students from a class of 30 students study one night to find the average study time per night for the students in your class

_____ c. The entire freshman class at Texas State University, San Marcos

_____ d. Because you are doing a report on the school cafeteria, you pass out surveys randomly to students as they walk into lunch on Monday

_____ e. The grade-point average for every student in a class for a study on the characteristics of the students in that class

_____ f. The exam scores for the students in an English class when computing the characteristics of that exam

_____ g. The age of every person in the United States when calculating the average age of Americans

_____ h. The number of students living in the freshmen dormitories

_____ i. In order to compare last year's 5th-grade math curriculum to the new 5th-grade curriculum, you gather data from one 5th-grade classroom

_____ j. The shoe sizes for all of the male professors on your campus

2. Which of the following are parameters, which are statistics, and which could be either? (Mark **P** for a parameter, an **S** for a statistic, and an **E** for either.)

_____ a. The average age of the students in your class for a report on the characteristics of that class

_____ b. The average reading level for the members of your 3rd-grade class as an estimate of the average reading level for all 3rd graders in your school district

_____ c. The average standardized test scores for the students in your 4th-grade class for a report on the standardized test scores for all 4th-grade students

_____ d. Researchers surveying a random sample of American households for the number of people per American family

_____ e. The average hours of football practice per week for a newspaper article on that particular high school

_____ f. The average height of all of the players on the varsity basketball team for the team roster

_____ g. While finding certain characteristics of every student at your college, the computer information system calculates the most common age of the students is 19

_____ h. The average snowfall, in inches, that your town received in January

_____ i. The average number of shoes that the students in your fifth-period English class own

_____ j. The average IQ score of all the students in your honors program for a report to the school board on the new honors program in your school

3. Determine whether each example is dealing with measurement on a nominal scale, an ordinal scale, an interval scale, or a ratio scale. (Mark **N** for nominal, **O** for ordinal, **I** for interval, and **R** for ratio.)

_____ a. Manuel is the third student to finish the test.

_____ b. Rob is now 48 inches tall.

_____ c. Sam scored a 530 on the SAT verbal exam.

_____ d. On her way home from school, Sarah drives 35 mph.

_____ e. Ben will be the second to the last student to give a speech.

_____ f. A gym class is divided into four groups and Janice is on the blue team.

_____ g. Joe is the youngest in his class.

_____ h. Janice has an IQ score of 106 and Raymond has an IQ score of 98.

_____ i. Tyler had 15 out of 20 items correct on his math test.

SPOTLIGHT ON THE CLASSROOM

Mai Ling is a teacher at Highlands High School, and is the boys' varsity tennis coach. She recently developed a boys' tennis program in her school because previously it was only available to girls. She feels that her program is very strong and that the students involved display a balance between academics and sports. She would like to gather data to show that this is true, but needs your help. What type of data could she gather to demonstrate that the tennis program has not had a negative impact on the academic focus of the boys involved in her program? What would you recommend that she do?

STUDY TIPS

How to Read a Measurement and Statistics Text

One mistake that many students make is that they try to deal with every reading assignment in exactly the same way. They sometimes try to read a physics textbook the same way that they read a novel. However, more experienced and more successful students recognize that reading in one subject matter must be approached differently from reading in another subject matter. Novels that you read for leisure, and even most high school textbooks, have relatively few ideas on each page. College textbooks frequently contain many more ideas per page. Here are some suggestions for reading a measurement and statistics text.

- Although you can easily read 20 or more pages of a novel without a break, a measurement and statistics chapter should probably be broken down into several 8- to 10-page sections. Reading shorter sections of the text will keep you focused and improve your comprehension of the material.
- Read through the technical terminology and the definitions before you read the chapter or section to familiarize yourself with the material. Make word cards to learn the technical terminology.
- This type of material requires a high level of concentration. Read in a quiet place, free from distractions.
- Use a reading/study system that involves previewing the chapter before reading and reviewing the material after reading.
- Examples and box features are frequently as important as, or sometimes even more important than the text.
- Use a text-making system (e.g. highlighting) as you read. It is best to read a full paragraph before you go back and mark the most important material. Mark meaningful phrases rather than whole sentences or key words.
- Mark headings, main ideas, and supporting points.
- Formulas and examples also need to be marked.
- Taking notes from the text can be very helpful. You can take notes in place of highlighting.
- Predict questions that you think the instructor might ask in the margin of your textbook and underline the answers in the text.
- Do the exercises after reading the section or the chapter to apply what you have learned.[1]

NOTE

1. This material has been adapted from Van Blerkom (2009).

19

FREQUENCY DISTRIBUTIONS AND GRAPHS

INTRODUCTION

You are the head of your high school math department and are asked to help the new high school principal better understand the courses that your department offers. The principal is especially interested in knowing which math courses are being taken by the freshmen. You list the various math courses taken by freshmen and include the number of students in each course. However, in reviewing your list, you come to believe that there should be a better way to present these data to the principal. Perhaps you could use some type of chart or graph.

In this chapter, you will learn how to organize data, such as students' scores from a classroom test or the number of students enrolled in each course, in the form of a frequency distribution. Once you create the frequency distribution, the typical next step is to develop a graphic representation of the data in the form of a bar chart, a pie chart, a histogram, or a frequency polygon. It is also important to learn how to describe the form of the frequency distribution—to be able to determine what it looks like. Finally, you will need to know when it is helpful to use either a grouped frequency distribution or a cumulative frequency distribution.

FREQUENCY DISTRIBUTIONS

Frequencies

Statistics is primarily concerned with summarizing data. A good first step when presented with a set of data is to organize it into a table known as a frequency distribution. Frequency distributions are used with both population and sample data. In general, frequency distributions and graphs often allow us very quickly to obtain an overall view of the data.

How do you develop a frequency distribution? Let's start with some data. Let's use scores for 20 students who each took a 15-item quiz; the 20 scores are as follows: 13, 12, 14, 10, 9, 15, 8, 6, 11, 12, 14, 13, 11, 12, 9, 13, 10, 11, 12, and 8.

We will take a step-by-step approach to learn how to produce a frequency distribution.

Step 1. List all possible scores in a column with the highest scores at the top. Since these quiz scores are variables, let's give them a label like "Quiz Scores" or a more generic label like "X." Since this is a 15-item quiz, the scores could range from a high of 15 to a possible low of 0 (see Figure 19.1).

Step 2. Tally the scores using tally marks. The first score is a 13, so put a tally mark by the 13. The next score is a 12, so put a tally mark by the 12. Continue until all 20 scores are recorded and your table looks like the one in Figure 19.2.

Step 3. Count up the tally marks. To do this we will need to develop a frequency column. By *frequency* we mean how many times did a score of 15 appear, a score of 14, a score of 13, and so on. We use the lowercase letter f to indicate frequency for a sample

X
15
14
13
12
11
10
9
8
7
6
5
4
3
2
1
0

Figure 19.1 A list of possible quiz scores.

X	
15	I
14	II
13	III
12	IIII
11	III
10	II
9	II
8	II
7	
6	I
5	
4	
3	
2	
1	
0	

Figure 19.2 Quiz scores with tally marks.

and the uppercase letter F to indicate frequency for a population. Since our classroom is the population of interest, we can use the uppercase F (see Figure 19.3).

When you add up the frequency column, it should always equal the number of scores you had. In this case $N = 20$. This can be shown by using the summation notation Σ. It would look like this. $\Sigma F = N$. The sum of F equals N (the sum of the frequencies equals the number of observations [scores] in the population). This is also true for samples where the notation would be $\Sigma f = n$. This is a good way to check to make sure that you recorded all of the observations. The sum of the frequencies should always equal N or n.

Definition

Frequency refers to how often a score occurs in a set of scores.

Proportion and Percentages

There are other ways in which data can be represented other than as frequencies. Two analogous ways to count data are as *proportions* and *percentages* of the observations. For example, in our frequency distribution 1 out of 20 students scored 15. We can represent that as a proportion, a two-digit decimal. Since 1 out of 20 students had a score of 15, this represents 1/20 of all the students, or .05 of all the students had a score of 15. We use the uppercase P to represent the population proportion and the lowercase p to represent the sample proportion. A proportion can be calculated using the following formula (Equation 19.1):

$$P = \frac{F}{N} \text{ or, for our example, } P = \frac{1}{20} = .05 \qquad (19.1)$$

X		F
15	I	1
14	II	2
13	III	3
12	IIII	4
11	III	3
10	II	2
9	II	2
8	II	2
7		0
6	I	1
5		0
4		0
3		0
2		0
1		0
0		0

Figure 19.3 A frequency distribution.

Therefore, .05 of all of the students scored 15. Four students received a score of 12. That can be converted to a proportion as follows (Equation 19.2):

$$P = \frac{4}{20} = .20 \tag{19.2}$$

This means that .20 (or 1/5) of the students had a score of 12.

The third way to represent frequencies is as a percentage of the observations. To compute percentages use the following formula (Equation 19.3):

$$\% = 100 \times \frac{F}{N} \text{ or, for our example, } \% = 100 \times \frac{1}{20} = 5\% \tag{19.3}$$

Five percent of the students had a score of 15.

Definitions

Proportion refers to the proportion of the students who had a certain score.
Percentage refers to the percentage of students who had a certain score.

Listed below (see Figure 19.4) is our frequency distribution with additional columns for proportions and percentage.

You should remember that the sum of F equals N, the number of observations (or, in this case, scores). When we convert frequencies into proportions and percentages we can use similar checks (Equations 19.5 and 19.6).

X		F	P	%
15	I	1	.05	5
14	II	2	.10	10
13	III	3	.15	15
12	IIII	4	.20	20
11	III	3	.15	15
10	II	2	.10	10
9	II	2	.10	10
8	II	2	.10	10
7		0	0	0
6	I	1	.05	5
5		0	0	0
4		0	0	0
3		0	0	0
2		0	0	0
1		0	0	0
0		0	0	0
		20	1.00	100

Figure 19.4 A frequency distribution with columns for proportion and percent.

$$\Sigma P = 1.00 \qquad\qquad (19.5)$$

$$\Sigma\% = 100 \qquad\qquad (19.6)$$

The sum of the proportion column should add up to 1.00, whereas the sum of the percentage column should add up to 100%. If you have an N that does not divide evenly into 100 (e.g. $N = 28$), then these two sums could vary somewhat from 1.00 and 100. With rounding errors you could obtain a $\Sigma P = .996$, for example. If you would carry the decimals out to four or five places you should get very close to 1.00 and 100.

There are several other issues to keep in mind when developing a frequency distribution. Values for data under the "X" column should be complete, yet mutually exclusive; that is, the list should be complete without any duplication. You should be able to place each observation into one and only one category. This becomes especially important and, at times problematic, when listing categorical data (described in Chapter 18). If this is unclear, try developing a frequency distribution for hair color in a college classroom. Do you choose the students' natural hair color or the color of their hair today? Do you have a third party to rate each person's hair color or do you ask each student to tell us the color of his or her hair. What about my hair color? I used to be a red head, but recently one of my students told me that my hair color could now be best described as "cinnamon and sugar." I think that by the time you finish the exercise you will have a better feel for what I mean by a list that is complete, yet mutually exclusive.

Grouped Frequency Distributions

Suppose that you are a physics professor teaching an introductory course where test scores could go from 1 to 50. For the sake of simplicity with numeric data, it is often advisable to keep the number of categories at fewer than 20. It is a good idea to avoid long columns of data that take more than one page because multi-paged frequency distributions are often difficult to read and interpret. Therefore, if you have exam scores between 1 and 50, you might want to group the data as listed below (see Figure 19.5). This is what is known as a *grouped frequency distribution*. A grouped frequency distribution uses intervals to group the data. I have listed the midpoints of

Exam Scores	Midpoint of Intervals
48–	50
43–47	45
38–42	40
33–37	35
28–32	30
23–27	25
18–22	20
13–17	15
8–12	10
3–7	5
–2	0

Figure 19.5 A grouped frequency distribution for test scores.

the intervals (which we will discuss later) to help you see why I have selected the intervals that I chose. Actually, the intervals can be set up in any reasonable way.

Now, let's talk about *end points, interval width,* and the *midpoints* of the interval. Let's take the interval of 13–17 as an example. The nominal end points (those listed) of the interval are 13 and 17. This means that this interval contains all scores between 13 and 17. However, you may remember from Chapter 18 that we are treating discrete data as if it were continuous data. For example, let's say that it were possible to obtain a score of 12.63 on this examination. Therefore, although our lower limit of the interval (abbreviated *ll*) is nominally listed as 13, the real lower limit is 12.50. In the same respect the real upper limit (abbreviated *ul*) of the interval is not 17, but is 17.4999 (which we could round off to 17.5). Therefore, the size of the interval width (abbreviated *i*) is the distance from the real upper limit to the real lower limit, which is expressed as the following equation (19.7):

$$i = ul - ll \qquad\qquad (19.7)$$

interval width = real upper limit − real lower limit

For our example (Equation 19.8):

$$i = 17.5 - 12.5 = 5 \qquad\qquad (19.8)$$

Another way to determine the size of the interval is simply to count the scores within the interval: 13 (1), 14 (2), 15 (3), 16 (4), 17 (5).

The midpoint of the interval can often be determined by inspection. However, if there is any doubt there is a useful formula (Equation 19.9):

$$\text{Midpoint} = ll + \frac{i}{2} \qquad \text{(Remember that } ll \text{ is the lower limit).}$$

For our example it would be:

$$\text{Midpoint} = 12.5 + \frac{5}{2} = 12.5 + 2.5 = 15. \qquad\qquad (19.9)$$

Actually, when grouping data for a frequency distribution, there are few rules. In general, grouping is done in a way that makes it easier for the reader to understand. When necessary, it is even permissible to vary the interval widths, although doing so means that the grouped frequency distribution may be more often misinterpreted. Consider the following example of a grouped frequency distribution with unequal intervals. Here is one way we sometimes group family incomes (see Figure 19.6).

As you can see, the distribution begins with a $10,000 increment at the bottom but increases the interval width with each successive higher interval. If we continued with the original $10,000 increments, we would need 100 intervals to reach the $1,000,000 income. With some practice, people can read this type of grouped frequency distribution and interpret it appropriately.

Yearly Family Income
> $1,000,000
$500,001–$1,000,000
$250,001–$500,000
$100,001–$250,000
$50,001–$100,000
$25,001–$50,000
$10,001–$25,000
$0–$10,000

Figure 19.6 Possible groupings for a grouped frequency distribution for yearly family income.

GRAPHING FREQUENCY DISTRIBUTIONS

There are a variety of ways of pictorially representing frequency distributions. We will discuss four types here: bar charts, pie charts, histograms, and frequency polygons. The first two—bar charts and pie charts—are used with categorical data, whereas the last two—histograms and frequency polygons—are used with numeric data.

Bar Charts

Categorical data can be represented in a bar chart. Let's suppose that we have a class-room with 25 students, 14 boys and 11 girls. This data can be represented in a bar chart as in the following example (see Figure 19.7).

There are several basic components to a bar chart. First, the vertical axis (the y-axis) represents frequency, proportion, or percentage (since they are all analogous with one another). Second, the categories are represented on the horizontal axis (the x-axis). Third, the data are represented as discontinuous bars. That means that the bars should not touch one another since they represent discrete categories. Finally, both the vertical

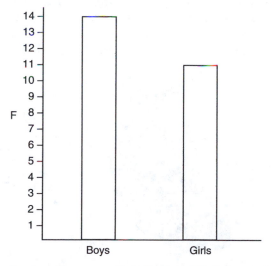

Number of boys and girls in Ms. Schmidt's 3rd-grade class

Figure 19.7 A bar chart.

and horizontal axes should each be clearly labeled. Using these four simple rules and the example, you should now be able to prepare a bar chart.

Pie Charts

Another way to represent categorical data is by use of a circle known as a pie chart. Remembering that there are 360° in a full circle, categories can be represented as slices of the circle or the pie. In our previous example, a class of 25 students consisted of 14 boys. The boys represent 56% of the classroom population. A simple calculation reveals that 56% of 360° is 202°. Therefore, we can represent the boys by indicating a slice of the circle with an arc of 202°. The girls will be represented by the remaining slice with an arc of 158° (see Figure 19.8). To make a pie chart by hand, you will need an inexpensive protractor and compass. However, today it is becoming increasingly more common to find computer packages that will produce beautiful pie charts. With some practice, they can be produced both quickly and easily.

When constructing a pie chart there are again several basic rules. First, be certain to label each piece of the pie. Sometimes this is accomplished by using different shadings or colors for each slice, and making a key to show what each shade or color represents. Second, be sure to clearly label the chart.

Histograms

One way to represent numeric data is as a histogram. In many aspects, histograms are similar to bar charts in that frequencies are represented on the vertical axis (y-axis), values are represented on the horizontal axis (x-axis), and vertical bars are used to represent the data. However, there are several ways in which histograms differ from bar charts. Let's use the example of quiz scores from earlier in the chapter to make a histogram (see Figure 19.9).

Of course, there are several rules involved in developing a histogram. First, place frequencies, proportions, or percentages on the vertical axis (y-axis). Second, place the values of the scale on the horizontal axis (x-axis) with lower numbers toward the origin (on the left). Third, place a vertical bar to indicate the data. The width of the vertical bar extends from the lower limit of the interval to the upper limit. Therefore, the bar representing scores of 9 should extend from 8.5 to 9.5. The bars are also continuous

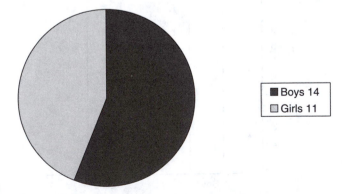

■ Boys 14
☐ Girls 11

Number of boys and girls in Ms. Schmidt's 3rd-grade class

Figure 19.8 Sample pie chart.

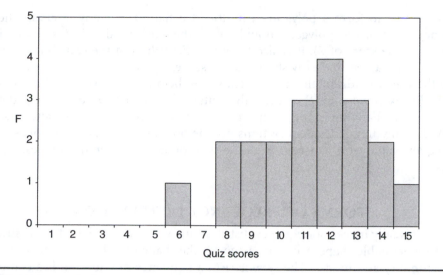

Figure 19.9 A histogram of quiz scores.

(that is, they touch one another) when the data warrants. In this example, there were no scores of 7. Therefore, that is missing in the histogram. However, since there were scores between 8 and 15, those bars are touching one another. Finally, be sure to label both the horizontal and vertical axes.

Frequency Polygons

An alternative way to represent numeric data is with a frequency polygon. An example of one is shown in Figure 19.10. A frequency polygon starts out much like a histogram with frequencies (or proportions or percentages) on the vertical axis and the scale of interest (e.g. exam scores) on the horizontal axis. Then you place a dot over the mid-point of each interval to represent the respective frequencies. Finally, you connect the

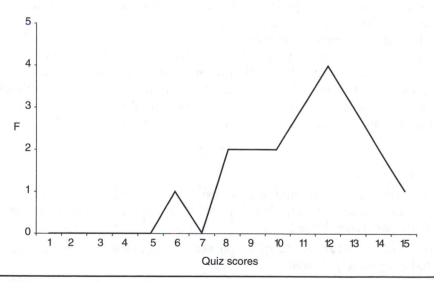

Figure 19.10 Frequency polygon.

successive dots to form a polygon (a multi-sided figure). For any interval where the frequency is zero, the polygon should touch the horizontal axis (as it did in this example for the score of 7). It is also helpful to list values of the scale both above and below those obtained to clearly show that no student scored at those values. I included a 5 on the scale to indicate that no student scored below a 6. However, I did not include a 16 in this example since the quiz only contained 15 items. Unfortunately, that does leave the graph hanging in the air, not returning to the horizontal axis after a score of 15. (With many frequency distributions no one obtains the highest possible score and the frequency polygon can return to the horizontal axis after the highest observed score.)

FORMS OF FREQUENCY DISTRIBUTION

When we visually inspect a frequency distribution, we often notice that the distribution takes on a definable shape. You can categorize the shape of a distribution according to both symmetry and modes. The *symmetry* of a frequency distribution is a comparison of the left and right sides of the distribution. If you make a vertical fold in the center of the distribution, would the right side be a mirror image of the left side? If so, then we say that the distribution is symmetrical. For example, a bell-shaped distribution is symmetrical. Real-life distributions are rarely exactly symmetrical. Therefore, if a distribution is even close to being symmetrical, we may still label it as symmetrical.

> *Definition*
> If the left and right sides of a graphed frequency distribution are mirror images of one another, we say that the distribution has **symmetry**.

Distributions that are not symmetrical are said to be *skewed*. In a skewed distribution, most of the observations are piled up on one side, with many fewer on the other side. The side with the fewer observations will visually form what has frequently been referred to as a tail. If most of the observations are low scores with relatively few high scores (as would occur with a very difficult exam), the tail will form on the right (the high scores). In this case the distribution is said to be positively skewed, or skewed to the right. On the other hand, if most of the observations are high scores with relatively few low scores (as would be seen with a very easy exam), the tail would form to the left. In that case the distribution would be labeled as negatively skewed, or skewed to the left.

> *Definition*
> If a graphed frequency distribution is not symmetrical, it is said to be **skewed**.
> If most of the scores are on the left and a tail forms to the right, the distribution is said to be **positively skewed**.
> If most of the scores are on the right and a tail forms to the left, the distribution is said to be **negatively skewed**.

Another way to describe a distribution is in terms of *modes* or humps. The mode is the score that occurs most frequently. On a graph it is represented as a high point. In the case of the quiz scores that we plotted earlier, the mode was 12. This could be determined directly from inspecting the frequency polygon. Distributions that have one mode are said to be *unimodal*. Examples of unimodal distributions are those that are bell-shaped, triangular, or J-shaped. If the distribution has two modes it is said to be *bimodal*. Even if the second hump is not as high as the first, the distribution is still labeled as bimodal. Examples of bimodal distributions are those with two humps and those that are U-shaped (see Figure 19.11). If a distribution has more than two modes, it is described as *multi-modal*. If a distribution is relatively flat, it is said to be *amodal* (without a mode). Amodal distributions are also sometimes referred to as rectangular or uniform distributions.

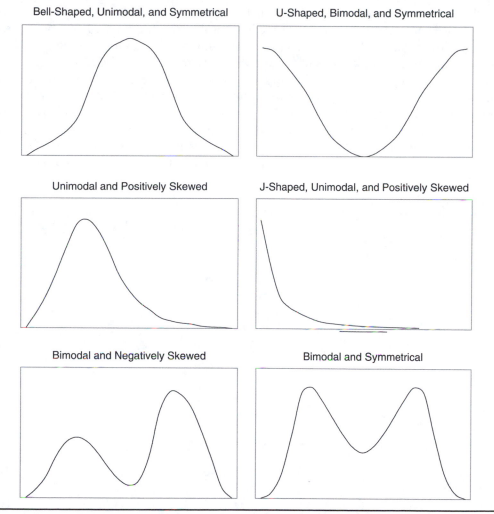

Figure 19.11 Various frequency distributions.

Definitions

The score that occurs most frequently is labeled the **mode**.

A **unimodal** frequency distribution has only one mode.

A **bimodal** frequency distribution has two modes.

A **multi-modal** frequency distribution has three or more modes.

An **amodal** frequency distribution has no apparent mode.

CUMULATIVE FREQUENCY DISTRIBUTIONS

Another type of distribution is a cumulative frequency distribution, which will be required to understand and compute medians and percentile ranks. Let's look at the frequency distribution that we used at the beginning of the chapter (see Figure 19.12). However, here I have added a column for cumulative frequency (labeled *CF*).

Cumulative frequency answers the question, "How many individuals had this score or lower?" To complete the count, start at the bottom of the frequency distribution and work up to the top. You can see that the frequencies accumulate until all of the observations have been counted. The top cumulative frequency must equal the number of observations (N), which in this case is 20. How do we read this? Well, if we use a score of 10 as our example, the cumulative frequency column tells us that 7 students had scores of 10 or less.

Definition
Cumulative frequency—How many individuals had this score or lower.

X		F	CF
15	I	1	20
14	II	2	19
13	III	3	17
12	IIII	4	14
11	III	3	10
10	II	2	7
9	II	2	5
8	II	2	3
7		0	1
6	I	1	1
5		0	0
4		0	0
3		0	0
2		0	0
1		0	0
0		0	0

Figure 19.12 Cumulative frequency distribution for quiz scores.

We can also convert cumulative frequencies into cumulative proportions and cumulative percents (also known as percentile ranks). You can calculate cumulative proportions and cumulative percents by using the formulas shown earlier in this chapter. However, if you have proportion and percent columns on your frequency distribution, you can calculate cumulative proportions and cumulative percents using the same procedure that we used to calculate cumulative frequency by starting from the bottom and working up one step at a time.

To plot a typical frequency distribution, place the dot over the midpoint of the interval to create a frequency polygon. In the previous example, two students had a score of 10, so we placed the dot over the 10—the midpoint of the interval. We do that because we are using the rounding convention. Here the 10 represents all possible scores between 9.50 and 10.49 (if such scores were possible). However, when we make a cumulative frequency polygon, we place the dot at the upper limit, which in this example would be at 10.49. We do that because a cumulative frequency represents all scores at that point or lower. Although that may appear to be a minor point, it will become an important issue in helping us calculate medians and percentile ranks in the next chapter.

SUMMARY

A common first step in organizing a set of raw data is to develop a frequency distribution which lists all possible scores and how frequently each occurs. For data sets with a very large range of possible scores, it is often preferable to set up a grouped frequency distribution. We can often interpret a frequency distribution more easily if we convert it into a graph. Categorical data are often represented as either bar charts or as pie charts. Numeric data are often represented as either histograms or as frequency polygons. Finally, we often want to describe our frequency distributions according to their form, their symmetry, and the presence of one or more modes. At times, we also want to go an additional step and develop a cumulative frequency distribution, which is often required in order to calculate the median and/or percentile ranks.

EXERCISES

Part A

The following are scores from an educational psychology exam given recently. The maximum score was 40. Each student's gender and the score from the first exam is listed below.

Gender	Score
F	27
F	30
F	33
F	27
F	27
F	28
M	38
F	27
F	31

Gender	Score
F	39
F	29
F	35
F	25
F	30
F	27
F	36
F	31
F	36
M	33
M	30
M	38
F	33
M	30
F	33
F	28

1. Prepare separate frequency distributions for "gender" and "score."
2. Graph each frequency distribution using an appropriate graph and f. (Do not group data.)
3. Redo the "gender" distribution twice using p and % on the vertical axis.
4. Redo the "score" distribution by grouping into 8–10 intervals.

Part B
The following is a frequency distribution of spelling test scores from 25 students in a 5th-grade class. The maximum score on this test was 20.

Score	F
20	2
19	3
18	3
17	4
16	3
15	3
14	1
13	0
12	1
11	2
10	1
9	1
8	1
7	0
6	0
5	0
4	0
3	0

2	0
1	0
0	0

1. Draw a frequency polygon based on this distribution.
2. Is this distribution symmetrical, positively skewed, or negatively skewed? Why?
3. What is the mode of this distribution? Is the distribution unimodal, bimodal, or amodal? Why?

SPOTLIGHT ON THE CLASSROOM

Juan Chavez is a dedicated 4th-grade teacher at Hillcrest Elementary School in San Antonio, Texas. Every day when Mr. Chavez comes home from school his wife, Betty, asks him how his students are performing in his class. Although Betty does not know much about classroom testing, she is very interested in her husband's career. Juan needs to find an easy way to describe how his students are doing.

Mr. Chavez began his explanation to his wife that 15 students are passing his reading class, but did not give her any other details. However, since he realized that this explanation was inadequate, he decided that he needed to use another technique.

Mr. Chavez is currently doing a unit on *Charlotte's Web* and gave a test last week on Chapters 1 through 5. He plans to use the results of the test to explain to his wife how the students are progressing through the unit. He prepared the following frequency distribution.

Test Score	F
20	1
19	1
18	3
17	3
16	5
15	4
14	2
13	1
12	0
11	0
10	2
9	0
8	1

No student had a score lower than 8.

How can Mr. Chavez use and expand upon this frequency distribution to describe to Betty how his students are performing on this unit?

STUDY TIPS

How to Take Lecture Notes in a Measurement and Statistics Class

Taking class notes is another important classroom skill. Over the years, when students struggle in one of my classes I have suggested a number of strategies to help them. I always ask the students to bring their notes with them to the office so that we can review how they take notes.

There are three general rules about taking class notes.

- Read the text chapter before going to class. Lectures make more sense when you have sufficient background information.
- Be actively involved in the class—be an active listener. Do not simply take dictation, which can be a very passive process.
- Review and edit your notes after class. Add examples and explanations where needed. Several weeks after the class you should be able to reconstruct what occurred in class from your notes.

There are a number of suggestions that could result in improved class notes from a measurement and statistics course.

- Begin by putting the date and the topic near the left margin.
- Put all main points near the margin; indent supporting details.
- Put all examples in your notes. If there is sufficient room, put the example on the left side of the page and put the instructor's comments and explanations on the right side of the page. If there is not enough room, put the instructor's comments right below the example.
- Leave plenty of room in your notes so that you can go back and fill in additional details later.
- If you miss a key word, draw a line and continue with the remaining information. Ask your professor or a classmate at the end of the class and fill in the blank.
- When editing notes, develop recall questions in the margin and underline the answers in your notes.[1]

NOTE

1. This material has been adapted from Van Blerkom (2009).

20

CENTRAL TENDENCY
What is a Typical Score?

INTRODUCTION

There are three basic characteristics of frequency distributions: form (the shape of the distribution, discussed in Chapter 19), central tendency (discussed in this chapter), and variability (to be discussed in Chapter 21). Now that you have learned to organize a set of data into a frequency distribution and describe its form, the next step is to learn to describe the other characteristics of that frequency distribution. One characteristic is central tendency, often referred to as a "typical score." In this chapter we will talk about three commonly used measures of central tendency: the mode, the median, and the mean, and you will learn how to calculate each. We will also discuss the characteristics of each of these measures and when each is appropriate to use in the classroom.

MEASURES OF CENTRAL TENDENCY

When we describe a set of data, we often like to use a single figure that represents a "typical" or "average" score. For example, you have probably heard statements such as: the average IQ is 100, the average verbal SAT score for incoming college freshmen is 495, or the average price for a new home is $245,000. These are all examples of ways to describe central tendency. Although there are a variety of measures of central tendency, we will be discussing the three most commonly used: the mode (discussed briefly in the previous chapter), the median, and the mean. All three of these indices can be used with either samples or populations.

Mode

Let's start with the mode since it is the easiest to understand. The *mode* is sometimes defined as the single score with the highest frequency; it is the score that occurs most often. However, there are frequency distributions that appear to possess several peaks. Therefore, another way to define the mode is as any significant peak in a frequency distribution.[1] As you learned in the previous chapter, the mode can be determined by developing a frequency distribution and using tally marks to count the number of times each score appears. The mode can often be determined by a simple visual inspection of either a frequency distribution or a graph of such a distribution. Let's try an example.

In Figure 20.1 we have a frequency distribution based on the number of books each student in Ms. Schmidt's 3rd-grade class read outside of school during the month of October. There are 22 students in the class.

From this frequency distribution you will notice that seven of the students had read 6 books during October. The score with the highest frequency is 6 books; therefore, the mode is 6.

Definition

The **mode** is the score that occurs most frequently.

Median

Another measure of central tendency is known as the *median*. The median is the score that divides the distribution in half: 50% of the scores are above it and 50% are below it. On a frequency polygon the median is that point that divides the area under the curve exactly in half. How do we compute the median? For some sets of data, computing the median is quite simple. However, for other sets of data, the computation can become more complex.

Simple Distributions

For a relatively small and simple distribution (without repeated scores in the middle) we can find *where the median belongs* by using the following formula (Equation 20.1):

$$\frac{N+1}{2} \tag{20.1}$$

For example, let's say that we have a very simple distribution with an *odd* number of scores, such as the science quiz scores for five students from Mrs. Potenkin's class. The scores are 8, 5, 7, 4, and 9. The first thing we do with any simple distribution is to arrange the scores in order from the highest to the lowest. See Figure 20.2.

No. of Books	Tally Marks	F
10	I	1
9	I	1
8	II	2
7	III	3
6	IIIIIII	7
5	IIII	4
4	II	2
3	I	1
2	I	1

Figure 20.1 Number of books each child read in October.

X
9
8
7
5
4

Figure 20.2 Five science quiz scores arranged in descending order.

Notice that the scores now range from 9 at the top to 4 at the bottom.

Since there are five scores, $N = 5$. To find the median you simply substitute the value of N for N in the formula (Equation 20.2).

$$\frac{N+1}{2} = \frac{5+1}{2} = \frac{6}{2} = 3 \tag{20.2}$$

Therefore, the median is the *third score* from the top of the distribution; the median of this distribution is 7.

> **Tip:** When determining the median in this manner, you can count down from the top of the distribution or up from the bottom. Either will work.

Now, let's say that we have a simple distribution with an *even* number of scores: 15, 17, 18, 12, 13, and 11, such as the quiz scores from Mr. Smither's 10th-grade math class. Again, we first arrange the scores in order from the highest to the lowest. See Figure 20.3.

We then apply our formula $N = 6$ (Equation 20.3).

$$\frac{N+1}{2} = \frac{6+1}{2} = \frac{7}{2} = 3.5 \tag{20.3}$$

Therefore, the median is halfway *between the third and fourth scores.* Since the third score is 15 and the fourth score is 13, the score halfway between those two scores is 14, which is the median. You will notice that the median of this distribution, 14, is not a score that was earned by any individual. However, it is the score that divides the distribution in half. Sometimes measures of central tendency are scores that were not earned by any of the students.

X
18
17
15
13
12
11

Figure 20.3 Six math quiz scores arranged in descending order.

> **Definition**
> The **median** is the middle score in a set of ranked scores.

Complex Frequency Distributions

Calculating the median for a large or complex distribution is somewhat more difficult. In this case you must recognize that the median is also the 50th percentile. You will have to develop a full frequency distribution and often will need to interpolate (estimate) to find the exact median. **Interpolation means to estimate where a theoretical score will fit between two real scores**. The interpolation formula is shown below (Equation 20.4).

$$\frac{X - X_{ll}}{i} = \frac{c\% - c\%_{ll}}{\%_{width}} \tag{20.4}$$

Here the X represents the raw score that corresponds to the 50th percentile, the score we want to find. The X_{ll} is the lower limit in the X (raw score) column. The i is the interval width in the X column. It will often be 1 unless you have a grouped frequency distribution. The $c\%$ is the cumulative frequency of 50, the 50th percentile (a value of 50). The $c\%_{ll}$ is the lower limit in the $c\%$ column, the highest value under 50. The $\%_{width}$ is the width of the interval in the $c\%$ column.

> **Definitions**
>
> | | |
> |---|---|
> | X | 50th percentile score—What you want to find. |
> | X_{ll} | lower limit of the interval in the X column |
> | i | width of the interval in the X column (frequently $= 1$) |
> | $c\%$ | 50th percentile—a value of 50 |
> | $c\%_{ll}$ | cumulative percent of the lower limit |
> | $\%_{width}$ | width of the interval in the $c\%$ column |

To solve for X, you need to rearrange the interpolation formula as follows (Equation 20.5):

$$X = \frac{i \times (c\% - c\%_{ll})}{\%_{width}} + X_{ll} \tag{20.5}$$

Take a look at Figure 20.4, which includes an expanded frequency distribution of the scores that Mrs. Wan's 20 chemistry students earned on their last chemistry quiz.

You will notice that columns for cumulative frequency (CF), cumulative proportion (CP), and cumulative percent (C%), also known as percentile rank, have been added. Each column was calculated using the procedures described in the previous chapter.

The CF column represents the number of students that had that score or a lower score. By examining the CF column from Figure 20.4, you will notice that 10 students had scores of 11 or lower. The CP column represents the proportion of students who

X		F	P	%	CF	CP	C%
15	I	1	.05	5	20	1.00	100
14	II	2	.10	10	19	.95	95
13	III	3	.15	15	17	.85	85
12	IIII	4	.20	20	14	.70	70
11	III	3	.15	15	10	.50	50
10	II	2	.10	10	7	.35	35
9	II	2	.10	10	5	.25	25
8	II	2	.10	10	3	.15	15
7		0	0	0	1	.05	5
6	I	1	.05	5	1	.05	5
5		0	0	0	0	0	0
4		0	0	0	0	0	0
3		0	0	0	0	0	0
2		0	0	0	0	0	0
1		0	0	0	0	0	0

Figure 20.4 Expanded frequency distribution of chemistry quiz scores.

had that score or lower. In Figure 20.4 the CP column tells us that .50 (or one half) of the students had scores of 11 or lower. The C% (also known as percentile rank) column represents the percent of students who had that score or lower.

> *Definitions*
>
> **CF (Cumulative Frequency)**—the number of students who had that score or lower.
>
> **CP (Cumulative Proportion)**—the proportion of students who had that score or lower.
>
> **C% (Cumulative Percent)**—the percentage of students who had that score or lower (also known as percentile rank).

Look again at the distribution in Figure 20.4. Since a 50 showed up in the C% column, we do not need to use the interpolation formula in this case. We can read the median (the 50th percentile) directly from the frequency distribution. At first glance you might guess that the median is a raw score of 11. However, an inspection of the frequency distribution will reveal that there were 7 scores less than 11 and 10 scores greater than 11. Since the score, 11, does not divide the distribution exactly in half, it cannot be the median. You might recall from the previous chapter, I mentioned that cumulative frequencies apply to the upper limit of the interval. The score, 11, really represents all potential scores from 10.50 to 11.4999. The upper limit of the interval (rounded off) is 11.5, which corresponds to the 50th percentile. The median, therefore, is 11.5. You can check that by counting the number of scores above and below 11.5. Ten scores are less than 11.5 and 10 scores are greater than 11.5. It is the median because it divides the distribution in half.

For that last frequency distribution, we did not have to use the interpolation formula. Now let's try a distribution where interpolation will be required. It is based on the

X	F	CF	CP	C%
50	1	25	1.00	100
49	2	24	.96	96
48	2	22	.88	88
47	1	20	.80	80
46	3	19	.76	76
45	4	16	.64	64
44	2	12	.48	48
43	3	10	.40	40
42	5	7	.28	28
41	1	2	.08	8
40	1	1	.04	4

Figure 20.5 Test scores for 25 students on an English test.

scores of 25 students who took a 50-point English test. The scores ranged from a low of 40 to a high of 50. See Figure 20.5.

Note that in this distribution there is no 50 in the C% column. Therefore, we will have to interpolate to find the median, the 50th percentile. In the C% column the two numbers closest to 50 are 64 and 48. These will represent our upper and lower limits in the C% column. We know that the 64th percentile corresponds to a raw score of 45.5 (the upper limit of the interval in the raw score column) and the 48th percentile corresponds to a raw score of 44.5 (the upper limit of that interval). Therefore the median (the 50th percentile) must be somewhere between 44.5 and 45.5. These two numbers represent the lower and upper limits in the raw score column. We can calculate the median by using the interpolation formula. See Figure 20.6.

In this problem the X is the median, the value for which we are looking. The i represents the interval in the raw-score column. We know that the median is between 44.5 and 45.5, so $i = 1$. The $c\%$ is the 50th percentile, a value of 50. The $c\%_{ll}$ is the lower limit in the $c\%$ column. In this case it is 48. The $\%_{width}$ is the interval width in the $c\%$

$$X = \frac{i \times (c\% - c\%_{ll})}{\%_{width}} + X_{ll}$$

X = the median (that for which we are looking)

i = the interval from 44.5 to 45.5, or 1.0

$c\%$ = the 50th percentile, or 50

$c\%_{ll}$ = the lower limit in the C% column, or 48

$\%_{width}$ = the interval width in the $c\%$ column, $64 - 48 = 16$

X_{ll} = the lower limit in the X column, or 44.5

As we substitute these values into the formula we get the following:

$$X = \frac{1.0 \times (50 - 48)}{16} + 44.5$$

$$X = \frac{1.0 \times 2}{16} + 44.5$$

$$X = \frac{2}{16} + 44.5 = .125 + 44.5 = 44.625$$

Therefore, the median is 44.625

Figure 20.6 Application of the interpolation formula to find the median.

column. It is the distances from the value just above 50 to the one just below 50. In this case it will be 64 minus 48 which equals 16. Finally, the X_{ll} is the lower limit in the raw score column. In this case it is 44.5. When we substitute each of these values into the formula, we compute that the median is 44.625.

You will be happy to know that you will not often be asked to calculate a median by hand. Most computer programs that handle data will do it for you.

Mean

The *mean*—or the arithmetic mean, to be exact—is what is most often meant when individuals use the generic word "average." Although the median divides the frequency polygon in half, the mean is the balancing point for the distribution, as if it were on a seesaw. To compute the mean we simply add up all of the scores and then divide that total by the number of scores. For a *population* we designate the mean using the Greek letter mu (μ).

The formula for determining the mean is as follows (Equation 20.6):

$$\mu_X = \frac{\Sigma X}{N} \tag{20.6}$$

This reads, the population mean of the scores (Xs, the individual scores) is equal to the sum of the scores (the Xs) divided by the number of scores (N). For a *sample*, today we most frequently see the sample mean designated by the uppercase letter M. The formula for the sample mean is as follows (Equation 20.7):

$$M = \frac{\Sigma X}{n} \tag{20.7}$$

The mean of a sample is the sum of the scores divided by the number of scores.

> **Definition**
>
> The **mean**, more correctly referred to as the arithmetic mean, is calculated by dividing the sum of all the scores by the number of scores.

Suppose that a small class of 10 students ($N = 10$) has the following scores on a history exam: 78, 85, 92, 81, 90, 88, 71, 75, 81, and 84. To compute the mean we must first add up all of the scores. In this case $\Sigma X = 825$. Since $N = 10$, the problem can be written as follows (Equation 20.8):

$$\mu_X = \frac{\Sigma X}{N} = \frac{78 + 85 + \ldots + 84}{10} = \frac{825}{10} = 82.5 \qquad \text{The mean is 82.5.} \tag{20.8}$$

You need to exercise more caution, however, when computing a mean from a frequency distribution. It is easy to become confused. Let me demonstrate with a simple frequency distribution on quiz scores from another science quiz (see Figure 20.7).

X	F
10	2
9	3
8	4
7	7
6	4
5	3
4	2

Figure 20.7 Frequency distribution of science quiz scores.

X	F	FX
10	2	20
9	3	27
8	4	32
7	7	49
6	4	24
5	3	15
4	2	8

Figure 20.8 Expanded frequency distribution of science quiz scores.

The first step in computing the mean is to compute the sum of the scores, ΣX. How do you compute the ΣX? You might be tempted to simply add up the X column: $10 + 9 + 8 + 7 + 6 + 5 + 4$. However, in that case, you would have added only seven scores. Two students had scores of 10; three students had scores of 9, and so on. If you add up the F (frequency) column, you will note that there are a total of 25 scores ($N = 25$). In order to obtain the ΣX you will need to add up 25 scores. Therefore, you need to develop a new column where you multiply the score (X) column by the number of students who had that score (F). We will label that new column FX (for frequency times the score). See the new column in Figure 20.8.

As you look at Figure 20.8 you will notice that multiplying the students' scores (from the X column) by the number of students who earned that score (from the F column) gives us a product that represents the sum of the scores for all of the students who earned that score. For example, three students earned scores of 9. The FX column gives us the sum of those three scores of 9. If you now add up this last column (FX) you will get the sum of all 25 students' scores. In this case $\Sigma X = 175$ and the mean is 7 (Equation 20.9)

$$\mu_X = \frac{\Sigma X}{N} = \frac{\Sigma FX}{N} = \frac{2(10) + 3(9) + \ldots + 2(4)}{25} = \frac{175}{25} = 7 \qquad (20.9)$$

In other chapters, you will learn that we can use the mean to help interpret and evaluate test scores and student performance.

DEVIATION SCORES

There is another type of score that is based on the mean and that we need to use in the next chapter to calculate variances and standard deviations. These new scores are known as deviation scores.

One of the most interesting characteristics of the mean is that the sum of all the deviations (distances) from the mean will always equal zero (Equations 20.10 and 20.11).

$$\Sigma(X - M) = 0 \qquad \text{for samples} \qquad (20.10)$$

$$\Sigma(X - \mu_X) = 0 \qquad \text{for populations} \qquad (20.11)$$

That is, if you take each score (X), subtract the mean (M or μ_x) from it, and sum all of the deviation scores, the sum will equal zero, as a result of the balancing property of the mean. The positive deviations will exactly balance the negative deviations. In other words, the sum of all of the positive deviations (all of the scores above the mean) will exactly equal the sum of all the negative deviations (all of the scores below the mean).

Definition

Deviation scores are based on the distance that each score is either above (+) or below (−) the mean.

Look at the following example to see how the balancing property works. Let's say that we have a simple distribution: 3, 4, 4, 5, 7, 9, and 10. First, we need to compute the mean using this formula (Equation 20.12).

$$\mu_X = \frac{\Sigma X}{N} = \frac{42}{7} = 6 \qquad (20.12)$$

Next, we can develop an abbreviated frequency distribution with a column for deviation scores (see Figure 20.9). In this example the X column represents the raw scores. The $X - \mu_X$ (raw score minus the mean) column represents the deviation scores.

The positive deviations ($4 + 3 + 1$) add up to 8, and the negative deviations ($-1-1-2-3$) add up to −8. The sum equals zero, as it always will.

X	$X - \mu_X$
10	$10 - 6 = 4$
9	$9 - 6 = 3$
7	$7 - 6 = 1$
5	$5 - 6 = -1$
4	$4 - 6 = -2$
4	$4 - 6 = -2$
3	$3 - 6 = -3$

Figure 20.9 Deviation scores example.

We use the script X (χ) to denote a deviation score. Therefore we can express the previous formula as (Equations 20.13 and 20.14):

$$\Sigma(X - M) = \Sigma\chi = 0 \qquad \text{for samples} \qquad (20.13)$$

$$\Sigma(X - \mu_X) = \Sigma\chi = 0 \qquad \text{for populations.} \qquad (20.14)$$

These read, the sum of each score minus the mean is equal to the sum of the deviation scores which equals 0 for either samples or populations.

Knowing how to compute deviation scores is important because we use them to compute variances and standard deviations, which we will use in many classroom settings.

CHARACTERISTICS OF CENTRAL TENDENCY MEASURES

Stability of Central Tendency Measures

We are frequently interested in populations even when only samples are available. We draw a sample, compute a statistic (e.g. the sample mean), and use that statistic to estimate the population parameter (e.g. the population mean). However, as was mentioned earlier, sample statistics display sampling fluctuation; that is, the sample mode, median, and mean will each vary from sample to sample. However, not all sample statistics fluctuate in the same way. Some are very unpredictable, whereas others vary little from sample to sample.

The sample mode is the least stable of the three measures of central tendency discussed in this chapter. The mode is the most common score, which frequently varies from sample to sample in a rather unpredictable manner (especially for small samples). Imagine that we are going from one 1st-grade classroom to another in an elementary school and we are to ask each 1st grader how many pets live in his or her home. The most common response (the mode) in one classroom might be three pets, whereas in another classroom the modal response might be only one pet. Unless we use very large samples, the mode frequently varies from one sample to another. The median, being a middle score, is somewhat more stable, varying less from one sample to another than will the mode. However, the most stable of the three measures is the mean. It is the least likely to be affected by sampling fluctuation. Because of its stability, the sample mean is the preferred measure of central tendency whenever a reasonable choice is available.

If you would like to see this stability characteristic in action you can try an experiment. Write out the numbers 1 through 10 on small index cards. Place all of the cards into a container and mix them up. Draw one card, record the number, and replace the card in the container. Repeat this procedure until you have a sample of eight numbers (you will get some repetition at times). This is your first sample. Continue repeating the same procedure until you have 10 samples of eight numbers. Then compute the mode, the median, and the mean for each sample. You will find that frequently the mode will vary the most from sample to sample, the median will vary somewhat less, and the mean will vary the least often.

Uses of Central Tendency Measures

Although the mean should be used whenever a choice of central tendency measures is reasonably available, there are times when it is more appropriate to use the other measures. The mode, for example, is sometimes used with numeric data. However, it is often the only reasonable way to simplify categorical data. Let's say that we have a class of 25 students. Fourteen students have brown hair, six are blonds, two are redheads, and three are unclassifiable. The most common hair color, the modal hair color, is brown. With categorical data we have names (here we used hair color) rather than numbers. We cannot compute medians and means without meaningful numbers.

The median is sometimes used because it has one distinct advantage over the mean. It is not affected very much by extreme scores. Let's say that you are visiting a friend's home and are impressed with the neighborhood in which he or she lives. So, you ask your friend, "What is the average family income of your neighbors?" Your friend tells you that there are 20 homes in the neighborhood. Nineteen of the families earn between $60,000 and $95,000 per year. However, the last family did very well last year and earned $1.5 million. The mean income for these 20 families is about $152,000 per year, a poor measure of the typical family income for the neighborhood. However, the median family income would be about $78,000 per year, much more indicative of the typical family income. Of course, this distribution displays a very powerful positive skew because of the one family that earned so much more than the other families. That very large income, the extreme score, makes a big difference when you compute the mean. The mean income, $152,000 per year, is not a very good representation of a typical income for the neighborhood since it is more than 1.5 times greater than the second highest income. Here, the median is a better measure of central tendency because it is more representative of a typical income. Therefore, with skewed distributions the sample median is often the preferred measure of central tendency. For this reason, we almost always report incomes using the median. You might also find that the median is a better measure of central tendency when you give a quiz or test that is highly skewed. If most students score quite high and only one or two score very low, the mean will be lower than anticipated because of the two very low quiz scores. In this case the median will be more representative of a typical score.

Table 20.1 A comparison of measures of central tendency

Mode	* the score occurring most frequently
	* often used with categorical and discrete data
	* displays the least stability from sample to sample
Median	* the middle score in a list of ranked scores
	* the 50th percentile
	* generally most appropriate with skewed distributions
	* displays moderate stability from sample to sample
Mean	* the balancing point of a distribution
	* frequently most appropriate for relatively symmetrical distributions
	* generally the preferred measure of central tendency
	* displays the greatest stability from sample to sample

Central Tendency and Form

You will remember that there are three characteristics of frequency distributions: form (the shape of the distribution, discussed in Chapter 19), central tendency (discussed in this chapter), and variability (to be discussed in Chapter 21). The three characteristics are generally independent of one another; however, there are some subtle relationships between central tendency and form. For example, the mean, median, and mode will all be equal to one another for any symmetrical, unimodal distribution (e.g. a bell-shaped distribution). In addition, the mean and median will always be equal for any symmetrical distribution (e.g. a U-shaped distribution). However, things change considerably for a skewed distribution.

With unimodal skewed distributions the three measures of central tendency will differ from one another. As we saw in the family income example, the mean will be the most affected by the extreme scores and will, therefore, be pulled out toward the tail of the distribution. Of course, the mode will be at the other end under the hump in the distribution. The median will fall between the mode and the mean.

These relationships are interesting and prove useful. For example, if I reported to you that the mean, median, and mode of a distribution were all 43, you would then know that the distribution is both unimodal and symmetrical. For another example, if the mode of a distribution is 79, the median is 75, and the mean is 70, we know that we are dealing with a negatively skewed distribution. You might find that with an easy test, where most students had high scores and relatively few students had very low scores. For a very difficult test the mode might be 45, the median 50, and the mean 55. Here, most students earned low scores and very few earned high scores. This would be a positively skewed distribution.

We have now examined how to organize data into frequency distributions, to display data in graphic form, and to summarize data in terms of central tendency. In our next chapter we will examine variability in frequency distributions.

SUMMARY

Measures of central tendency include the mode, the median, and the mean. The mode is the score that appears most frequently and can often be determined by inspection. The median is the middle score in a list of ranked scores and may require the use of a cumulative frequency distribution for its calculation. The mean, also frequently known as the average, is based on the sum of all of the scores divided by the number of scores. The mode is used most often with categorical data; the median is the most appropriate with a skewed distribution; whereas the mean is likely to be used most often in the classroom and is appropriate in many classroom situations. The mean also happens to be the most stable measure of central tendency when samples are used to estimate population characteristics.

EXERCISES

1. There are four separate distributions (sets of data) listed below (labeled A, B, C, and D). Each is a set of quiz scores. A, B, and C each represent quiz scores from a small class. Data set D represents quiz scores for three high school biology classes combined. For each distribution compute:

a. the mean;
b. the mode;
c. the median.

Note that distributions A, B, and C are unorganized raw data, whereas distribution D is an organized frequency distribution.

A	B	C	D	
7	3	12	X	F
4	5	15	9	3
3	12	17	8	6
3	9	13	7	7
6	4	15	6	9
9	7	11	5	12
5	6	15	4	7
8	8	19	3	3
	11	15	2	1

2. For distribution C, compute $\Sigma\chi$. [Remember $\Sigma\chi = \Sigma (X–M)$.]
3. Frank Jones, a high school math teacher from Dubuque, Iowa, read in his local paper about a national commission that looked at math achievement scores for high school students reported by the Department of Education of each of the 50 states. The article in the paper said that about two thirds of the states reported that their students were performing above the national average. The newspaper article also provided a web address where the entire report could be downloaded.

Mr. Jones became curious because he felt that there must be something wrong with how this report had been interpreted, although he wasn't certain why he felt that it was wrong. He decided to download the entire 175-page report to see if he could determine for himself what the report actually said and what it actually meant. Unfortunately, a thunderstorm had shut down the high-speed internet provider that Mr. Jones used and the provider reported that it would be several days until service was fully restored and Mr. Jones could download the report.

While he waited those several days until he could obtain the report, he frequently thought about it. He was certain that there was something wrong, but just couldn't put his finger on the problem. The third night after reading the newspaper article he slept restlessly, but suddenly awoke at 4:00 a.m. and realized that he had figured out what was wrong.

a. What was the problem that he detected?
b. What could have contributed to the problem?

SPOTLIGHT ON THE CLASSROOM

Anna Kline is a 6th-grade teacher in a suburban Maryland school district. Early in the year she teaches her students a unit on geometry (shapes and angles) that is a follow-up to a topic that they typically cover near the end of fifth grade. This year some of the students appear to be doing well, but a number of others are clearly confused. At the point that she would normally give her first exam on the topic, she decides to go forward with the exam even though she is aware that many of the students are still confused. She tells her class that this is a practice exam and will not affect their grade, but asks that they do their best. She has decided to use the test primarily as a diagnostic tool.

When Ms. Kline scores the 100-point test, she finds that the students display a wide variety of scores from a low of 15 to a high of 99. She computes the mean for the test which turns out to be about 50. Although that tells her by itself that the students, on average, performed poorly, it does not tell the full story. Then she computes the median which is 26.50. Since the median is well below the mean, she knows that she has a highly skewed distribution. Finally, she develops a grouped frequency distribution, which is the most revealing of all. Clearly, she has two fairly distinct groups of students. One group of students performed very poorly and does not appear to have much background knowledge about shapes and angles. The other group did very well on the test and appears to have considerably more background.

Ms. Kline discovers that the students who are struggling with geometry all came from the same 5th-grade class last year. As she checks into this she finds out that their 5th-grade teacher required emergency surgery late last year and was out for the last six weeks of school. It had taken a couple of weeks until the school district could get a fully qualified substitute to help the class complete the year. In the transition, the students were not taught the typical 5th-grade material on shapes and angles.

Now Ms. Kline realizes that she will need to provide the students who are struggling with a review unit on the material that they missed last year. She rearranges her schedule for her math lessons so that she will be able to provide the review material and still be back on her typical schedule by the beginning of the second marking period.

STUDY TIPS

Learning Technical Terminology

Many college courses, including courses on measurement and statistics, involve a great deal of technical terminology. Technical terminology involves words that are sometimes used in a specific field. It can also include terms that have a variety of meanings, but are used in a much more specific way in that field. Success in a technical course involves becoming proficient with the technical terminology.

One technique that many students have found to be useful is to develop and use word cards. Keep a stack of blank 3″ × 5″ index cards with you. As you come to a technical term while reading a chapter, prepare a word card. Put the word on the front of the card and the definition on the back. You can also make word cards on a computer. Set up a table with two columns and five rows per page. Put the words in the left column and the definitions in the right column. Then print, cut the rows into strips, and fold over each strip to form word cards. You can tape or staple them so that they form word cards. Word cards for each chapter can be kept together and bound with rubber bands. A stack of word cards is frequently small enough that you can carry it around with you in your pocket, your purse, or your back pack. Every now and then, when you have a few minutes to spare, you can practice your word cards. Read the word on the front of the card and try to say the definition from memory. Then check the back to see if you were correct. When reviewing the word cards, it is even more effective if you recite the definitions out loud or write them as you might do on a quiz. You should also shuffle the cards between practice sessions so you do not learn them in order.

For a topic like measurement and statistics, don't forget to make word cards for the many symbols such as μ_X or σ_x^2. They are also considered technical terminology.[2]

NOTES

1. Typically, a significant peak means any score that clearly stands out as occurring more frequently than surrounding scores.
2. This material has been adapted from Van Blerkom (2009).

21

VARIABILITY

How Spread Out Are the Scores?

INTRODUCTION

As I mentioned in the previous chapter, frequency distributions have three character-istics—form, central tendency, and variability—which are largely independent of one another. Knowing two of the characteristics does not typically tell you anything about the third. We have discussed both form and central tendency. We now need to discuss variability or dispersion.

We will discuss several measures of variability. These will include several forms of the range, the variance, and the standard deviation. We will also discuss how to compute each.

THE VARIABILTY QUESTION

The variability question is, "How spread out are the scores?" We can express central tendency as a single point on the score scale—"What is a typical score?" However, we express variability as a distance in the score scale—"How spread apart are the scores?"

Let's look at an example. I used to go bowling with two good bowlers, Steady Freddy and Wavering Wayne. Here are some recent scores for each bowler:

- Steady Freddy   180, 185, 170, 183, 190, 177, and 175;
- Wavering Wayne   180, 210, 150, 140, 220, 130, and 230.

If we plot the scores for each bowler, we will discover several similarities. Both distribu-tions are symmetrical. They also display the same mean, 180. However, if you had to choose between these two bowlers and needed someone who could bowl consistently better than 170, who would you choose?

The difference between these two bowlers is their variability. Freddy's scores are bunched up together. He consistently has bowling scores between 170 and 190.

However, Wayne's scores are considerably more spread out, with scores ranging from a low of 130 to a high of 230. Although this example may be somewhat exaggerated, it does point out the issue of spread—also known as "dispersion" or "variability." We have several measures of variability, which include several types of range, the variance, and the standard deviation.

Ranges

The Simple Range

There are several ways to measure the range of scores. The simplest measure is known as the *range* (or the simple range), which is the distance from the upper limit of the highest score to the lowest limit of the lowest score. For example, Steady Freddy's highest score was 190 and his lowest score was 170. Therefore, the real upper limit of his highest score is 190.5 and the real lower limit of his lowest score is 169.5. Now we can compute the range (Equation 21.1).

$$\text{Range} = 190.5 - 169.5 = 21 \tag{21.1}$$

Definition

The **range** is the distance from the upper limit of the highest score to the lower limit of the lowest score.

The range is very simple to compute. However, it is based on the two most extreme scores, which are frequently atypical. In the case of test scores, it is based on two students: the one who performed the best and the one who performed the worst. Perhaps the student who did the best put in an extraordinary amount of time into preparing for the exam, much more than he or she would do normally. On the other hand, perhaps the student who performed the least well actually forgot about the test and came to class totally unprepared. Since these two extreme scores can easily vary from one administration of a test to another, the range can display enormous variability from one sample to another. The range is most useful to give you a quick, but dirty, measure of spread.

D_9-D_1 (*The Distance Between the 90th Percentile to the 10th Percentile*)

Since extreme scores have a negative effect on the stability of the range, some statisticians have suggested alternative forms of the range that avoid the extreme scores. One suggestion is to measure the range of scores from the 90th percentile (also known as the 9th decile or D_9) to the 10th percentile (also known as the 1st decile or D_1). This eliminates the highest and lowest 10% of the scores and should be more stable than the simple range. However, I cannot recall ever having seen it used.

Semi-Interquartile Range

Another method, which sounds quite strange but is occasionally used, is known as the *semi-interquartile range*. The first quartile (q_1) is the 25th percentile. The second quartile (q_2) is the 50th percentile, also known as the 5th decile and the median. The third quartile (q_3) is the 75th percentile.[1] The semi-interquartile range is essentially the average of the distance from the median to the first and third quartiles. The formula is quite simple (Equation 21.2).

$$\text{Semi-interquartile range} = \frac{q_3 - q_1}{2} \qquad (21.2)$$

It will certainly be more stable than the other two types of range. Although it seems quite strange, I have actually seen it used several times. Perhaps some statisticians like it because it is very close in magnitude (size) to the standard deviation, which we will discuss next. Furthermore, it may have some distinct advantages when attempting to make certain interpretations from data. It has been suggested that the semi-interquartile range is the appropriate measure of spread when reporting a median.

> **Definition**
>
> The **semi-interquartile range** is the average of the distance from the median to the first and third quartiles.

Variance and Standard Deviation

Another approach to the spread of scores is to use deviation scores. On average, how far does each score deviate from the mean? You might remember, from the previous chapter, that we defined deviation scores (χ) as follows (Equation 21.3):

$$\chi = X - M \quad \text{(the raw score minus the mean).} \qquad (21.3)$$

You will also likely remember that the sum of the deviation scores equals zero. When added together, the positive and negative deviations will always cancel each other out (Equation 21.4).

$$\Sigma\chi = 0 \qquad (21.4)$$

Although it would be nice to be able to compute the mean of the deviation scores, it will always equal zero. To compute a mean we first need to sum the scores and, as I just mentioned, the sum of the deviation scores will always equal zero.

In reality, when considering variability, we are interested in how far the scores deviate from the mean, and not whether they are above or below the mean. Therefore, if we could simply get rid of those pesky negative signs in front of the negative deviations we could compute a mean. One approach would be to use absolute numbers and to compute the mean of the absolute deviations. The formula would look like this (Equation 21.5).

$$\text{Mean absolute deviation} = \frac{\Sigma|\chi|}{N} \qquad (21.5)$$

This would give us a nice interpretable deviation score. However, mathematicians and statisticians are reluctant to use absolute numbers because they become problematic when we use them in other formulas.

Variance

Therefore, we need to find another way to get rid of those pesky negative signs. Another way to do so is to square the deviation scores. You may remember that all numbers, whether positive or negative, become positive when squared. Therefore, we can simply square all of the deviation scores, find their sum, and compute a mean. The mean of the squared deviations is known as the *variance*. The formula for the population variance is as follows (Equation 21.6):

$$\sigma_X^2 = \frac{\Sigma(X - \mu_X)^2}{N} = \frac{\Sigma\chi^2}{N} \quad (\sigma \text{ is the Greek letter sigma.}) \tag{21.6}$$

We designate the variance as "sigma squared" since it is the mean of the squared deviations. This is known as the definitional formula, which is used only occasionally to actually compute the variance. Later, I will describe a computational formula, which is the one that I recommend using when actually computing a variance.

> **Definition**
> The **variance** is the mean of the squared deviations from the mean.

It turns out that there is a minor difference in the formulas for the population and sample variances. The formula for the sample variance typically has $n - 1$ in the denominator rather than just n. The reasons for this are quite complicated and are still debated. However, if we calculate the sample variance with the same formula used to compute the population variance, and if we wanted to use the sample variance to estimate the population variance, then using n in the denominator tends to give us a variance estimate that is too small. The basic reason for this is related to the sizes of populations and samples. As population and sample sizes increase, the variance tends to increase. We are more likely to get extreme scores with a large population than with a small sample. The $n - 1$ in the denominator is essentially a correction factor so that the sample variance is a better estimate of the population variance. Samples are typically much smaller than populations and are simply less likely to contain extreme scores. Therefore, the definitional formula for the sample variance is as follows (Equation 21.7):

$$s_X^2 = \frac{\Sigma(X - M)^2}{n - 1} = \frac{\Sigma\chi^2}{n - 1} \tag{21.7}$$

We use the lowercase s^2 to represent the sample variance.

Standard Deviation

The variance is a very powerful measure of variability, is widely used throughout measurement and statistics, and is used in several of the measurement chapters.

However, it is based on a squared scale and is therefore difficult to interpret directly. To bring it back to the original scale we simply have to take the square root of it. The square root of the variance is known as the *standard deviation*. The definitional formula for the *population* standard deviation is as follows (Equation 21.8):

$$\sigma_X = \sqrt{\sigma_X^2} = \sqrt{\frac{\Sigma(X - \mu_x)^2}{N}} = \sqrt{\frac{\Sigma\chi^2}{N}} \tag{21.8}$$

The definitional formula for the *sample* standard deviation is as follows (Equation 21.9):

$$s_X = \sqrt{s_X^2} = \sqrt{\frac{\Sigma(X - M)^2}{n - 1}} = \sqrt{\frac{\Sigma\chi^2}{n - 1}} \tag{21.9}$$

The standard deviation is a parameter (for populations) and a statistic (for samples). It can be interpreted as an average deviation and is an excellent measure of spread. Of course, a larger standard deviation represents a set of scores that are more spread out, whereas a smaller standard deviation represents a set of scores that are less spread out. We will find the standard deviation useful in many ways in both measurement and statistics.

Definition
The **standard deviation** is the square root of the mean of the squared deviations from the mean.

Computational Formulas for the Variance and the Standard Deviation

The formulas that I just gave you are definitional formulas. However, they are frequently rather cumbersome to use. In many cases, the mean is not a whole number. It is more likely to be a decimal, such as 12.584. To use the definitional formulas you must start out by subtracting the mean from each score. When the mean is a decimal number it makes the subtraction process more cumbersome, and we begin to introduce error because of rounding. There is a computational formula that uses only whole numbers and is, therefore, not subject to rounding error. In addition, it is easier to use with a hand-held calculator.

Essentially, the computational formula is for the numerator of the equation, for the computation of the sum of the squared deviation scores. It looks like this (Equation 21.10).

$$\Sigma\chi^2 = \Sigma(X - M)^2 = \Sigma X^2 - \frac{(\Sigma X)^2}{n} \tag{21.10}$$

The *computational* formula for the *population variance* therefore becomes (Equation 21.11)

$$\sigma_X^2 = \frac{\Sigma(X - \mu_X)^2}{N} = \frac{\Sigma X^2 - \frac{(\Sigma X)^2}{N}}{N} \qquad (21.11)$$

The *computational* formula for the *sample variance* becomes (Equation 21.12)

$$s_X^2 = \frac{\Sigma(X - M)^2}{n - 1} = \frac{\Sigma X^2 - \frac{(\Sigma X)^2}{n}}{n - 1} \qquad (21.12)$$

The numerators in both computational formulas are essentially the same. Only the denominators differ. We use N in the denominator for the population formula and $n - 1$ in the denominator for the sample formula.

The *computational* formula for the *population standard deviation* becomes (Equation 21.13)

$$\sigma_X = \sqrt{\frac{\Sigma(X - \mu_X)^2}{N}} = \sqrt{\frac{\Sigma X^2 - \frac{(\Sigma X)^2}{N}}{N}} \qquad (21.13)$$

Finally, the *computational* formula for the *sample standard deviation* becomes (Equation 21.14)

$$s_X = \sqrt{\frac{\Sigma(X - M)^2}{n - 1}} = \sqrt{\frac{\Sigma X^2 - \frac{(\Sigma X)^2}{n}}{n - 1}} \qquad (21.14)$$

Although these formulas look rather complex, they are really not difficult to use. Let's try a couple of examples. First, let's try a set of 12 scores based on a 20-item quiz. The scores are as follows (listed from highest to lowest): 20, 19, 18, 17, 16, 16, 15, 15, 14, 13, 12, 11.

Let's list these in a column and let's add a second column of each score squared, which we will need to compute the variance and standard deviation (see Figure 21.1).

You will notice that when we add up the X column we get the ΣX, which is 186. When we add up the X^2 column we get ΣX^2, which equals 2,966. Since this is a class of 12 students, we will consider it a population with $N = 12$. We now have everything that we need to compute the population variance and standard deviation (Equation 21.15).

$$\sigma_X^2 = \frac{\Sigma X^2 - \frac{(\Sigma X)^2}{N}}{N} = \frac{2,966 - \frac{(186)^2}{12}}{12} = \frac{2,966 - \frac{34,596}{12}}{12}$$

$$= \frac{2,966 - 2,883}{12} = \frac{83}{12} = 6.917 \qquad (21.15)$$

X	X²
20	400
19	361
18	324
17	289
16	256
16	256
15	225
15	225
14	196
13	169
12	144
11	121
$\Sigma X = 186$	$\Sigma X^2 = 2,966$

Figure 21.1 Computational example 1 for variance and standard deviation.

We now have found that the variance is 6.917. To find the standard deviation we simply find the square root of the variance. Using a calculator makes each of these steps much easier (Equation 21.16).

$$\sigma_X = \sqrt{\sigma_X^2} = \sqrt{6.917} = 2.63 \tag{21.16}$$

The standard deviation is 2.63.

How do we know that this is correct? A simple way to estimate the standard deviation is to remember that it will almost always be between 1/6th and 1/3rd of the range. In this example the range would be $20.5 - 10.5 = 10$. One sixth of 10 is 1.67. One third of 10 is 3.33. Since 2.63 falls between 1.67 and 3.33, we can feel rather confident that we have computed the standard deviation correctly. At least, we have not made any significant computational errors.

Now let's try another example with a frequency distribution. Let's say that we have the results of 55 students who took a 50-point exam. Since this is one of five classes that took the same English exam, we will assume that this is a sample. Below you will find the frequency distribution. However, I have added several columns. You will eventually need the ΣX and the ΣX^2. You might recall that in order to obtain the ΣX from a frequency distribution, you needed to create a new column, $f \cdot X$. If you examine the frequency distribution you will note that two students had scores of 49, three students had scores of 48, and so on. In order to obtain the sum of the scores we must count 49 twice, 48 three times, and so on. The easiest way to do that is with a new column with the scores multiplied by the frequency (how often the scores occurred). If you then add up that new column it will give you the sum of the scores. In a similar way, you will need columns for X^2 and $f \cdot X^2$ so that you can obtain the sum of the squared scores. Be careful in developing the $f \cdot X^2$ column. First develop the X^2 column. Then multiply the values in that column by the corresponding values in the frequency (f) column. Summing that new column will give you the sum of X^2. (Do not square the values of the $f \cdot X$ column. To do so would actually give you the value for $f^2 \cdot X^2$, which you do not want.) That frequency distribution is shown in Figure 21.2.

You now have everything that you need to compute the sample variance and standard deviation (Equation 21.17).

$$s_X^2 = \frac{\Sigma X^2 - \dfrac{(\Sigma X)^2}{n}}{n-1} = \frac{102,307 - \dfrac{(2,365)^2}{55}}{55-1} = \frac{102,307 - \dfrac{5,593,225}{55}}{54}$$

$$= \frac{102,307 - 101,695}{54} = \frac{612}{54} = 11.333 \qquad (21.17)$$

You now have computed the variance. To find the standard deviation, you simply find the square root of the variance (Equation 21.18).

$$s_X = \sqrt{s_X^2} = \sqrt{11.333} = 3.37 \qquad (21.18)$$

As a final check, you can now compare our calculated standard deviation with our estimate. Remember, the standard deviation will typically be between 1/6th and 1/3rd of the range (Equation 21.19).

$$\text{Range} = 50.5 - 35.5 = 15 \qquad (21.19)$$

Since 1/6th of 15 is 2.50 and 1/3rd of 15 is 5.00, and since the standard deviation that we calculated (3.37) is between those two, you can safely assume that you are close to being correct.

X	f	f · X	X²	f · X²
50	1	50	2,500	2,500
49	2	98	2,401	4,802
48	3	144	2,304	6,912
47	3	141	2,209	6,627
46	4	184	2,116	8,464
45	5	225	2,025	10,125
44	6	264	1,936	11,616
43	7	301	1,849	12,943
42	6	252	1,764	10,584
41	5	205	1,681	8,405
40	4	160	1,600	6,400
39	3	117	1,521	4,563
38	3	114	1,444	4,332
37	2	74	1,369	2,738
36	1	36	1,296	1,296
	$n = 55$	$\Sigma X = 2,365$		$\Sigma X^2 = 102,307$

Figure 21.2 Computational example 2 for variance and standard deviation.

The variance and the standard deviation are likely to be the two most often used measures of variability. In most situations, if you were expected to provide a description of a set of scores, you would likely be expected to use the standard deviation as the measure of variability. In fact, the American Psychological Association (2001) recommends that a standard deviation always be reported any time a mean is reported.

SUMMARY

Frequency distributions can be described by three characteristics: their form (shape), central tendency, and variability. A variety of variability measures have been developed. Perhaps the simplest to compute, but statistically the least useful, measure of variability is the range. There are also variations of the range, such as the range from the 9th decile to the 1st decile and the semi-interquartile range. Statisticians and psychometricians tend to prefer the variance and the standard deviation as measures of variability because of their mathematical properties. The variance is the mean of the squared deviations from the mean. The standard deviation is the square root of the variance. There are slight differences in the formulas for these two measures depending on whether you are dealing with populations or with samples.

EXERCISES

1. Consider the following set of 100 test scores from Mr. Moran's 9th-grade biology classes.

Scores	F
98	3
97	7
96	6
95	4
94	5
93	5
92	8
91	12
90	10
89	8
88	7
87	5
86	4
85	6
84	4
83	3
82	1
81	2

a. What is the mean?
b. What is the median?
c. What is the mode?

    d. What is the range from D_9 to D_1?

    e. What is the semi-interquartile range?

    f. Plot a histogram and a frequency polygon from the data above.

2. For this set of population scores, compute the mean, the range, the variance, and the standard deviation.

Population Scores

Population Scores
15
17
14
13
12
11
9
8
20

3. For this frequency distribution, compute the mean, range, variance, and standard deviation.

Population Scores	F
20	2
19	3
18	5
17	6
16	7
15	4
14	3
13	2
12	1

4. For this frequency distribution from a sample, compute the mean, range, variance, and standard deviation.

Sample Scores	f
10	2
9	4
8	5
7	8
6	6
5	3
4	2

SPOTLIGHT ON THE CLASSROOM

Mr. James is a 5th-grade teacher at McCullough Upper Elementary School. This year his classroom is rather unique. He has some very high-performing students and some rather low-performing students.

When Mr. James administers a test to his class he always computes the mean to see how the children performed. However, this term he would like to try something different because of the wide spread of the scores. He would like to find a better way to display the results of the math test that he gave last week. Here are the results.

Test Score	F
20	5
19	3
18	3
17	2
16	0
15	0
14	0
13	1
12	1
11	4
10	2
9	2
8	1
7	1
6	0

No student had a score lower than 7.

How do you think that Mr. James could display the results of this test? How would you describe the results of this test?

STUDY TIPS

How to Prepare for an Exam

Although there are general exam preparation strategies that work in most courses, students need to use some different strategies when preparing for an exam in a measurement and statistics course. The specific preparation strategies that you might use to prepare for history exam, a literature exam, or even a general psychology exam will typically not work well with this material.

Here are some **general exam preparation strategies**.

- Determine the types of questions that will appear on the exam.
- Develop a study plan.
- Begin preparing four to five days ahead, breaking the material down into smaller units such as chapters. Spread out your studying.
- Prepare from both the textbook and from class notes.

- Use active review strategies where you actually work on the material. An example is self-testing.
- Prepare study sheets, word cards, question cards, and so on.

Here are some **specific strategies** that you could use in a measurement and statistics course.

- The best way to prepare to solve math problems is to actually practice with real problems. Redo homework problems from scratch, make up your own problems, or ask your instructor for suggestions on how to find additional problems to use for practice.
- Treat formulas and other technical material as you would definitions. Be prepared to produce them from memory and be prepared to explain what each part of the formula means.
- Set up a study group with three to five members of your class. Review exercises together; use each other as resources to explain difficult concepts; and quiz one another. Students who prepare in study groups frequently do better in technical courses.[2]

NOTES

1. In some fields the 1st quartile refers to all of the students who had the lowest 25% of the scores, the 2nd quartile refers to the next 25% of the scorers, and so on. However, when psychometricians say the 1st quartile, they simply mean the 25th percentile, and not the students who scored below that. This also follows for the 2nd and 3rd quartiles.
2. This material has been adapted from Van Blerkom (2009).

22

CORRELATION

INTRODUCTION

In previous chapters we have examined frequency distributions and ways to describe them, including descriptions of form, central tendency, and variability. These concepts are all important for the discussion of measurement in the first 17 chapters. However, there is still one important statistical concept that we need to fully understand measurement. That topic is correlation.

In this chapter we will discuss correlation, which is a way of describing how two variables are related to one another. Therefore, we will need to discuss the nature of bivariate distributions where we look at two variables simultaneously. We will discuss the use of z-scores as a starting point in understanding correlation. We will learn about the Pearson Product-Moment Correlation coefficient, how to compute it, and how to interpret it. Finally, we will look at correlation as a step in making predictions.

BIVARIATE STATISTICS

Up until this point we have been discussing frequency distributions concerning one variable at a time. This is known as *univariate* statistics. However, there are many times when we are interested in how two variables relate to one another. For example, are scores on the first examination in a course related to the scores on the second or subsequent examinations? Do students perform consistently on the course?

> **Definition**
> **Univariate** statistics deals with one variable at a time.

When we are examining two variables simultaneously, we are then dealing with a *bivariate* distribution. Of course, the two variables must be related to one another. Typically, the variables are related because we measured two characteristics from the same group of individuals. Each member of the group is measured on two different characteristics. We can label one variable X (sometimes known as the *predictor* variable) and the other variable as Y (sometimes known as the *criterion* variable). A correlation is a way to describe the relationship between the two variables.

Definition

Bivariate statistics deals with two variables simultaneously.

Let's say that we are collecting data on the first two exams in a course. Do students who obtain high scores on the first exam (X) also obtain high scores on the second exam (Y)? Do students who obtained low scores on the first exam also obtain low scores on the second exam? In other words, are scores on the first exam predictive of how students will perform on the second exam? Are the scores co-related to one another—hence, the term *correlation*.

We can plot a bivariate distribution with a diagram known as a scatter plot. Let's consider an example using scores from 10 students from an introduction to psychology course that I taught several years ago. Each exam had a total of 50 points (see Figure 22.1).

To plot this data, draw Cartesian coordinates with X (Exam 1) on the horizontal axis and Y (Exam 2) on the vertical axis. Next, place a point on the plot to represent each pair of scores. For example, student 1 had a score of 34 on Exam 1 and a score of 32 on Exam 2. Therefore, on the horizontal axis locate 34 (in this case you must estimate). Then move up until you are at 32 on the vertical axis. Place a dot at that point. That dot represents the first student. Then, repeat that procedure for each of the other students. When you have placed a point for each student, you have created a scatter plot.

The scatter plot may appear to be a set of randomly placed dots that show no discernable pattern, or they may reveal some type of pattern. If the dots form a random, circular, or rectangular pattern, then there is no relationship between the variables and there is no correlation. However, if the dots form a rather straight, diagonal line pattern

Student	Exam 1 X	Exam 2 Y
Andrea	34	32
Clark	37	31
Erin	29	36
Geof	24	19
Inez	31	36
Kwame	26	24
Maddy	23	29
Oprah	29	34
Quinn	48	47
Sarah	28	29

Figure 22.1 Scores from Exams 1 and 2 for 10 psychology students.

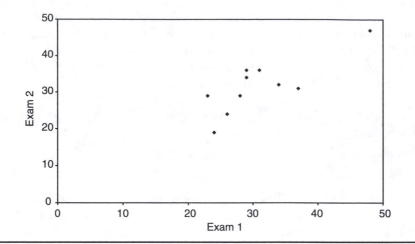

Figure 22.2 Psychology exam scores.

from the lower left-hand corner to the upper right-hand corner, then the variables are positively correlated. On the other hand, if the dots form a rather straight, diagonal line pattern from the upper left-hand corner to the lower right-hand corner, then the variables are negatively correlated.

This example (Figure 22.2) shows a positive correlation. That means that high scores on one variable are related to high scores on the other. Low scores on one variable are also related to low scores on the other. This means that students who performed well on the first exam also tended to perform well on the second, and students who performed poorly on the first exam tended to perform poorly on the second. For example, in Figure 22.1 Quinn scored high on Exam 1 and again high on Exam 2, whereas Geof scored low on Exam 1 and again low on Exam 2.

The value of the correlation coefficient is directly dependent on two characteristics of the scatter plot: (1) the slope of the best-fitting straight line through the points, and (2) their spread. The difference between a positive and a negative correlation derives from the slope of the best-fitting straight line. The magnitude (size) of the correlation is dependent on the spread of the points. If all of the points fall on or near that best-fitting straight line, then the correlation will be of great magnitude. However, as the points begin to spread, the correlation is of lesser value.

You can use a computer to complete what is known as a regression analysis that determines a best-fitting straight line. As you can see from Figure 22.3, most of the actual data points fall very close to the line. Therefore, we can expect a fairly strong positive correlation. If the vertical distance between the straight line and the data points is larger, the correlation will be smaller.

The correlation coefficient is somewhat easier to understand if you learn about z-scores.

z-SCORES

As we will learn throughout this course, raw scores are not always the best way to represent data. Raw scores are often difficult to interpret without some type of legend or key—some way to make sense of the scores. Therefore, psychometricians have

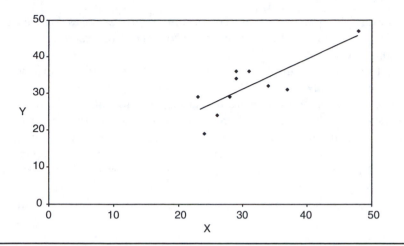

Figure 22.3 Best-fitting straight line.

developed a variety of derived scores—alternative ways to represent raw scores. These are discussed elsewhere in the text. However, one way to interpret raw scores is to use z-scores.

If you received a 37 on your last biology test, I would need to ask you at least two questions to be able to know how well you did. The two most important questions would be "What was the mean?" and "What was the standard deviation?" However, if instead you report your z-score, you will be telling me how you performed in relation to both the mean and the standard deviation. z-scores have a mean of zero (0) and a standard deviation of one (1). If you report that your z-score was positive, then I know that you scored above the mean. However, if your reported z-score was negative, then I know that you scored below the mean. Also, if your z-score is +1.5, not only do I know that you scored above the mean, but I also know that you scored 1.5 standard deviations above the mean (Good job!). Therefore, we say that z-scores are reported in standard deviation units, above (+) or below (−) the mean.

The calculation of z-scores is rather simple. A z-score is simply a deviation score (the raw score minus the mean) divided by the standard deviation (Equation 22.1).

$$z = \frac{X - \mu_x}{\sigma_x} \tag{22.1}$$

The mean of the z-scores will always equal zero (0) and the standard deviation will always equal one (1). For most distributions, scores will rarely be more than three (3) standard deviations from the mean. Therefore, z-scores will typically range from a low of about −3.0 to a high of +3.0.

> **Definition**
>
> **z-scores** represent scores in standard deviation units either above or below the mean.

Let's use an example to make certain that you understand z-scores. Figure 22.4 contains a set of quiz scores for 15 students. In the second column, each raw score has been converted to a z-score.

For this set of 15 quiz scores the mean is 16.13 and the standard deviation is 2.36. To find the z-scores, simply subtract the mean (16.13) from each raw score and divide the difference by the standard deviation (2.36). You will notice that raw scores above the mean have positive z-scores, whereas raw scores below the mean have negative z-scores. How do you interpret a z-score of 1.22? It simply means that anyone who had a raw score of 19 scored 1.22 standard deviations above the mean. In a similar fashion, a z-score of −2.17 means that anyone who had a raw score of 11 scored 2.17 standard deviations below the mean.

Now that you understand z-scores, you are ready to learn about correlation coefficients.

PEARSON PRODUCT-MOMENT CORRELATION COEFFICIENT

Over the past 100 years, psychometricians have developed a number of mathematical formulas for quantifying correlation. The most useful and general of these was developed by the classic statistician, Karl Pearson (Magnello, 2001). The coefficient is known as the Pearson Product-Moment Correlation Coefficient. However, it is typically referred to as the Pearson Correlation coefficient; by the abbreviation PPMC Coefficient; or, at times, generically as the Correlation Coefficient. Most times, when people refer to a correlation coefficient they do mean the PPMC. However, we need to be more explicit since there are a number of other correlation coefficients.

The PPMC coefficient for populations uses the Greek letter ρ (rho) and is designated ρ_{xy}, which means the correlation between variables x and y. The sample statistic uses the designation r_{xy}, which again stands for the correlation between variables x and y. The definition of the PPMC coefficient is the mean of the cross-products of the z-scores. The definitional formula looks like this (Equation 22.2):

$$\rho_{xy} = \frac{\Sigma z_x z_y}{N} \tag{22.2}$$

Although the formula may appear complex, it is rather simple. Let's use the example that we developed earlier in this chapter concerning the 10 students and their scores on the two examinations. In order to convert the raw scores into z-scores we have to calculate the mean and standard deviation for each examination. Let's start with Exam 1. I calculated that the mean is 30.9 and the standard deviation is 6.77. For Exam 2, the mean is 31.7 and the standard deviation is 7.16. The next step is to convert each raw score to a z-score by subtracting the mean from it and dividing the difference by the standard deviation. For example, the first student, Andrea, had a score of 34 on the first exam. To convert that to a z-score, plug it into the formula (Equation 22.3).

$$z_{Exam1} = z_x = \frac{X - \mu_x}{\sigma_x} = \frac{34 - 30.9}{6.77} = \frac{3.1}{6.77} = .46 \tag{22.3}$$

Raw Quiz Score	z-score
20	1.64
19	1.22
19	1.22
18	0.79
18	0.79
17	0.37
16	−0.06
16	−0.06
16	−0.06
15	−0.48
15	−0.48
15	−0.48
14	−0.90
13	−1.33
11	−2.17

Figure 22.4 Raw quiz scores converted to z-scores.

The raw score of 34 on Exam 1 converts to a z-score of .46 which means that Andrea scored about one half of a standard deviation above the mean on Exam 1. Label Exam 1 as X and Exam 2 as Y. Now we can calculate Andrea's z-score for Exam 2. Her raw score was 32, and is designated Y rather than X (Equation 22.4).

$$z_{Exam2} = z_y = \frac{Y - \mu_y}{\sigma_y} = \frac{32 - 31.7}{7.16} = \frac{0.3}{7.16} = .04 \tag{22.4}$$

The raw score of 32 on Exam 2 converts to a z-score of .04. This means that Andrea scored slightly above the mean on Exam 2. To find the cross-products of the z-scores, simply multiply z_x by z_y. These calculations, prepared on a computer, are summarized in the following figure (Figure 22.5). The values from the above examples are slightly altered on Figure 22.5. In the above example, the values are rounded off to two decimal places. The computer, however, carries many more significant digits, although in Figure 22.5 they are rounded off to three decimal places.

Student	Exam 1 X	Exam 2 Y	z_x	z_y	$z_x \times z_y$
Andrea	34	32	.458	.042	.019
Clark	37	31	.901	−.098	−.088
Erin	29	36	−.281	.601	−.169
Geof	24	19	−1.019	−1.774	1.808
Inez	31	36	.015	.601	.009
Kwame	26	24	−.724	−1.075	.778
Maddy	23	29	−1.167	−.377	.440
Oprah	29	34	−.281	.321	−.090
Quinn	48	47	2.526	2.137	5.398
Sarah	28	29	−.428	−.377	.161

Figure 22.5 Correlation example using z-scores.

The last column of the table represents the cross-products of the z-scores, z_x multiplied by z_y [(.458)(.042) = .019]. To calculate the PPMC coefficient, add up the cross-products (which add to 8.266) and divide by the number of students, 10 (Equation 22.5).

$$\rho_{xy} = \frac{\Sigma z_x z_y}{N} = \frac{(.019) + (-.088) + \ldots + (.161)}{10} = \frac{8.266}{10} = .83 \qquad (22.5)$$

A correlation coefficient of .83 is considered a strong positive correlation. This means that those students who scored well on Exam 1 also did well on Exam 2. Similarly, those who scored poorly on Exam 1 also tended to score poorly on Exam 2. The sign of the correlation coefficient (+ or −) can be better understood by looking closely at the z-scores. A positive correlation means that high scores on one variable are associated with high scores on the other variable. It also means that low scores on the one variable are associated with low scores on the other. If the scores are positively correlated, students who scored above the mean on Exam 1 (a positive z-score) should score above the mean on the other variable, Exam 2 (also a positive z-score). Similarly, students with negative z-scores on one variable (because they scored below the mean) should have negative z-scores on the other variable. The cross-products of two positive z-scores will be positive, as will the cross-products of two negative z-scores. Only cross-products of unlike signed z-scores will be negative (one score above the mean and the other score below the mean). Therefore, we can estimate the correlation coefficient by simply examining the column of cross-products. If the cross-products are largely positive, the correlation coefficient will be positive. If the cross-products are a mix of positive and negative, then the correlation coefficient will be near zero. Finally, if the cross-products are largely negative, then the correlation coefficient will be negative.

A positive correlation means that individuals tended to score similarly on the two variables: if high on the one variable then high on the other, if average on the one variable then average on the other, and if low on one variable then low on the other. A zero (or near zero) correlation essentially means that there is no relationship between the variables: scoring well on one variable is unrelated to how one will score on the other. A negative correlation essentially means that high scores on one variable are associated with low scores on the other variable. Figure 22.6 includes examples of scatter plots for several different correlations.

Actually, the sign of the correlation is relatively unimportant. A positive correlation between two variables can be turned into a negative correlation by redefining one of the variables. For example, in my research, I have found a positive correlation between class attendance and course grades. The two variables are the final course grade (represented in the total points that the students attained) and the number of classes attended. However, I could just as easily obtain a negative correlation if I counted the number of classes missed rather than the number of classes attended. So, as you can see, the sign of the correlation coefficient is primarily dependent on how we define the variables.

Much more important than the sign of the correlation is its magnitude. The PPMC coefficient can range from −1.00 to +1.00. As you can now see, our correlation of .83 is high. If you ever calculate a correlation coefficient greater than 1.00, it means that you made a mathematical error.

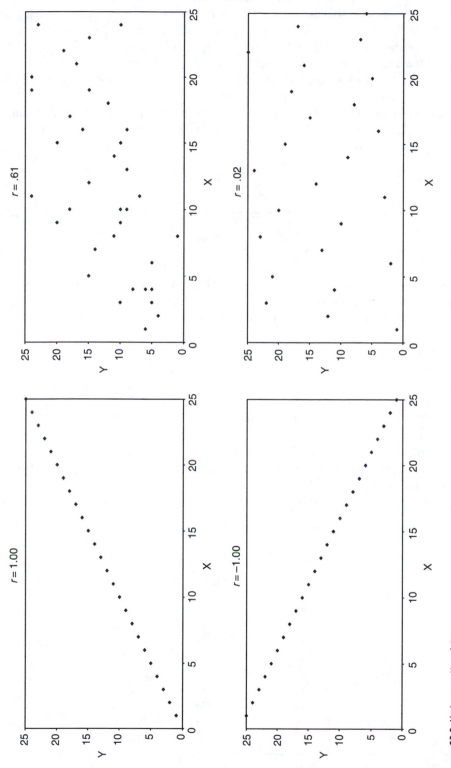

Figure 22.6 Various scatter plots.

Computational Formula for the PPMC

We do not typically use the definitional (z-score) formula to compute PPMC coefficients. The main problem with this type of formula is that we have to calculate the means and standard deviations, which frequently involve decimals. The use of decimals is problematic in that it often results in rounding errors. Therefore, it is preferable to calculate the PPMC coefficient with raw scores, which are most often whole numbers.

I will not go through the derivation of the computational formula here, although it can be derived directly from the definitional formula. However, here is the computational formula (Equation 22.6).

$$\rho_{XY} = \frac{\Sigma XY - \dfrac{\Sigma X \Sigma Y}{N}}{\sqrt{\left[\Sigma X^2 - \dfrac{(\Sigma X)^2}{N}\right]\left[\Sigma Y^2 - \dfrac{(\Sigma Y)^2}{N}\right]}} \qquad (22.6)$$

Although this formula may appear complex, it has advantages over the z-score (definitional) formula. When using the raw score formula, we typically deal only with whole numbers, so it is easier to compute the coefficient than it is when using the z-score formula.

You may also note that parts of this formula are similar to the computational formula for the variance that you learned in Chapter 21. Correlation and variance are similar since correlations simply look at how two variables *co-vary* together. The numerator of the correlation formula is essentially the numerator of the variance formula, but for two variables, rather than one. In addition, each section of the denominator of the correlation formula is simply the numerator of the variance formula.

To demonstrate the use of this formula, we can use the numbers from our previous example. We are going to need columns for X, Y, X^2, Y^2, and the cross-products of our raw scores, XY. In Figure 22.7 I have calculated the values for the X^2, Y^2, and XY columns. I have also calculated the sum of each column.

Student	X	Y	X^2	Y^2	XY
1	34	32	1,156	1,024	1,088
2	37	31	1,369	961	1,147
3	29	36	841	1,296	1,044
4	24	19	576	361	456
5	31	36	961	1,296	1,116
6	26	24	676	576	624
7	23	29	529	841	667
8	29	34	841	1,156	986
9	48	47	2,304	2,209	2,256
10	28	29	784	841	812
Sums	309	317	10,037	10,561	10,196

Figure 22.7 Computation of correlation with raw scores.

Now, let's plug these sums into our formula (Equation 22.7)

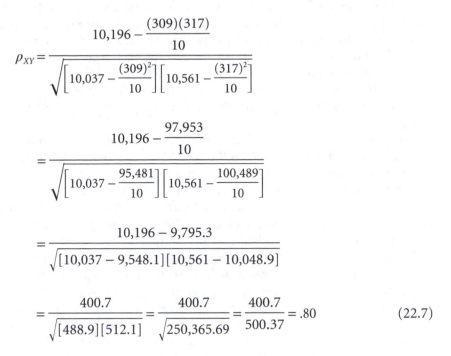

$$\rho_{XY} = \frac{10,196 - \dfrac{(309)(317)}{10}}{\sqrt{\left[10,037 - \dfrac{(309)^2}{10}\right]\left[10,561 - \dfrac{(317)^2}{10}\right]}}$$

$$= \frac{10,196 - \dfrac{97,953}{10}}{\sqrt{\left[10,037 - \dfrac{95,481}{10}\right]\left[10,561 - \dfrac{100,489}{10}\right]}}$$

$$= \frac{10,196 - 9,795.3}{\sqrt{[10,037 - 9,548.1][10,561 - 10,048.9]}}$$

$$= \frac{400.7}{\sqrt{[488.9][512.1]}} = \frac{400.7}{\sqrt{250,365.69}} = \frac{400.7}{500.37} = .80 \qquad (22.7)$$

You might note that when we used the definitional formula, we obtained a PPMC coefficient of .83. However, with the raw score formula, we obtained a PPMC coefficient of .80, the correct value. When using the definitional formula, you can have rounding errors that can result in a slightly inaccurate coefficient value. (By the way, computer programs typically use the definitional formula, but do not run into rounding errors since they carry numbers to eight or more decimal places.)

CORRELATION AND PREDICTION

Correlation is useful in many ways. If two variables are correlated with one another, and if we know the value of one variable, then we are able to make a prediction about the value of the other variable. In fact, this is one of the most practical reasons to compute correlations. For example, since SAT scores are correlated with the freshman grade-point-average (GPA), college admissions officers are able to make a reasonable prediction about a college applicant's likelihood of having a successful freshman year based simply on the applicant's SAT scores. Thus, for a selective college, where they receive many more applications than they can accept, they often offer admission to those students most likely to be successful. (In reality, colleges use several predictors, not just SAT scores.)

The stronger the correlation coefficient, the better the prediction we can make. For example, if the correlation between two variables is either 1.00 or −1.00, then knowing the value of one variable allows us to exactly predict the value of the other. However, as the magnitude of the correlation decreases, then our ability to predict is less exact. For example, if the correlation between two variables is .42, then knowing the value of one variable allows us to make a prediction about the likely range of values for the second variable. For example, if the correlation between SATs and freshman GPA is .42, and we know that a student's combined Verbal and Math SAT score is 1,100, then we may be able to predict the probability that this student's freshman GPA would fall somewhere between 2.25 and 3.25. However, when the correlation between two variables is near zero, then knowing the value of one variable does not help us in any way in predicting the value of the other. This use of the correlation coefficient becomes important when discussing issues such as validity, covered elsewhere in the text (see Chapter 5).

Before we leave our discussion of correlation, there are two important points that should be made. First, the Pearson Product-Moment Correlation coefficient and several of the other popular correlation coefficients are measures of the linear relationship between two variables. They are each concerned with the best-fitting straight line. However, there are times when a curved line better describes the relationship between two variables, and there are techniques for discovering the best-fitting curvilinear relationship between two variables. However, that is beyond the scope of this text.

The second issue has to do with correlation and causation. Typically, it is argued that correlation does not necessarily imply causation. Simply because two variables are correlated with one another does not imply that one variable is causing the other. Although the relationship between the two variables may be causal, we have no way of telling that for sure. Sometimes two variables are correlated with one another, but the causal factor is a third variable. For example, in some research that I performed a number of years ago (Van Blerkom, 1992), I discovered a moderate positive correlation between class attendance in college courses and final grades in those courses. Those students who attended class the most often tended to obtain the highest grades. Although I would like to believe that when students attend my classes they learn more and, therefore, perform better on my tests, there is no guarantee, however, that is what actually happens. It is possible that a third, unmeasured variable, such as motivation, affects each. Perhaps the best motivated students attend more classes and prepare better for exams, whereas the less motivated students attend fewer classes and do less well on exams.

SUMMARY

When we examine two variables at the same time, we refer to this as bivariate statistics. We often use bivariate statistics to compute correlations to see if the two variables are related to one another. One of the most common ways to compute correlations is with the Pearson Product-Moment Correlation (PPMC) coefficient. The PPMC is defined as the average of the cross-products of the z-scores. Z-scores are standard scores where raw scores are adjusted by the mean and standard deviation of the data set. In addition, there is a raw score formula for computing the PPMC which is preferred in most situations. Once we have established that two variables are correlated with one another, we can use the value of one variable to predict the other.

You now know many of the basic characteristics of both univariate and bivariate descriptive statistics. With these tools you should be well able to tackle the principles of measurement, which are discussed in Part I on Measurement.

EXERCISES

1. Dr. Van Blerkom feels that class attendance is often associated with learning. Find the correlation between total points students earned in the course from exams and class attendance (taken during eight random classes during the term). This is based on a sample from an introduction to psychology class.

Points	Attendance
91	5
129	8
134	8
113	8
116	7
96	8
84	6
79	5
113	6
82	4
57	1
70	6
98	8
118	8
111	6

2. Create a scatter plot from the above data.
3. The following is a set of scores from a 7th-grade math test.

   a. What is the mean?
   b. What is the standard deviation?
   c. Convert each raw score into a z-score.

Raw Score	z-score
25	
25	
24	
23	
23	
23	
23	
22	
20	
20	
19	
18	
18	
18	
18	
16	
15	

SPOTLIGHT ON THE CLASSROOM

Dr. Welsh is a new professor at a small university. She teaches statistics to a group of college freshmen. She is frustrated because she is having a hard time getting her students to show up for class each day. She would like her students to be accountable for class attendance. She would not like to put a strict attendance policy in place because she feels that college students should be responsible for their actions. The students are currently learning about correlations in her statistics class, so she thought this was a good opportunity to accomplish her goals of extending their understanding of correlations and, at the same time, motivating them to come to class.

After the first exam, Dr. Welsh decides to show the students a correlation between exam scores and their attendance throughout the first few weeks of class. The test was out of 100 points. The following is a list of the test scores and the number of days each student was absent.

Points	Absent
85	1
68	3
91	0
77	3
89	1
90	1
76	3
73	3
59	7
70	5
90	1
74	4
92	0
84	2
87	1
90	1
91	2
86	1
77	3
62	6
81	2
79	3
93	0

Discuss the correlation and what her students could learn from her study.

STUDY TIPS

How to Learn from an Exam

Students sometimes think that once they have finished an exam they are finished with that material. However, in a measurement and statistics course, and in many similar courses, material that is learned early in the term is needed and used again later in the term. In addition, you can get a lot of feedback after an exam that can help you perform better on subsequent exams in the same course.

One thing that you can learn about when you go over an exam in class is your level of preparation. If you performed very well on the exam, you can safely assume that you were probably well prepared. However, if your score was lower than you had anticipated or lower than you had hoped for, then you should probably assume that you were not as well prepared as you had planned. As you were taking the exam, were the questions ones that you had anticipated seeing or were there many items that were a surprise to you? For example, were you prepared for items that required you to interpret concepts that you were taught, or apply concepts to new circumstances provided on the exam? Perhaps you performed well on items that simply required the recall of knowledge but not as well on items that required you to show that you fully understood the concepts or could apply to concepts to real-life situations. After the exam is returned, you can determine whether you performed better on material that was presented in class or that was presented in the textbook. If 75% of the items were from class and 25% were from the textbook, then you should have allocated about 75% or your study time to class material and 25% to textbook material. Did you?

You can also learn from your mistakes, although this may take some help from fellow students or from your professor. If you are uncertain about why you got a particular item wrong, you may need to discuss it with a classmate or your professor to determine where you are confused. Perhaps you misunderstood a particular concept or did not fully understand it. If you have particular questions in mind when you go in to see your professor, she or he is more likely to be able to help you. By analyzing your errors, you can often determine whether your mistakes were the result of careless errors or poor test preparation.

Finally, after reviewing your test, you need to know where to go for help. Some of my students wait until they have performed poorly on two or more tests before they try to get help. Unfortunately, by that time it is often too late in the term to salvage the course grade. You should seek help immediately after your first disappointing test score. Often the first person you should see is your professor. He or she can often offer suggestions about seeking additional help from a tutor or through your college learning center. I typically suggest that students get together in small study groups with other members from the class. These groups work very effectively but work best when they meet, at least, weekly.[1]

NOTE

1.   This material has been adapted from Van Blerkom (2009).

REFERENCES

American Association for the Advancement of Science (1993). *Benchmarks for science literacy*. New York: author.

American Psychological Association (2001). *Publication manual of the American Psychological Association* (5th ed.). Washington: author.

Anderson, L. W., & Krathwohl, D. R. (Eds.) (2001). *A taxonomy for learning, teaching, and assessing: A revision of Bloom's taxonomy of educational objectives*. New York: Longman.

Andrade, H. G. (2000). Using rubrics to promote thinking and learning. *Educational Leadership, 57* (5), 13–18.

Bloom, B. S. (Ed.) (1956). *Taxonomy of educational objectives: Cognitive and affective domains*. New York: David McKay.

Cronbach, L. J. (1951). Coefficient alpha and the internal structure of tests. *Psychometrika, 16,* 297–334.

Cronbach, L. J. (1984). *Essentials of psychological testing* (4th ed.). Boston: Allyn and Bacon.

Downing, S. M. (2006). Selected-response item formats in test development. In S. M. Downing & T. M. Haladyna (Eds.), *Handbook of test development* (pp. 287–301). Hillsdale, NJ: Erlbaum.

Gagné, R. M. (1984). Learning outcomes and their effects. *American Psychologist, 39,* 377–385.

Gagné, R. M. (1985). *The conditions of learning and theory of instruction* (4th ed.). New York: Holt, Rinehart, & Winston.

Gagné, R. M., Briggs, L. J., & Wager, W. W. (1992). *Principles of instructional design* (4th ed.). Fort Worth: Harcourt, Brace, Jovanovich.

Games, P. A., & Klare, G. R. (1967). *Elementary statistics: Data analysis for the behavioral sciences*. New York: McGraw-Hill.

Gronlund, N. E. (2004). *Writing instructional objectives for teaching and assessment* (7th ed.). Upper Saddle River, NJ: Pearson, Merrill, Prentice Hall.

Impara, J. C. (2007). 2006 Presidential address: Errors and omissions: Some illustrations from unpublished research. *Educational Measurement: Issues and Practice, 26*(1), 3–8.

Kuder, G. F., & Richardson, M. W. (1937). The theory of estimation of reliability. *Psychometrika, 2,* 151–160.

Likert, R. (1932). A technique for the measurement of attitudes. *Archives of Psychology, 22* (140), 1–55.

Linn, R. L., & Grondlund, N. E. (1995). *Measurement and assessment in teaching* (7th ed.). Englewood Cliffs, NJ: Prentice-Hall.

Linn, R. L., & Miller, M. D. (2005). *Measurement and assessment in teaching* (9th ed.). Upper Saddle River, NJ: Pearson, Merrill, Prentice Hall.

Locke, E. A., & Latham, G. P. (2002). Building a practically useful theory of goal setting and task motivation. *American Psychologist, 57,* 705–717.

Lord, F. M. (1952). The relation of the reliability of multiple-choice tests to the distribution of item difficulty. *Psychometrika, 17* (2), 181–194.

Mager, R. F. (1962). *Preparing instructional objectives*. Belmont, CA: Fearon-Pitman.

Magnello, E. (2001). Karl Pearson. In C. C. Heyde & E. Senta (Eds.), *Statisticians of the centuries* (pp. 248–256). New York: Springer-Verlag.

Mead, A. D., & Drasgow, F. (1993). Equivalence of computerized and paper-and-pencil cognitive ability tests: A meta-analysis. *Psychological Bulletin, 114,* 449–458.

Messick, S. (1995). Validity of psychological assessment: Validation of inferences from persons' responses and performances as scientific inquiry into score meaning. *American Psychologist, 59,* 741–749.

Miller, R. B. (1962). Analysis and specification of behavior for training. In R. Glaser (Ed.), *Training research and education: Science edition,* New York: Wiley.

Montgomery, K. K., & Wiley, D. A. (2008). *Building E-portfolios using PowerPoint: A guide for educators* (2nd ed.). Thousand Oaks, CA: Sage.

National Council for the Social Studies (1994). *Expectations of excellence: Curriculum standards for social studies.* Washington: author.

National Council of Teachers of Mathematics (2000). *Principles and standards for school mathematics.* Reston, VA: author.

Oosterhof, A. (2001). *Classroom applications of educational measurement* (3rd ed.). Upper Saddle River, NJ: Merrill / Prentice Hall.

Popham, W. J. (2005). *Classroom assessment: What teachers need to know* (4th ed.). Boston: Pearson / Allyn & Bacon.

Riley, J. P. (1986). The effects of teachers' wait-time and knowledge comprehension questioning on science achievement. *Journal of Research in Science Teaching, 23,* 335–342.

Rodriguez, M. C. (2005). Three options are optimal for multiple-choice items: A meta-analysis of 80 years of research. *Educational Measurement: Issues and Practice, 24*(2), 3–13.

Stevenson, H. W., Stigler, J. W., & Lee, S. (1986). Achievement in mathematics. In H. Stevenson, H. Azuma, & K. Hakuta (Eds.), *Child development and education in Japan* (pp. 201–216), New York: Freeman.

Sweet, D. (1993). Student portfolios: Classroom uses. *Education Research Consumer Guide,* (OR Publication No. 93–3013). Washington, DC: U.S. Department of Education.

Van Blerkom, D. L. (2009). *College study skills: Becoming a strategic learner* (6th ed.). Belmont, CA: Wadsworth.

Van Blerkom, M. L. (1992). Class attendance in undergraduate courses. *The Journal of Psychology, 126,* 487–494.

Wang, S., Jiao, H., Young, M. J., Brooks, T., & Olsen, J. (2007). A meta-analysis of testing mode effects in grades K–12 mathematics tests. *Educational and Psychological Measurement, 67,* 219–238.

INDEX